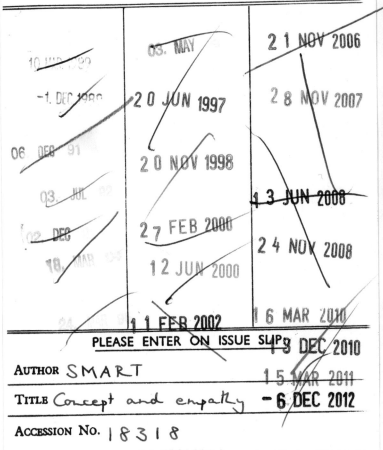

LIBRARY OF PHILOSOPHY AND RELIGION

General Editor: John Hick

Danforth Professor, Claremont Graduate School, Claremont, California

This series of books explores contemporary religious understandings of humanity and the universe. The books contribute to various aspects of the continuing dialogues between religion and philosophy, between scepticism and faith, and between the different religions and ideologies.

The authors represent a correspondingly wide range of viewpoints. Some of the books in the series are written for the general educated public, and some for a more specialised philosophical or theological readership.

Already published

Masao Abe	ZEN AND WESTERN THOUGHT
William H. Austin	THE RELEVANCE OF NATURAL SCIENCE TO THEOLOGY
Paul Badham	CHRISTIAN BELIEFS ABOUT LIFE AFTER DEATH
Paul and Linda Badham	IMMORTALITY OR EXTINCTION?
Patrick Burke	THE FRAGILE UNIVERSE
Margaret Chatterjee	GANDHI'S RELIGIOUS THOUGHT
William Lane Craig	THE KALAM COSMOLOGICAL ARGUMENT
	THE COSMOLOGICAL ARGUMENT FROM PLATO TO LEIBNIZ
Stephen T. Davis	LOGIC AND THE NATURE OF GOD
Lynn A. de Silva	THE PROBLEM OF THE SELF IN BUDDHISM AND CHRISTIANITY
Padmasiri de Silva	AN INTRODUCTION TO BUDDHIST PSYCHOLOGY
Ramchandra Gandhi	THE AVAILABILITY OF RELIGIOUS IDEAS
J. C. A. Gaskin	HUME'S PHILOSOPHY OF RELIGION
H. A. Hodges	GOD BEYOND KNOWLEDGE
J. Kellenberger	THE COGNITIVITY OF RELIGION

Hywel D. Lewis	PERSONS AND LIFE AFTER DEATH
Julius J. Lipner	THE FACE OF TRUTH
Eric Lott	VEDANTIC APPROACHES TO GOD
Geddes MacGregor	REINCARNATION AS A CHRISTIAN HOPE
Hugo A. Meynell	AN INTRODUCTION TO THE PHILOSOPHY OF BERNARD LONERGAN
F. C. T. Moore	THE PSYCHOLOGICAL BASIS OF MORALITY
Dennis Nineham	THE USE AND ABUSE OF THE BIBLE
D. Z. Phillips	BELIEF, CHANGE, AND FORMS OF LIFE
Martin Prozesky	RELIGION AND ULTIMATE WELL-BEING
Bernard M. G. Reardon	HEGEL'S PHILOSOPHY OF RELIGION
John J. Shepherd	EXPERIENCE, INFERENCE AND GOD
Patrick Sherry	RELIGION, TRUTH AND LANGUAGE GAMES
	SPIRITS, SAINTS AND IMMORTALITY
Ninian Smart	CONCEPT AND EMPATHY
Wilfred Cantwell Smith	TOWARDS A WORLD THEOLOGY
Shivesh Chandra Thakur	RELIGION AND RATIONAL CHOICE
Robert Young	FREEDOM, RESPONSIBILITY AND GOD

Further titles in preparation

Series Standing Order

If you would like to receive future titles in this series as they are published, you can make use of our standing order facility. To place a standing order please contact your bookseller or, in case of difficulty, write to us at the address below with your name and address and the name of the series. Please state with which title you wish to begin your standing order. (If you live outside the United Kingdom we may not have the rights for your area, in which case we will forward your order to the publisher concerned.)

Standing Order Service, Macmillan Distribution Ltd,
Houndmills, Basingstoke, Hants, RG21 2XS, England.

CONCEPT AND EMPATHY

Essays in the Study of Religion

Ninian Smart

Edited by
Donald Wiebe

MACMILLAN

First published 1986

Published by
THE MACMILLAN PRESS LTD
Houndmills, Basingstoke, Hampshire RG21 2XS
and London
Companies and representatives
throughout the world

Printed in Hong Kong

British Library Cataloguing in Publication Data
Smart, Ninian
Concept and empathy: essays in the story of
religion.—(Library of philosophy and religion)
1. Religion—Philosophy
I. Title   II. Wiebe, Donald   III. Series
200'.1   BL51
ISBN 0–333–38793–7

For Bryan Magee
whose friendship started in the year of
the first article in this collection

Contents

Preface   ix
Acknowledgements   x
Introduction by Donald Wiebe   1

PART I   PHILOSOPHY AND THE STUDY OF RELIGION

1 The Comparative Logical Analysis of Religious
   Doctrines   9
2 God, Bliss and Morality   11
3 The Criteria of Religious Identity   25
4 Numen, Nirvana, and the Definition of Religion   40
5 Myth and Transcendence   49
6 The Concept of Heaven   61
7 The Philosophy of Worldviews: The Philosophy of
   Religion Transformed   72

PART II   THE COMPARATIVE STUDY OF RELIGION

8   Living Liberation: Jivanmukti and Nirvana   89
9   Interpretation and Mystical Experience   98
10 Problems of the Application of Western Terminology to
    Theravada Buddhism   113
11 Nirvana and Timelessness   119
12 Precept and Theory in Sri Lanka   125
13 Beyond Eliade: The Future of Theory in Religion   131
14 Religion, Myth and Nationalism   143

PART III   METHODOLOGICAL ISSUES IN THE STUDY OF RELIGION

15 Religion as a Discipline?   157
16 Towards an Agreed Place for Religious Studies in Higher
    Education   163

Contents

17 What is Comparative Religion?   176
18 Social Anthropology and the Philosophy of Religion   184
19 The Principles and Meaning of the Study of Religion   195
20 Methods and Disciplines in the Study of Religion   207
21 The Exploration of Religion and Education   220

Notes   231
Index   241

Preface

The appearance of this volume owes a great deal to Don Wiebe, who kindly undertook to select and edit the papers from among many that I have written in the fields of the history and philosophy of religion. His introduction sets them in their context. I am most grateful to him for the very considerable labours involved in getting the book ready for the press. The papers, naturally, range over differing phases of my thinking, and I hope reflect some of the important conceptual and other issues arising in regard to the modern study of religion and, more widely, worldviews.

Santa Barbara and Lancaster NINIAN SMART

Acknowledgements

I am grateful to Professor Smart for the opportunity to assemble this collection of his essays and thank him for his contribution of time and effort in its preparation. I wish also to thank Trinity College for its generous support of my research and preparation, acknowledging especially the encouragement of the Dean, Professor John Cole. The Social Sciences and Humanities Research Council of Canada also assisted in the work by making funds available for travel undertaken on this project.

On behalf of the author and publisher I would like to thank those listed below for their kind permission to reprint the materials included here:

E. J. Brill Publishers for 'The Comparative Logical Analysis of Religious Doctrines', which appeared in the proceedings of the VIIIth IAHR Congress held in Rome (April, 1955); *The Sacral Kingship*, (*Studies in the History of Religion*, 4), 1959.

The Aristotelian Society for 'God, Bliss and Morality', which appeared in its *Proceedings*, Vol. 58, 1957–8; pp. 59–78.

The Philosophical Quarterly for 'The Criteria of Religious Identity', Vol. 8, 1958; pp. 328–341.

The Church Quarterly Review (Epworth Press) for 'Numen, Nirvana, and the Definition of Religion', Vol. 160, 1959; pp. 216–25.

The Monist for 'Myth and Transcendence', Vol. 50, 1966; pp. 475–87.

The Macmillan Press for 'The Concept of Heaven' in G. N. A. Vesey (ed.), *Talk of God*, 1969; pp. 226–38.

Neue Zeitschrift für Systematische Theologie und Religionsphilosophie for 'The Philosophy of Worldviews – that is, the Philosophy of Religion Transformed', Vol. 23, 1981; pp. 212–24.

Manchester University Press for 'Living Liberation: Jivanmukti and Nirvana' in E. J. Sharpe and J. R. Hinnells (eds), *Man and His Salvation*, 1973; pp. 281–90.

Religious Studies (Cambridge University Press) for 'Interpretation and Mystical Experience', Vol. 1, 1965; pp. 75–87.

Religion (Academic Press) for 'Problems of the Application of Western Terminology to Theravada Buddhism, with Special Reference to the Relationship between The Buddha and the Gods', Vol. 2, 1972; pp. 37–41: and 'Precept and Theory in Sri Lanka', Vol. 3, 1973; pp. 74–78.

Journal of Dharma for 'Nirvana and Timelessness', Vol. 1, 1976; pp. 318–23.

Numen for 'Beyond Eliade: The Failure of Theory in Religion', Vol. 25, 1978; pp. 171–83.

The Scottish Journal of Religious Studies for 'Religion, Myth and Nationalism', Vol. 1, 1980; pp. 5–15.

Universities Quarterly (Basil Blackwell Publishers) for 'Religion as a Discipline', Vol. 17, 1962; pp. 48–53.

Theoria to Theory (Gordon & Breach Science Publishers Ltd) for 'What is Comparative Religion?', Vol. 1, 1967; pp. 138–45.

Inquiry (Universitetsforlaget) for 'Social Anthropology and the Philosophy of Religion', Vol. 6, 1963; pp. 287–99.

Oxford Review of Education (Carfax Publishing Co.) for 'The Exploration of Religion and Education', Vol. 1, 1975; pp. 99–105.

'Towards an Agreed Place for Religious Studies in Higher Education' is the unpublished E. Savell Hicks Memorial Lecture delivered at the Mansion House, Dublin, on 1 November 1967.

'The Principles and Meaning of the Study of Religion' is the Inaugural Address delivered at the University of Lancaster on 14 February 1968 (and printed in booklet form by the University Library).

'Methods and Disciplines in the Study of Religion,' is an unpublished lecture delivered at the University of California, Santa Barbara.

DONALD WIEBE

Introduction

Donald Wiebe

This volume of essays in the study of religion makes available some of the important but not easily accessible (or previously unpublished) papers of one of the more influential students of that phenomenon. Professor Smart, who established the first department of religious studies in the United Kingdom, has achieved an enviable international reputation for his work in this field. In his professorial role he has donned a variety of identities such as that of philosopher of religion, historian of religion, and theologian and has held a wide variety of academic appointments including University College of Wales, the University of London, and Lancaster University in the UK; Yale and Princeton Universities, the University of Wisconsin and the University of California at Santa Barbara in the USA; and Banaras Hindu University and the University of Otago in New Zealand. In addition he has delivered lectures in numerous other universities around the world and has presented several prestigious lectureships including the Gifford Lectures for 1979–80. His influence on religious studies, however, ranges far beyond the boundaries of his professorial activities as extensive as they are. His role as consultant to the immensely successful film series 'The Long Search' and other broadcasting ventures have made an impact on the role of religion in education both inside and outside the University community. In writing, moreover, Professor Smart has been prolific, with a score of books and somewhere near to a hundred essays, papers, addresses and the like.

The significant role which Professor Smart has played in the shaping of religious studies in universities around the world would in itself constitute sufficient justification for making his thought more readily available to a new generation of students and scholars. Such justification, moreover, is enhanced in that the essays included here have lost none of their edge or relevance; they are still valuable contributions to the contemporary debate on the topics discussed.

1

Furthermore, they will also be of great value to those interested in the development of Professor Smart's own thinking on the nature of religious studies over the last quarter century. However, the selection of essays for inclusion in this volume concerns more than their individual value; as arranged here they are meant to constitute a unity even though the unity is more implicit than one might expect in a book or monograph. The unity is 'thematic': the essays, although written over a period of twenty years or more and concerned with a variety of topics and issues, 'embody' a philosophy for religious studies. The essays do not, for the most part, focus our attention explicitly on such a 'philosophy' but rather exemplify that philosophy in the way that Professor Smart proceeds in his study of religious phenomena. The essays in the first two sections of this volume for example, focus attention quite narrowly on two foci of religious studies: conceptual clarity (understanding) and phenomenological understanding – hence the title *Concept and Empathy*. The essays in parts one and two highlight the phenomenological and comparative approaches to the study of religion and show how such approaches are enhanced by a proper focus on the conceptual – something too often neglected in empirically oriented studies today. The essays in section three extend the argument in more general terms in discussing questions of method and of the place of religious studies in higher education. In some sense the essays in this final section present explicitly and abstractly the pattern of the approach to understanding religion exemplified in the work contained in sections one and two.

What should be of primary interest to readers here is Professor Smart's emphasis on the role of philosophy in the field of religious studies. In distinguishing itself as a separate field of academic inquiry from theology, the 'new discipline' also eschewed philosophy, since it shared with theology an interest in the question of the truth of religion. Although in agreement with the central thrust of the movement's aim of distinguishing research in religion as an enterprise distinct and independent from theology, Smart nevertheless refuses to identify theology with philosophy in any such simple fashion. Philosophy as conceptual analysis, he repeatedly insists, can be of invaluable assistance in coming to understand the meaning of religion. To understand the logical status of religious concepts and ideas is to have increased one's factual understanding of religion according to Smart; it is to have improved one's historical, empirical, descriptive understanding of religion rather than, as with theology, to have compromised it.

This emphasis upon philosophy is, I think, unique amongst contemporary students of religion; it certainly runs counter to the general assumptions held in the field of study and few of its practitioners undertake such an analysis as is to be found in the work of Professor Smart. Nevertheless, Smart is still very much in the centre of that field, for a second central concern throughout all his work is with understanding the phenomenon of religion through careful, objective descriptions of religious traditions in all their individuality and particularity. The essays in section two of this volume make that abundantly clear. Philosophy here is not rejected but it is certainly seen to be ancillary to the main work of history and phenomenology. If the essays in section one suggest that the history of religions can be improved by undertaking philosophical analysis those in section two show the reader that no 'philosophy of religion' is of any value without a solid historical understanding – a philosophy of religion bereft of historical understanding is no more plausible than would be a philosophy of science ignorant of the history of science. This rare 'symbiosis' of history and philosophy in Smart's theory and practice is precisely that which lends his work such credibility and makes his work a model for religious studies research. Professor Smart shows us that the student of religion must forego narrow specialisms without denigrating them, *and* open herself/himself to theoretical interpretations of the data provided by such disciplines. Only in combining both the 'ideographic' and the 'nomothetic' frames of mind is the meaning of religion ever likely to be uncovered.

Later deliberations on the nature of religious studies (the essays in each section of this volume being in roughly chronological order) reveal a 'twist' in Professor Smart's use of philosophy; philosophy of religion becomes more than conceptual analysis (and presumably less than an outright speculative metaphysics) in that it is extended to become a philosophy of worldviews. The 'twist' comes in the fact that, for Smart, such a philosophy implies that the history of religions has a more general destiny than heretofore conceived. (See especially the concluding essays of sections one and two). Such a 'philosophy-of-religion-cum-philosophy-of-worldviews' might to some, however, indicate a *return* to a theologically oriented study of religion. A kind of theological intention, in any event, is not foreign to Smart's work. And indication of that fact is not present simply in his having held a chair in theology at the University of Birmingham. Professor Smart has always maintained, for example, that it is more important to 'be religious' than to 'study religion' (see here his inaugural address at the

University of Lancaster and also his *The Phenomenon of Religion* and *The Science of Religion and the Sociology of Knowledge*). And his sympathy for M. Eliade's 'creative hermeneutic' in those same essays shows his hope for a more global value, so to speak, for religious studies. Indeed, his Gifford Lectures, it could be argued, constitute a step in that direction for the discipline; in a *Times Higher Education Supplement* (1982) he wrote: 'The formation of a worldview which will synthesise elements from the religious, political and cultural past of the West is a sort of theology, and I have attempted it in my Gifford Lectures.' (In this he seems to have fulfilled his own call for a new, although 'soft', natural theology voiced in his inaugural lecture in taking up the chair of theology at the University of Birmingham: 'Theology, Philosophy and the Natural Sciences' and it seems that religious studies as a 'science' plays a dominant role in that exercise.) Whether this 'move' in Professor Smart's thought amounts simply to a return to an earlier theological mode of investigation or rather to a post-critical fulfillment of Eliade's call for a 'creative hermeneutic' that still guarantees the autonomy of religious studies, need not, of course, be resolved here. It is, however, likely to stimulate even more methodological discussion in this field.

The provision of a brief overview of the essays selected for publication here may be of some help in seeing the 'implicit method' in the wide array of tasks undertaken in them by Professor Smart.

Section one opens with a very brief 'note' that merely sounds the theme embodied in the essays to follow. Professor Smart clearly points out the value that philosophy as analysis can have for the empirical and comparative study of religious traditions. In doing so he obviously places great emphasis upon the element of doctrine/belief in religion. The essays that follow take up the kind of analysis this note calls for.

In 'God, Bliss and Morality' he tackles the question of the relationship of 'religious' to 'moral discourse'. This analysis results in the formulation and clarification of two key notions that are extremely valuable in succeeding analyses: the concept of 'doctrinal schemes' and 'strands of spiritual discourse'. 'Criteria of Religious Identity' and 'Numen, Nirvana and the Definition of Religion' are concerned with the misperceptions of religion that derive from a failure to 'locate' properly the context or framework (scheme) in which superficially weird belief claims can make sense. Both essays are concerned with properly identifying the particular nature of religion and religious identity by paying attention to the range of utterances, beliefs, rituals, and practices with which any particular belief or doctrine is associated. A similar exercise is undertaken in the next two essays – 'Myth and Transcendence' and 'The Concept of Heaven' – for concepts peculiarly related to the context of theism and particularly Christian theism. The essay on the philosophy of worldviews, of which I have made so much in this introduction, concludes the first section. As I have already intimated, the article attempts to extend the scope of philosophy of religion beyond mere analysis.

The essays in section two show the other, and possibly dominant, side of Professor Smart's approach to the understanding of religion; they reveal his passion for the historical/empirical and comparative study of religious traditions in all their particularity. He works here with such 'comparative problems' as the application of western terminology in the study of non-western religious traditions; with religious experience and mysticism underlying all religions; and, more specifically, with the meaning of liberation, nirvana, etc. Included in these discussions are Professor Smart's responses to other major figures in this field of enquiry. This section closes with a more recent analysis by Smart of 'traditions of thought' that are not, strictly speaking, religious and it bears some correspondence to his call for 'worldview analysis' at the end of section one.

The final section of this book contains several essays that, to varying degrees, make explicit the philosophy 'embodied' in the work of sections one and two. In a sense, this section provides a kind of commentary on those preceding it – discussing in a more general way questions of method and of the place of religious studies in higher education.

Two essays in this final section, it must be noted, have not previously been published: 'Towards an Agreed Place for Religious Studies in Higher Education' and 'Methods and Disciplines in the Study of Religion'. The former, I suggest, puts in more abstract terms the possible tension in Smart's own methodology adverted to above for it argues that the study of religion must not itself be a religious exercise, (it must be 'trans-religious' and so distinguishable from theology and even from 'dialogue of religions'), and yet that it requires 'engagement' in order to do good history of religions, so to speak. The same theme is sounded in the latter paper but it extends the argument in interesting ways and also provides a review of the 'stages in the evolution of the study of religion' as Smart sees it, and seems to press for even further 'creative' development. 'Religion as a Discipline' is a very early piece that briefly presents the mind set behind the establishment of the first department of religious studies in England and 'What is Comparative Religion' treats of the nature of one of the most important sub-disciplines of the field. 'Social Anthropology and the Philosophy of Religion' focusses on the relationship of religious studies to the social sciences and also raises directly the question of reductionism in that study. 'The Principles and Meaning of the Study of Religion' is the inaugural lecture delivered by Smart on taking up the chair at the University of Lancaster and it provides a concise methodological overview of the field. In this piece he describes religious studies as a polymethodic discipline that espouses a method-ological pluralism. This essay comes closest to describing in an explicit way not only Smart's view but also the range of his own activities. The final essay, 'The Exploration of Religion and Edu-cation' closes this section and the volume. In it, Professor Smart attempts to untangle a variety of confusions regarding theory and practice both in the study and in the teaching of 'religion'.

These essays are presented essentially as they were first printed. Only minor editorial changes and corrections have been made. Occasionally some passages have been deleted where they simply repeat a point already made. Some thematic overlap, however, still remains but acts to reinforce key notions and concepts in Professor Smart's thought. The reader will find in these essays an excellent introduction not only to religious studies (both theoretically in the abstract methodological discussions and, more importantly, practi-cally in the actual studies carried out) but also to Professor Smart, one of its most interesting and creative practitioners.

Part I
Philosophy and the Study of Religion

1 The Comparative Logical Analysis of Religious Doctrines

I wish to argue that the philosophy of religion is a factual enquiry closely bound up with the study of comparative religion.

The philosopher is a logician, whose job is to explore the logic of different types of proposition, including religious ones, and not to establish or overthrow particular beliefs (e.g., that God exists). The essence of a proposition's logic lies in the mode whereby the truth or falsity (correctness, propriety, etc.) of that type of proposition is attested, and the canons appealed to: and thus is intimately coupled with the function, which is seen in the setting, of that type of proposition (e.g., the logic of mystical utterance can only be luminous in the setting of spiritual training and behaviour).

We must attach a rider to all this: the field of religious discourse should be regarded as autonomous, and the investigator's assumption must be that religious utterances have a meaning; their own. His enquiry, then, is in its own strange fashion a factual one, and not normative, for he avoids legislating about logic.

Now we find that religious propositions occur within, or are connected with, doctrinal systems or *schemes* (a better term: they are not tautly systematic like, say, Euclidean geometry), from which they cannot be severed. For the sense of such a proposition is in part determined by what other propositions are conjointly asserted. But some schemes contain propositions of differing logics (e.g., there are differing canons of propriety relevant in respect of propositions about a Creator and of those about mystical experience), and this is connected with the fact that there are diverse sorts of religious activity (e.g., worship and asceticism). When the logician wishes to separate out the varying types of propositions, he meets a grave obstacle, for the propositions, being woven into a scheme, are mutilated if cut apart. He must honestly recognise that he is bound to distort, and

9

justify the dissection by appeal to comparative religion. A doctrinal scheme containing one strand serves as a model of the strand where it appears in another scheme in conjunction with, and influenced by, a second strand.

Thus, for instance, Brahmanism seems to contain two strands: propositions about Brahman as source and sustainer of the world, and mystical propositions about the Atman (to be sought within). Sānkhya, on the other hand, does without the first strand, as does early Buddhism (the anattā doctrine is largely directed against the concept Atman as influenced by Brahman).

Thus historical comparisons will help to give logical distinctions content; and so another name for the philosophy of religion is: 'the comparative logical analysis of religious doctrines'. This should count as a specialised, and I think, important, factual enquiry within comparative religion. By rejecting metaphysical controversy and the desire to indoctrinate, the philosopher can gain enlightenment from the historian, and may even offer something in return.

2 God, Bliss and Morality

I wish here to review rather generally the relations between religious and moral discourse. At first sight, such an enterprise might seem odd or objectionable on a number of counts. First, some might think that there is no real distinction between the two; for is not such a commandment as 'Love thy neighbour as thyself' an integral part of spiritual discourse? Yet it is at least doubtful whether any moral principles or rules are entailed by specifically religious doctrines, except trivially (e.g., where we have 'God's Will is . . .' and 'One ought to conform to God's Will: therefore one ought to . . .'). One does not require religious insight to see that lying or stealing is wrong; or, to put it a little more formally, one can justify such pronouncements without asserting anything which refers to a religious entity. It is therefore convenient to make a rough distinction between specifically religious utterances and those which are specifically moral: thus 'God created the world' would fall into the former class, 'adultery is wrong' into the latter. Perhaps, however, it will be questioned whether there is any clearly discernible field of discourse to be described as 'moral language'. For though moral philosophers have traditionally addressed themselves to such problems as the justification of social rules and the nature of (so-called) moral judgement, it is by no means clear which practical affairs are to count as falling under the aegis of morality and which judgements about people are to count as 'moral'. Is to commend someone as happy to make a moral pronouncement? And while most folk would say that the Wolfenden report is about morals, what pigeon-hole would a report on pensions fit into? Nevertheless, though it is unclear what the limits are, and though within the area there is great variegation in kinds of assertion, a rough indication of the sort of discourse which we can call moral is possible: those assertions which concern the dispositions and conduct to be cultivated by individuals so that their and their neighbour's lives will benefit or at least not avoidably suffer – these would hold a pretty central place in this sphere of language. Next, some may complain on the other side: 'It is foolish to talk about religious language – there is Christian, there is Buddhist, there is Hindu – very different sorts.' True; and it is grossly mistaken for philosophers (as they have so frequently done) to pretend to discuss something called 'religion' when they have merely been speaking about Christianity or Judaism.[1]

Nevertheless, there is at least a family resemblance between religions, and phenomenologists of religion have not been utterly frustrated in their attempts to adduce similarities: thus one does not always have to speak with incurable particularity. And though in this essay I shall confine attention largely to examples drawn from Western religions, some of the remarks will have wider relevance. Finally – and this is the most powerful objection to my project – since both fields display much subtlety and variety, it would seem shockingly crude, in so short a space, to try to characterise the relations between the two. But I think that it does no harm to try to present a rather general picture, which can function as a kind of plan if one wishes to deal with individual and knotty problems in this area. Thus the intention of this paper is to provide certain preliminaries to the investigation in more detail of problems (e.g., those clustering about *grace* and analogous concepts) which arise at the boundary between ethics and the philosophy of religion. As such, I wish to give something like a *description* of the relation between religious and moral concepts: I shall not therefore be indulging in philosophical *arguments*. These, perhaps, come later.

My task requires the exposition of certain points about religion which I shall have to state somewhat dogmatically. To this I now proceed.

I

A striking aspect of spiritual discourse is its variegation. However hard it may be to translate into a foreign tongue common words for colours, shapes, objects, feelings, etc., the difficulty is small in comparison with that which besets attempts to give the meaning of key expressions occurring in the discourse of an alien faith. This is mainly because each religion has a doctrinal system – or *scheme*, a word I prefer because it is less rigour-suggesting – and the propositions thereof have, so to speak, a mutual effect, such that not merely does one have to understand a proposition by reference to its neighbours, but the comprehension of a key expression requires the exposition of a number of central propositions at least. But further, even within a faith, the language is far from homogeneous. For example, in Christianity certain assertions are made about a Creator God Who is, so to say, beyond or behind the visible world; while others concern a divine human being Who lived within the world. Again, some propositions in Buddhism concern nirvana, which is neither God nor man nor both. Already, therefore, we have three types of doctrinal proposition: those dealing with invisible and mysterious objects of worship, those concerning incarnate deities and those which deal with a mystical path and goal. These types of propositions (and it is sufficient for our purposes here to consider these three varieties) I propose to call respectively the *numinous*, the *incarnation* and the *mystical* strands of spiritual discourse.[2] And some doctrinal schemes are woven together from different strands and so are in a special way complex. But further, not all propositions in a strand are of the same logical sort: for example, those about nirvana are sometimes expressions of its joys, sometimes recommendations on how to attain it, and so forth.

An illustration of the weaving together of strands into a complex doctrinal scheme is to be found in Brahmanism. Here two disparate concepts are identified: Brahman, the Sacred Power lying behind the visible world, and the Atman or Self, lying within man and attainable through mystical endeavour. Again, in Christianity, Jesus, the sinless human Teacher, is identified with the Father in heaven. These points prompt such questions as: Why should the mystical goal and the object of worship be one? Why should a certain human be one with the Creator?

The first of these questions may be put in a sharper way by asking why the Christian mystic should consider his nirvana-like state to be union with God while the agnostic Buddhist does not, so to speak?[3] An account which covers both the similarity between some of the things said by Buddhists and by Christian contemplatives and between their doctrinal differences is this: that there are certain loose resemblances between the mystical state and the object of worship – both are timeless, glorious, transcendent, liberating and imperceptible.[4] Again an incarnate deity may have likenesses to the Creator – He has the power to save (by teaching and performatively through self-sacrifice); is miracle-working (a sign of omnipotence); is good – and so forth. The moral here is that the similarities justifying identifications in religion are looser than those criteria which would justify a mundane claim that A and B are identical (consequently, while there may be a case for asserting a given identity in religion, it is not absurd to deny it). And, briefly, a complex doctrinal scheme has a certain artistic composition, so to speak, which makes the disparate elements hang together.

This point is relevant to the way moral propositions are incorporated into the fabric of spiritual discourse. That is, moral discourse, in the context of religion, functions like one of the strands of specifically religious discourse mentioned above. Thus (i) the justification for integrating moral and religious discourse lies in a somewhat loose agreement between certain moral concepts and certain specifically religious ones, an agreement which I wish to illustrate here; and (ii) the moral strand and the others have, as do the latter reciprocally, an effect on each other: crudely, the moral attitudes of the religious man differ in flavour from those of the secular, while religion itself is moralised. It may be thought that the first of these points is hardly relevant to a descriptive project such as this; but it is often hard to penetrate to the meaning of an utterance without considering the sort of backing it would have. Actually, however, I shall be dealing not so much with the explicit justifications ordinary men might give for such claims as that morality in some sense presupposes religious doctrine,[5] as with the reasons why the integration has such convincingness as it may possess; though it is not to be thought that the considerations I shall describe have no place in explicit religious arguments. (Unfortunately, religious language itself is bedevilled in at least two ways: first, through having been mixed up with philosophical metaphysics, and secondly, because the logical status of religious concepts has been far from clear even to their employers – so that, for instance, certain spiritual doctrines have been inappropriately taken as straightforward empirical pronouncements.)

II

A central activity for one who is the adherent of a numinous faith is worship. For a God is by definition to be worshipped.[6] That is, the recognition of X as a God is a recognition that X is to be worshipped. An object of worship is holy and the adherent conversely unclean and sinful; and he expresses this profanity of his in awe-struck abasement, which is given ritual shape in formal worship. However, we discover that the notion of worship is considerably extended, so that the service of God in everyday life, through being virtuous and charitable, counts as a kind of worship. Thus it is written: Pure religion and undefiled before God and the Father is this, to visit the fatherless and widows in their affliction, and to keep himself unspotted from the world.[7] And in a somewhat similar vein: Take my life, and let it be Consecrated, Lord, to Thee; take my moments and my days, let them flow in ceaseless praise.[8] But this kind of worship can only count as such if there is worship in the primary sense (i.e., the religious ritual): otherwise we cannot know what it means to say that it is actions performed *in the right spirit* that count as worship. It may be objected that even if we had lost the notion and institution of ritual worship, there might still be a use for the word 'worship' – as in, for example, 'the worship of the State'. But the important example here is: suppose we still spoke of 'worshipping God', but all that would count as this would be visiting the fatherless, etc. It seems to me extremely doubtful whether we could understand this as a religious concept, nor could we easily comprehend the sense of the word 'God' as used here. It would doubtless have the same status as 'ether' in such locutions as 'The programme came over the ether' – a mere element in a stereotyped phrase: and so 'Visiting the fatherless is a way of worshipping God' would be equivalent in import to 'Visiting the fatherless is a way of doing good'. But it would hardly have the same sense as it would in a *serious* religious context.

But though the existence of formal worship would be a necessary condition for counting daily conduct seriously as a form of worship, it is hardly a sufficient one. What would make the extension of the concept plausible?

(i) In any case, the concept *worship* is extended within the sphere of the specifically religious, so that more than a public ritual perform- ance counts as worship. Private devotions of a certain pattern – these count as a kind of worship: it being seen that the so-called 'external' performances without proper humility before God are useless, even though this humility is taught in part *through* the rituals. But further, in a monotheistic faith, God is given the most exalted value, is infinitely to be praised – so that it is insufficient to worship Him on fixed occasions (more will be said below on this).

(ii) More vitally, humility is an important moral disposition, since the common tendency among humans towards pride is liable to issue in conflict and suffering, while conversely humility involves a compara- tively high prizing of others and so brings greater interest in their welfare. Personal abasement, then, before the All-Holy fits in with the disposition of humility which is important in moral conduct. The solidarity between the two is enhanced in monotheistic faiths by the above-mentioned infinite praiseworthiness of God. His utter transcendence is expressed by saying: We never sufficiently praise Him. But at least we can increase the quantity and intensity of our praise when daily actions performed in the right spirit count as worship. In speaking of 'quantity' and 'intensity' here I am formulating crudely two aspects of expressive speech. For in the non-expressive giving of plain information, for example, repetition only has a marginal use – to drum facts into the obtuse or hard of hearing, say; and intensity of manner and verbal expression has no obvious function here. On the other hand, in the expressing of gratitude, for instance, repetition and intensity do count for something: to repeat one's thanks is not otiose, and to say seriously and sincerely 'My *immense* gratitude' is to express more, *ceteris paribus*, than is done by 'My gratitude'. A further point: *sincerity* is what may be termed a 'pattern concept', for though it may be applied to particular actions the criteria for its application spread over a much wider area; and to say that an action is sincere is to imply (roughly) that it fits consistently into a pattern of actions. Consequently, once the notion of worship is extended to cover daily actions performed in the right spirit, the idea of intensity in worship is affected: fervent praise will not be thought to be truly so if it fails to fit into a pattern of worshipful behaviour.

The performance of duties and services in a humble spirit can, then, be presented as a form of worship. By consequence, moral blemishes and inadequacies are to be regarded not merely as failings, but as sins. The latter notion is, indeed, incomplete without reference to some numinous entity. Thus the Psalmist can say: 'Wash me throughly from mine iniquity, and cleanse me from my sin. For I acknowledge my transgressions; and my sin is ever before me. Against thee, thee only, have I sinned.'[9] Sin, then, is here moralised, inasmuch as it is not merely the uncleanness of a profane creature before the All-Holy, but covers his moral wickedness (and this becomes a sort of uncleanness). Both *worship* and *sin* are thus given extended scope, beyond their specifically religious applications.

Another example of the way in which religious concepts (in the numinous strand) and moral ones exhibit a certain solidarity is as follows. Sacrifice is a religious ritual which is fairly closely linked, for a number of reasons, with worship. But, like other rituals, it can become mechanical and indelicate; so that, by way of protest, it is said: 'The sacrifices of the Lord are a broken spirit.'[10] Here already there is a wide extension of the concept beyond its specifically religious use, leading to the notion that good conduct, or at least the dispositions leading thereto, are a kind of sacrifice. Now although sacrifices have often been offered to the gods in order to buy them off, much as one might give presents to the powerful to sweeten them, the deeper spiritual point of sacrifice is that it is a gesture of expiation, and the object sacrificed a token. (In speaking of a deeper spiritual point, I am aware that herein lies a value-judgement, and there are many objections to using valuations when one is engaged on a descriptive task; but the deeper point mentioned does exist, and it is not entirely unphilosophical to be charitable in matters of interpretation.) Sacrifice is a gesture of expiation, for words alone are not sufficient to express properly man's abasement before the numinous and the sincerity of his worship. This idea of something's 'going beyond mere words' is interesting to investigate, and is connected with what was said above about repetition and intensity. For whereas it might well be deemed absurd to speak of some factual matter as inexpressible, as eluding description – since language defines, so to speak, the realm of the possible[11] – when we come to expressive (and some other) modes of speech, it is by no means suspect. For here the notion of something's being 'too much to express' has a use, for already we are in an area where quantitative expressions have (in a peculiar way) application. Nor, since here speech is often in a narrower sense a way of doing something, is it absurd to speak of non-linguistic performances as transcending speech. Thus a gesture, for instance, is a manner of transcending language when there is, say, a felt necessity to render a situation morally tolerable. If A saves the life of B's child, B can only make the situation tolerable by performing a gesture as a pledge of his continuing and overwhelming gratitude: for instance, he can invite A's children on a long summer holiday. But what counts as an appropriate gesture is governed by the most delicate rules – many such gestures seem gross and unfeeling, as with the rich man who repays kindnesses by gifts of money.[12] Hence indeed the Psalmist's protest. For though by giving up a prized possession – a ram or a bullock – one performs a gesture of expiation, it may not be a good one. But a broken spirit? How is this a sacrifice? What plausibility is there in holding that a moral disposition counts as an expiatory gesture?

Nothing is a sacrifice unless something is being given up; and holy conduct is a sort of giving up for the following reasons: (i) There are many occasions on which the performance of duty conflicts with self-interest. Indeed, if it were not so there would hardly be a practical use for the word 'duty' and its cousins – a point which is probably responsible for the idea that nothing counts as a duty *unless* it so conflicts. (Though also this idea is in line with the ascetic outlook of Puritanism: on asceticism, see below.) And failing to attain one's interests is a sort of loss, even if not always of the sort we call 'tangible'. (One might draw a distinction between tangible and intangible sacrifices: and compare visible and invisible exports – the latter need not be 'ex-' and cannot be ported, but it is still useful to have the word.) (ii) Ascetic training – the giving up of certain pleasures – is sometimes thought to conduce to virtue, inasmuch as dispositions are created which facilitate the correct decision in the event of a conflict of interest and duty. Although asceticism plays a more prominent spiritual rôle in mystical rather than numinous religion, it has a part to play in the latter, both as a way of atoning for sins and as a method of directing our thoughts and inclinations away from the world towards the things of God. (iii) Self-indulgence, it is often thought, leads to unhappiness, both first- and second-order, i.e., the unhappiness directly occasioned by indulgence and that which accrues upon recognition of one's own wickedness and weakness. In such ways, then, moral conduct aimed at the production of others' and one's own happiness is considered to involve some degree of giving up. Thus is the path open for an extension of the notion of sacrifice so that a man's life or stream of conduct can count as a holy and living sacrifice to the Lord. And so he can do something to expiate his sinfulness and moral unworthiness. (Note that even in the quotation with which we started, which might be used out of context to show that religion is simply or mainly a matter of doing good, there is the requirement not merely that we should visit the fatherless and widows but also that we should 'keep ourselves unspotted from the world'.)

I have given two instances of the superimposition of religious upon other concepts. The effects are often subtle and difficult briefly to explicate. But one point worth mentioning is that, though there is an independent application for the notion of happiness, the major goal of life is thought to be salvation. (Here, by the way, the conflation of morality and numinous religion results in disputes about faith versus works as being necessary or sufficient or both conditions for salvation.) Further, specifically religious duties remain, so to speak, at the centre of life; and in themselves constitute the chief difference in content between secular and religious morality. Often, by consequence, a believer's path will diverge widely from that of the nonbeliever's – as when a man dies for his faith. Another effect is that since a supremely Holy entity is regarded as being the source, in some way, of all that is holy, holy conduct has as its source God, Who is held to grant grace to His devotees. And it is not just that God is supposed to have the power to release the worshipper from his religious uncleanness, but given that sin comprises moral unworthiness as well, He can give him grace to do good and avoid evil. (And it is a good indication of the difficulties besetting analysis of this notion that grace is connected with a numinous object of worship, whose status, so to speak, is already obscure.) Two further points. (i) The superimposition of religious upon moral concepts as illustrated above gives the latter a different flavour: (a) because a moral action will have a double significance (not mere kindness, but consecrated kindness; not mere self-control, but a sacrifice, etc.); (b) because the solemnity of moral utterances becomes considerably increased: it is not merely that murder is wrong, but that life is *sacred*; and a bad action is *sinful* and *impious*; discrimination against black folk in South Africa is not merely a great injustice, but it is (to quote a Churchman's recent pronouncement) *blasphemy*; marriage is more than a fine institution, it is a *sacrament*. (ii) The presentation of morality as part of numinous religion involves it in the conservatism of the latter (which is due to two main factors: first, the inexcogitability of revelation means that the ordinary man is discouraged from formulating his own beliefs and so must take doctrines on authority; and secondly, there are social causes for the entrenchment of religious organisations.) Hence, although there are ways and means of reforming the moral teaching of a faith in accordance with scientific, technical and social changes, there is much greater difficulty here than where moral beliefs are thought not to have divine sanction.

Finally, two general remarks on the preceding. First, it might be objected that when one 'does all to the glory of God' one is performing many actions which lie outside the area of morals – for instance, in doing one's daily work 'to the glory of God' one is not performing works of charity. Are not discussions of humility and asceticism beside the point here? A brief answer: roughly, we tend to regard the spirit of what we do (of whatever sort this is) as falling within the purview of moral judgement and training. Thus, we praise a man for playing a game fairly and enthusiastically, and this is a kind of moral praise: though the rules of the game could not be thought to be *moral* rules, and success in the game is not thought to be, in normal circumstances, morally praiseworthy.[13] Second, the foregoing illustrations of the extension of religious concepts should not lead one to suppose that the performance of duties, etc., in the right spirit is simply to be justified as being religious acts. The good is not good because it is the Will of God, but because it is good. On the other hand, the good is not the Will of God just because it is good, but because it has divine qualities. Much of the structure of independent moral discourse remains, even though morality is integrated with religion; just as much of the characteristic language of mysticism remains even when it is woven into discourse about God.

III

Because of its convenience and familiarity I shall use the Christian doctrine of the Incarnation to illustrate briefly the relation which this sort of belief bears to morality. (i) The doctrine involves a deepening of the points already made about humility and sacrifice. For the teaching here is that only the self-sacrifice of God could be enough to expiate the enormous weight of sin upon mankind and to bring about atonement.[14] But God could only achieve this in a state of solidarity with mankind: hence the obstinate rejection by the Church of any form of docetism – it must insist on the humanity of Christ as well as on His divinity. This seeming paradox that Christ is both God and man[15] brings new light to the religious demand for humility. Christ himself seems to exhibit the most profound humility; and He is, because divine (and uniquely so among humans) the central model for imitation. (ii) The abasement and suffering of Christ is on behalf of mankind: our most luminous evidence that God is Love (a point foreshadowed in doctrines of grace; and one which finds some, though ambiguous, backing in the claim that God is creator.) Hence there accrues a tighter knitting together of the moral demand 'Love thy neighbour as thyself' and the spiritual one 'Love God'. (iii) As mentioned above, the belief that a human is divine, and uniquely so, implies that there is one supreme life to model our conduct on (models are one main method of inculcating moral insight). This, incidentally, has both an advantage and a defect: for while it harnesses the resources of worship and meditation to the task of self-improvement, a single main model is likely to be hard to apply to the varied circumstances of many lives. Note also that the life to be imitated is a religious one (though the religion of Christ might be thought to differ in certain particulars from that expected of the ordinary adherent) and this serves to cement the moral and religious requirements in the faith. (iv) The Teacher founded a Church, membership of which is thought necessary or conducive to salvation: this creates special loyalties and obligations for the faithful. These are given supernatural expression in such notions as 'fellowship in Christ'. (v) Finally, certain concepts concerning Christ are given application to individual lives. Thus: 'Like as Christ was raised up from the dead by the glory of the Father, so we also should walk in newness of life'.[16] Christ's resurrection, though claimed to be a physical fact, has a significance beyond the marvel of man's rising from the dead. It is a demonstration that Christ has overcome death, though this is a peculiar sort of victory (and a peculiar sense of 'death'). For the victory is so described partly at least because Christ has saved mankind. But this saving is only hypothetical: if such-and-such conditions are fulfilled you will be saved (not: you are saved in any case). And one of the conditions is a change of heart: you must repent and believe. This conversion is a 'new birth'. What might at first glance appear a merely metaphorical use of a phrase can hardly be considered as such in view of the ramified nexus of analogical expressions connected with this one (the converted die unto sin; this also through grace, wherefore Christ is life – which is borne out, so it is said, in the spiritual life: for me to live is Christ.)[17] Again: 'And they that are Christians have crucified the flesh'.[18] The notion 'crucifixion of the flesh' is applicable to expiatory asceticism in virtue of the extension of the concept *sacrifice* as explicated above and of the history of the divine model's career.

In such ways, then, certain spiritual concepts prominently instantiated in Christ's life are applied also to individual lives.

Briefly, then, while the main point of Christ's career is his specifically religious rôle as Saviour of men, his words and conduct illustrate in a profound manner the way numinous religion and morality hang together.

IV

Mysticism is usually or always associated with some degree of ascetic training. Through such endeavour (known variously as 'the Path', 'the Way', etc.) one attains a blissful goal (in this life). The purest form of this goal – inasmuch as there is no theistic complication of doctrine – is the Buddhist aim of nirvana. This is given such epithets as 'The Other Shore', 'Peace', 'The Immortal', 'The Unshakeable', etc. For in gaining bliss we go beyond the impermanent and painful world, attain calm and detachment, lose the fear of death, etc. These epithets serve to indicate, perhaps, that there is (as claimed earlier) a pattern of loose resemblances between nirvana and an object of worship; but it is not of course a God. It is this principally that makes agnostic Buddhism so unlike Christianity, Judaism and Islam – the faiths we have the greatest acquaintance with in the West. And even the traditional gods of Indian religion are assigned the status merely of somewhat remarkable items in the furniture of the impermanent universe. These facts account for the disinclination felt by some to calling Buddhism a religion. Nevertheless, the mystical quest occurs also in theistic faiths, and there are certain other resemblances we can point to; and so we are justified in giving it the title of a spiritual system. There are two aspects of agnostic Buddhism which I wish to draw attention to, since they throw light on two general points about mystical religion.

First, the *anicca* doctrine, that all things are impermanent, is a mild form of those idealistic doctrines commonly associated with mysticism in which the world is declared to be unreal or not fully real.[19] At first sight, we might wish to dismiss such doctrines as being, metaphysics-wise, vacuous through lack of contrast (all life, surely, cannot be a dream, for the concept *dream* gains its force from the contrast of dreaming and waking). But such criticism would pass the mystic by, for there is, so to speak, an *inner* life which is real. The world is illusory or impermanent: but not the Atman, not nirvana. And a sense can be given to 'inner' here (whether or not a sense can be given to the rather different philosophical inner-outer distinction enshrined in such phrases as 'the external world'), because a method of training is laid down as conducive to spiritual well-being, and this involves the rejection of ordinary interests and pleasures: it is, roughly, this range of enjoyments that delimits the 'external world'. This mystical ascetic training has, incidentally, a likeness to the abnegation practised by worshippers to atone for their sins, and is peripherally one of the considerations making the identification of the numinous object with the mystical goal convincing. It may be mentioned also that a full-blown mystical idealism fits easily into the theistic picture: the inner state is outside the web of reality, and so is God – the one on the hither, the other on the farther side, so to speak; and this may help to explain the moderate idealism of early Buddhism, for indeed the extreme Mahayanist idealists paved the way for theistic forms of the faith. Briefly then, the idealistic beliefs function as a picture advertising the mystical quest. Normally, there-fore, since many moral issues concern the so-called outer world, a mystical faith will tend to pay little attention to these, and will be quietistic. On the other hand, this tendency is mitigated by three factors: (a) idealistic doctrines are not likely to affect the content of ordinary moral rules to any great degree, since practical affairs nearly all fall within the orbit of the illusory world, and there is no special reason to abandon ordinary moral distinctions within that sphere – any more than there is to abandon colour-contrasts. (And certain mystical theologians make a contrast between higher and lower knowledge: thus Śankara distinguishes between the two in a manner which corresponds with his distinction between the higher and lower Brahman – the former being without attributes (*nirgunam*), the latter with attributes (*sagunam*); the latter is the Lord and object of worship, and the performance of moral duties goes with the ceremo-nial worship, etc., due to Him: in such ways characteristically theistic doctrines and practices have a place even though 'in the highest truth' the world is illusory. (b) Belief in rebirth takes an edge off the rigorous demands of mystical religion, since the ordinary adherent who does not tread the monk's path can hope to raise himself in a future existence to within striking distance of the supreme spiritual goal. (c) It is generally considered that no-one can attain the goal who is not morally good: the cultivation of benevolent dispositions and others is part of the spiritual training. This indeed is the second aspect of agnostic Buddhism I wished to draw attention to: that moral training is built into the Noble Eightfold Path.[20] This is understand-able in two ways. First, the mystical goal is, after all, merely a very peculiar *summum bonum*: herein, it is claimed, lies the highest joy, and therefore the truly wise man will tread the Path. So a moral code containing a recommendation of this as the right aim would not differ in structure, one would expect, from that with more mundane goals: one aims at happiness (of whatever quality) in accordance with virtue. Secondly, the dispositions to be cultivated as morally import-ant are in line with the ascetic requirements of the mystic, though the latter involve more rigour (hence the difference in rules laid down for the layman and the *bhikkku* respectively in Buddhism). In addition, detachment from worldly interests is assisted by the cultivation of impartiality.[21] Finally, the picture of the saintly *arhat* who has at-tained nirvana is that of one who has undergone a transfiguration of character, and the calm and radiant peacefulness of such a man is presented as a glorious example to follow.[22]

V

The outline that I have given will, I hope, help to throw light on the peculiarities of such passages as the following (written by a theistic mystic):

> You must understand that, as Saint Gregory says, there are two ways of life in Holy Church through which Christians may reach salvation; one is called active and the other contemplative. One or the other of these is necessary to salvation. The active life consists in love and charity shown outwardly in good works, in obedience to God's Commandments, and performing the seven corporal and spiritual works of mercy for the benefit of our fellow-Christians . . . Another requirement of the active life is the disciplining of our bodies through fasting, vigils and other severe forms of penance. For the body must be chastised with discretion to atone for our past misdoings, to restrain its desires and inclinations to sin, and to render it obedient to obey the spirit. Provided that they are used with discretion, these practices, although active in form, greatly assist and dispose a person in the early stages of the spiritual life to approach the contemplative life.[23]

Gestures of atonement, the cultivation of good character and mystical asceticism can plausibly be thought to hang together. Probably it is the convincingness of the pattern of doctrine and moral teaching that would tend to justify those who loosely assert that morality presupposes religion, rather than any dry arguments about the objectivity of ethics or the evolution of conscience. In any case I hope to have given enough description to have shown (what is perhaps obvious) that an analysis of religious moral language requires an investigation of such concepts as *atonement, worship, sacrifice, sin, grace, holiness,* and so on: it is not just that religious people, while sharing principles, have different factual or metaphysical beliefs. There may, however, be those who would be indifferent to such investigations because of a prior rejection of religious beliefs. Yet these enquiries ought to have some interest even for them. For instance, if my cursory attempt at sketching some of the relations between spiritual and moral concepts is in any degree accurate, it may help to show the kind of absurdity which (on their view) characterises religious morality.

3 The Criteria of Religious Identity

I

Religious doctrines are often weird, though sometimes we fail to notice this, for familiarity banishes surprise. One of the stranger features of them is the manner in which on occasion one spiritual entity is identified with another. For instance, in the Christian creed three such entities are held to be one; in the Upaniṣads there is the doctrine that Brahman, the Reality behind the visible world, is identical with Atman or Self; while in Mahāyāna Buddhism we discover that all Buddhas are united in the *dharmakāya*, their Truth-Body which is the same as Absolute Reality (*tathatā*). At a more primitive level we find such assertions as this:

> They speak of Indra, Mitra, Varuna and Agni,
> Also of the heavenly fair-winged Garutman;
> In various ways they are referring to one Reality
> They speak of Agni, Yama and Mātariśvān.[1]

Also it is not uncommon for polytheists to identify foreign gods with their own. With these latter two types of identity-statements, however, I shall not be concerned here, since they are relatively easy to understand: the first kind is a consequence of the urge to be more systematic and ultimately to evolve a doctrine of one God rather than many, [2] while the second is straight-forwardly based upon similarities in mythology – some of which are due in any case to common descent; and these are similarities which obtain between entities of the same type. This kind of identity, incidentally, is exemplified in modern times by such claims as that Christians and Muslims really worship the same God. But one comment on these two kinds is opposite: that they also illustrate a feature of doctrinal thinking – to a search for identities where in other realms of discourse one might be

25

more inclined to seek classifications. It is, however, the other examples which are of more immediate interest and difficulty. My object is to describe the sort of grounds upon which they rest. But I do not propose to go on to the further question as to whether the sort of grounds described should be considered adequate.

II

I shall begin with the most familiar of the three examples mentioned above, namely the identification of Christ with the Father. Its oddness can be brought out as follows: (i) The location of Jesus during his life was Palestine, whereas the Father has always existed in heaven. Admittedly the latter is no ordinary place, but nevertheless it looks superficially as though the two Persons identified are in different places, and this would, in ordinary identity-statements about people, entail the falsity of the claim. (ii) Jesus possessed personal characteristics in a literal sense, whereas the Father only has them in an analogical sense (and, moreover, Jesus had physical properties). (iii) Jesus was in time, the Father not. And so on. It is true that Christ is held to be the Logos, to sit on the right hand of the Father in heaven, etc., and thus to possess other-worldly attributes. But these are not, so to speak, data upon which an identification could be based but rather are consequences of such an identification. The problem I wish to discuss is: What are the criteria of such identity-statements in religion? Clearly, Christ's supra-mundane position (in heaven) is not a ground for asserting that He and the Father are one, but rather, as I have said, a consequence (or part) of that claim.

The third example mentioned has some similarities to the Christian case. For a full explication of it, one must advert to the so-called *trikāya* doctrine, namely the doctrine that a Buddha possesses three bodies. First, a Buddha has his *nirmāṅ-akāya* or Transformation Body: this is the form in which he appears on earth – the most important instance being that of the historical Buddha Gautama.[3] In this form he works for the salvation of all creatures. The name of the Body is due to the belief that the eternal Buddha appears in an unreal physical form for the edification of mankind, this being part of his *upaya-kauśalya* or skilfulness in means (of leading men to salvation): thus the earthly appearance is a kind of magical transformation. But although the picture presented here of the historical Buddha is thoroughly infected with docetism, and although the Mahayanist theologians rejected the Hindu notion of *avatāra* or divine descent (i.e. incarnation), nevertheless there remain analogies between the Buddhist and Christian beliefs. From the logical point of view there remains the problem of determining the grounds upon which an historical figure is to be counted the Transformation Body of the eternal Buddha. Next, a Buddha possesses a *sambhoga-kāya* or Bliss Body, in which, for instance, he appears to assemblies of Bodhisattvas (Buddhas-to-be) and which is radiant and glorious. This celestial manifestation of the Supreme Buddha-hood assimilates the Buddhas to Hindu deities and provides the basis for worship of and devotion to a heavenly figure – such as Amitābha in the Pure Land sects. Third, there is the most important aspect of all: the *dharma-kāya* or Truth Body, which is identical for all Buddhas and is indeed the same as ultimate Reality (*tathatā*). This is called the support of the other Bodies and is in fact the fundamental spiritual entity in the world. The problem about identity, then, is how one could support the claim that certain human beings are in an intimate fashion manifestations of his *dharma-kāya*.

The third example I am going to consider is the more familiar one of the famous identification, in the *Upaniṣads*, of Brahman with the Atman. This is summed up in the text *Tattvamasi*, 'Thou art thou',[4] that is, that Brahman is identical with the Self[5]. Here Brahman on the one hand is that mysterious Power lying behind or within the visible world[6] and upon which the world depends,[7] while the Atman is the *antaḥ puruṣa* or inward person,[8] beyond that empirical self which has a name and ancestors: it is, that is to say, the inner spiritual entity. Now these dark pronouncements will require some illumination later. But already this much is clear, that the divine object of worship lying beyond the world is somehow identical with something lying within the individual; and so we get such seemingly self-contradictory assertions as this: Than whom there is naught else higher, than whom there is naught smaller, naught greater . . . .[9] And there is here also an apparent difference in location between the two entities asserted to be one. But whereas in the Christian case only one of the places is analogical, in this example both are.

These weird identifications, then, are the ones I am going to discuss, with the object of determining what criteria are used to make them. Since, however, these are rarely made explicit, what I say may seem misleading; but they nevertheless appear to be the inner grounds upon which the identity statements are asserted. I intend to discuss first the Brahman-Atman example as being in some ways the easiest, and then the Christian one. With the results thus obtained it may be possible to give an account of the Mahayana Buddhist example. Incidentally, I shall not discuss the Third Person of the Trinity when considering the Christian example, since the status of the Holy Spirit is rather obscure and I am most unsure as to what to say here.

III

(i) First, what is the nature of Brahman? The most important point about It is, I think, Its numinousness. This is clear from the meaning of the word, which can be rendered as 'sacred energy'. This was a concept applied to the power inherent in magic formulae in the Veda, and was then used more generally of the holy power which sustains the world. A consequence of Its being numinous is that It is to be treated with awe and circumspection, and indeed Brahman appears as an object of worship. This is evident in the more theistic *Upanisads*, such as the *Īśa, Katha* Śvetāśvatara.[10] Here there is a tendency to speak of Brahman in more personal terms, as the Lord (*Īśvara*), and it is characteristic of objects of worship to be described thus. The reason for the more impersonal accounts of Brahman elsewhere will later become apparent. Second, Brahman is the Imperishable, the Eternal Reality behind the shifting world about us. To attain Brahman is thus to gain immortality.[11] Third, Brahman is in some sense the cause of the world, since the world evolves out of Brahman.[12] These three points about Brahman may be linked together as follows.

A numinous entity is mysterious and hidden, for ever apart from the profane. Hence its description as the Other.[13] And thus, when the belief in a single *numen* is developed, the primitive arrangement whereby the holy or sacred object is literally screened from the gaze of the profane is extended cosmically, so that now the visible world itself is regarded as a screen concealing the divine Mystery. Thus the numinous acquires the status of the Reality behind appearances. Second, an entity's holiness is reflected in the sinfulness and profanity of the worshipper. These two points rather naturally generate a doctrine about the origin of the world. For first, the reality behind the phenomena is likely to exist when phenomena do not (and indeed in being Other is, unlike things we see, immutable), and consequently to be the sole candidate for being the cause of the visible world's having arisen in the first place; and second, abasement felt by the profane when confronted by the holy is well expressed by the notion of dependence on the latter. We need not then be surprised at the type of answer given to that awful question: 'Why does anything exist at all?' Similarly, since the object of awe and worship lies beyond phenomena it is timeless, immortal; and the more so because the worshipper wishes to reduce the width of the gap between himself and the divine: for in coming close to the Holy One he overcomes his fears and thereby attains deathlessness. Thus Brahman corresponds in large measure to the one object of worship with which we are familiar in the Judaic religions. But this point requires qualification in that, as we shall see, there is another important element in Brahmanism which affects the way Brahman is described: the concept Brahman is woven together, so to speak, out of concepts in different strands of religious discourse, since It is identified with the Atman, which in origin has a very different flavour. And the conflation of the concepts of two strands involves the modification of each.

(ii) What is the nature of the Atman? First, as I have said, it is the *antaḥ puruṣa*, the inward person beyond even the empirical self. This might be a hard saying and it would be easy to dismiss it as sounding like confused metaphysics – and especially so when it is noticed that Indian theologians from the earliest times have on occasion argued for its existence on philosophical grounds that would not appear convincing, namely that there is a metaphysical subject beyond anything that can be introspected in the ordinary way, since when I know myself the first I is itself unknown. But the Atman is essentially a spiritual concept and we must view it in its proper setting, just as we must view the concept God in its proper setting and not in its unfortunate appearances in conclusions of metaphysical arguments. Now the main setting for the notion of the Atman or Self is that of mysticism. By 'mysticism' here I mean something more precise than is often meant: namely, a method of achieving an inner spiritual goal. On this usage, St. John of the Cross, Eckhart, Gotama Buddha and countless Indian yogis would count as typical examples of mystics, for they have practised a certain sort of physical and mental training during their lives, and the treading of this path has brought them to an inner attainment. There is, of course, obscurity in the word 'inner' here; but its meaning will later become clearer.

Now the goal which the mystics attain is, putting it roughly, a state of bliss; and this is:

Not that which knows external objects, not that which knows internal objects, not that which knows both sorts, not a mass of cognition, not cognitive. It is unseen, incapable of being spoken of, without any distinctive marks, unthinkable, unnameable, the essence of the knowledge of the one Self, that into which the world is resolved, the peaceful, the auspicious, the non-dual . . . .[14]

By this is meant: in the mystical state one neither perceives objects around one nor does one visualise any such objects ('internal objects' here are, in our jargon, mental images). Hence also it is said to be unseen. Its unthinkability arises from the fact that in mystical meditation one does not think (i.e. cogitate or day-dream) and also from its ineffability. The latter springs from two causes, first its indescribability (i.e. it is not describable the way a dream or a perceptual experience is describable), and second its utter exaltation (it is unspeakable the way gratitude and joy are sometimes unspeakable). And it is non-dual because here there is – to put it in an old-fashioned way, no distinction of subject and object. That is to say, it is not a sort of observation (where you are aware of being in one spot seeing something which is a distinct entity from yourself). (It is true that mystics sometimes speak of seeing God or Brahman; but this is, briefly, a concession to the mixed nature of their doctrinal systems, for a numinous entity is separated from the worshipper. And, of course, it is no ordinary seeing.)

It is now possible to see why this experience of the Self generates a doctrine that this Self is beyond the empirical self. For the mystical state lies outside all *ordinary* experience (the flow of which constitutes the empirical self): it lies beyond mere seeing or touching or imagining or feeling angry and pleased. The contrast between the Atman and the person does not wither away through the Atman's being beyond all experience whatsoever; just as the idealism commonly associated with mysticism does not wither away though there being nothing to contrast the unreal or impermanent world with: all life is a dream – all life, that is, save the spiritual life. In this respect, spiritual idealism differs from its philosophical counterpart. Again, we can see why the Atman is held to be *within*. For first, the search to realise the Atman involves a mystical discipline which leads one away from interest in the world about one and more particularly which has as its core meditative practices wherein one banishes unwanted perceptions, visualisations, cogitations, etc., thereby attaining the right spiritual voidness of mind. A second reason for the picture of the Atman as lying within is that in the mystical experience there is ineffable bliss. Now joy, bliss, remorse, etc., are often in common parlance said to be within one, because (a) such an experience belongs to the experiencer thereof in a way it can belong to no-one else; (b) behaviour, though it reveals feelings, also masks them (hence the model of their lying beyond the surface of the organism); (c) they could not in any intelligible sense be said to lie *outside* the organism. And also, of course, in some cases the having of certain feelings is accompanied by our being aware of events happening which occur *literally* inside (heartbeats, etc.). But it must be noted that the interiorness of the Atman is deeper than that of mere joy, since it lies beyond, as we have said, certain events like visualisations which are also pictured as occurring within.

Further, it must be added that (a) the mystical experience is timeless: hence such peculiar utterances as Vaughan's 'I saw Eternity the other night'.[15] It is timeless because there is in the mystical state no awareness of time passing (how, under the circumstances, could there be?), and it has, so to speak, its own time-scale as dreams too have their own. Moreover, the surpassing peace attained banishes all fear of mortality. One has arrived at the immortal.[16] And (b) the effect of the divine vision is an establishment of holiness and purity of character; and the behaviour of the mystic betrays a strange power and other-worldliness.

(iii) Now we are in a better position to answer the main question, viz., What plausibility is there in the famous identification of Brahman and Atman? Why should it be asserted that

> This is my Self within the heart, smaller than a grain of rice, smaller than a barley corn, than a mustard seed, than a grain of millet or than the kernel of a grain of millet. This is my Self within the heart, greater than the earth, greater than the atmosphere, greater than the sky, greater than these worlds. Containing all works, containing all desires, containing all odours, containing all tastes, encompassing the whole world, without speech, without concern, this is the Self of mine within the heart; this is Brahman?[17]

First, we must point to some general facts about spiritual discourse. It appears to be the case that systems of doctrine[18] arise from different strands of discourse and in some cases are woven together out of these strands. Thus, propositions about a God are generated out of the numinous strand, that is, that segment of religious language

which expressed awe and abasement before the intimations of divinity in the world, language which has its central place in the activity
of worship: the doctrines of early Islam are very largely drawn from
this strand, for example. On the other hand, propositions about the
attainment of nirvana, about release, about inner bliss, are expressive of mysticism, the practice of which is rather a different sort of
spiritual activity from that of worship: Hinayana Buddhist doctrines,
for example, are drawn largely from this strand, and the numinous
belief in a God is absent. In some cases it turns out – as in the
Brahman-Atman instance – that a doctrinal scheme contains strong
elements of both strands, woven together. Similarly, the logical bases
of propositions about an incarnate deity are different from those
about a transcendent God, and so we have a third strand. (This way
of presenting doctrinal schemes is, of course, very crude and highly
schematic, but it can be used, I think, to throw a little light on their
structure.) A second general point about religious discourse is this:
because it tends to possess a capacity appropriate to the numinous,
because one of its chief functions is expression and thus must be
loosely moulded to fit the expressive utterance of diverse people,
because there is an intrusive ineffability in religion, and because
many key religious expressions are used in an analogical rather than a
literal sense,[19] spiritual discourse tends to be somewhat imprecise.
This imprecision and analogicality allows of an interweaving between
different strands of discourse which would be merely absurd in
precise discourse. For on the one hand, imprecision obviously leaves
room for manoeuvre, and on the other the analogical use of expressions mitigates the paradoxes which we discover and which are consequences of the interweaving of the initially disparate.

The paradox, for instance, that Brahman is both far and near,[20]
that it lies beyond the visible world and yet within the person. How
do we justify this saying? Our general remarks above merely prepare
the ground, but give no positive reason for the identity-statement.

There exist, however, certain similarities between Brahman and
the Self. (a) Both are unseen, imperceptible, veiled: and indeed the
picture often generated by the mystical goal, of the world as insub-
stantial and unreal in comparison with the deathlessness within, fits in
also with the model of the divine lying the other side of the visible
world. Moreover, to gain the mystical bliss is like travelling to the
other shore, crossing over, going beyond (to use a simile popular in
Buddhism[21]). Thus both Brahman and the Atman are 'outside'
phenomena. (b) Brahman is immortal and unshifting; while similarly

the mystical experience is timeless and a release from the bonds of mortality. (c) Brahman is holy; but also the mystic's character is (albeit in a secondary sense) holy and it is pure – the attainment of release is regarded often as the source of this unshakeable power of character; and thus the mystical state is like the divine in being a source of holiness and salvation (for in the worshipper's religion the object of worship is not only holy but the source of holiness: hence doctrines of grace – for any other ascription of the capacity to uplift the sinner would be presumptuous). (d) Brahman has supreme mystery-value, is, in being the supreme numinous entity, utterly glorious; so too the mystical goal overwhelms the saint in its fulness, and is only palely conveyed by the words *summum bonum*. (e) Connectedly, both Brahman and the realisation of the Atman are ineffable in some degree (Brahman, since one can never fully express the wonder to be displayed before a Supreme Being and can never adequately express the praise due, the Atman, since the mystical experience is both void of content, so to speak, and unutterably eirenic). Briefly, then, both are imperceptible, transcendent, timeless, liberating, supreme and ineffable. These provide the justifications for weaving together the two concepts (though I do not wish to suggest that having these points explicitly in mind led spiritual teachers such as Yajnavalkya to formulate the identity; and indeed most often such points as I have made can only be made *ex post dicto* – here the critic of spiritual doctrines and the theologian are in some measure parasites upon revelation).

The effect of the identification can be described as follows. (i) The concept of deity is a good deal more impersonal than it would be in a doctrinal scheme built largely round the numinous strand. Thus in Sankara's interpretation of Brahmanism a distinction is made between the *nirguṇam* and the *saguṇam* Brahman, Brahman, that is, without and with attributes. The latter corresponds to the Creator in Judaic religions and is similarly described in personal terms, as having a will, as being omnipotent, etc., and as having created the visible world. But the former is largely ineffable and is without those attributes ascribed to the *saguṇam* Brahman – *Īśvara* or Lord. According to Śankara, the impersonal Absolute is prior, and the Lord is infected, as in the world, by illusion. The picture of God as *Īśvara* is not the highest truth. For this distinction compare the similar one made by Eckhart between Godhead and God (*Deitas* and *Deus*).[22] We may note that the mystical aspect of Brahman is described very much ontologically (for ontological terms play a central part in much mystical discourse).[23] (ii) The creation of the world is less 'contingent' in the Upaniṣads than it is in the monotheistic religions of the West, where the existence of the world is due to a clear-cut divine decision controlled by a general purpose. The impression of necessity, of logical evolution, in cosmic events is more characteristic of the mystically-minded.[24] (iii) As the divine becomes more like the mystical entity, so the Self becomes more divine: thus, the Atman is regarded as the World Soul. So much then for the first example.

IV

This next example is a harder one, for many of the statements about Christ which appear inconsistent with statements about the Father, with Whom He is held to be one, are not analogical.

First, some remarks on what I term the incarnation strand of spiritual discourse. An incarnate deity is in some respects merely a limiting case of the saintly prophet: that is, he possesses in a preeminent degree two gifts found in lesser degree elsewhere, namely (i) that holiness we expect to see in the saint's life; and (ii) the spiritual wisdom with which the prophet or religious teacher is endowed. Regarding the former, it tends to include not merely strength and depth of character born of religious experience, but also marvellous powers associated therewith, the capacity to work miracles. However, these characteristics are hardly sufficient by themselves to establish a claim to be identical with God; at any rate where the requirements for such an identification are at all stringent. For, of course, religions vary in the number of incarnations which they allow. In Mahayana Buddhism as we have seen there are many Buddhas and in Vaisnavite Hinduism there are many *avatāras* of Visnu; while Christianity cleaves fast to the principle that there should be but one such incarnation. This principle may be defended on the grounds of simplicity and propriety – for on the one hand, though the doctrinal scheme containing the incarnation strand is more complex than that which is strictly unitarian, like Islam, the case of a unique incarnation is, so to speak, the spiritually most elegant; while on the other hand, the wrench that has to be made in allowing that anyone of human form should be one with the Supreme Being causes less offence at the seeming blasphemy if but one incarnation is allowed. However, it is not in place here to press any defence or attack on the principle; but to point out the consequences flowing from its application. Briefly, they amount to this: that the emphasis placed upon one human being's life requires that very special attention be paid to the historical circumstances of that career. To this we shall return after making a further preliminary point.

One of the principles of spiritual reasoning (if we may call it such), is that, as we have mentioned in another connection, saving power flows from the divine (for it is a fitting expression of the wonder and marvellousness of That which is numinous to ascribe thereto the power to release the worshipper from his reflected sinfulness). Now, it would not seem unlikely that a candidate for divinity[25] should also have to possess this power. This can be displayed in two main ways – first, by saving teaching (together with conduct illustrating that teaching) – as in the case of Christ as in the exemplarist interpretation of, say, Abelard; or more mysteriously, for instance, through providing an adequate expiation for the sins of mankind (as according to the so-called 'objective' theory of Anselm).[26] And this latter inasmuch as the appropriate response on the part of sinful man to the holiness of the divine is abasement and contrition. Now the expression of such abasement linguistically (as also often with, say, gratitude) appears most inadequate: more is required, namely a gesture. Nevertheless the supreme exaltedness of the Godhead in a monotheistic and morally conditioned faith[27] is such that even although the concept of expiatory gestures is extended to daily conduct, so that: The sacrifices of God are a broken spirit . . . Then shalt Thou be pleased with the sacrifices of righteousness, with burnt offering and whole burnt offering.[28] Yet the enormous yawning gap between the divine and the human remains intolerable, despite these gestures. On the Christian view the gap can only be closed by God: only He can perform a sufficient gesture – through His sacrificing Himself (again, in an extended sense of 'sacrifice'). But of course a gesture is of no value for the human race unless it is made on its behalf: unless the performer thereof is identified with the human race. Hence the point upon which Christianity is centrally based: the gap between God and man can only be made tolerable for man by an adequate sacrifice, and this can only be performed by God in a state of solidarity with man. This, it is held, is done by Christ, being both God and man, in his self-sacrifice on the Cross.

But this raises the point that the saving of mankind (i.e. making the gap tolerable and providing the possibility of salvation for those who have faith in Christ) can only be thought plausibly to have occurred at a suitable juncture of history, and it is mainly hence that springs the importance of the historical facts both of the incarnate human's career and of the previous setting thereof. Do they present a convincing pattern?

We may now sum up the grounds for counting Christ as identical with the Father.

To be divine (if this is allowed about any human) the candidate ought to be similar to the Creator in certain respects and can be so in the following ways. (i) In being morally pure and so sinless, unlike the ordinary worshipper; (ii) in displaying power of character and the capacity to perform miracles: these are intimations of omnipotence (a special case is the Resurrection, which as well as being supremely wondrous, also has a doctrinal setting as being a demonstration that man is freed from death); (iii) in possessing deep spiritual knowledge and the power to convey this: here are intimations of omniscience; (iv) in having the power to save, first as under (iii) through the teaching and the conduct illuminating it, but second performatively, for instance in constituting an adequate expiatory sacrifice which will make the gap between man and God tolerable. It is to be noted too that all these points must be fitted together into a convincing pattern of divine conduct set in an appropriate historical environment.

The consequences of the identification are that Christ is now considered the Logos and so having creative powers; and as sitting on the right hand of the Father and so dwelling in that divine place beyond the world that well expresses the otherness of the numinous. But the Father's nature too undergoes a change, so to speak: it is seen that God is Love.

V

In the Buddhist examples we meet elements which we have already examined. First, the historical Buddha possesses some of the marks of an incarnate deity (though it may be mentioned that in the Pali Canon, where there is of course no *trikāya* doctrine, since the Theravada, like early Buddhism, is agnostic – there is little distinction between the *arhat* or saint (one who achieves *nibbāna*) and the Buddha, except that the latter is the originator of the Path).[29] (i) Gautama was possessed of something close to omniscience;[30] (ii) he was free from error and full of compassion (*karuṇā*) – thus being morally perfect;[31] (iii) he taught men the road to salvation and founded an order and so is in one respect (though not performatively) a saviour;[32] (iv) he had wondrous powers.[33] So in these respects he has affinities with a numinous being beyond the world. However, even in Mahayana the numinous other-worldly beings have a restricted function, for in Buddhism there is no ordinary doctrine of creation. For the question whether the world was eternal or not (i.e. whether it was created or not) was pronounced by the Buddha to be an undetermined question.[34] On the other hand, there was a doctrine of a sort of evolution of phenomena from an original Reality: for instance, the latter is described (by the *Vijñānavādin* school) as the *ālaya-vijñāna* or store-consciousness, for the world is nothing but mind (*cittamātra*). But an apparent world arises through transformation of this original consciousness into individual minds, a move which causes individuals to conceive of the external world as really existing.[35] However, the more obviously numinous entities in the Mahayana are such Buddhas as Amitabha and such Bodhisattvas as Avalokitesvara. Amitabha, for instance, is the object of worship and devotion for countless adherents, and dwells in another world, his famous Pure Land in the West which gave its name to the Pure Land sects. This land was in effect created by him, being his *Buddhakṣetra* or Buddha-field – it is being a belief that Buddhas are capable of such creative activity[36] (it is of course limited, in that no Buddha created the whole universe). Hence, the weaving together of the concept appearing in his *nirmāṇa-kāya* upon earth with that of a celestial lord to be addressed with words of praise and petition is not dissimilar to that occurring in the Christian example – with two modifications: (i) the capacity to save performatively is reserved, for historical reasons, for the *Bodhisattvas*, who by putting off their *nirvāṇa* use the merit acquired hitherto in coming close to this final tranquility to raise up the sinners who have no merit (thus we have the story in the Lotus Sutra of the famous Bodhisattva Avalokitesvara who undergoes the direst afflictions and the most strenuous labours and who uses the merit so acquired on behalf of others out of deep compassion for them: he is a divine example of compassion and humility for the edification of the faithful); (ii) there are countless Buddhas, so far as the *sambhoga-kāya* and the *nirmāṇa-kāya* are concerned – though they are ultimately all one in their *dharma-kāya*. And this last point reminds us that the *dharma-kāya* or Absolute is held to be the ultimate basis for the other two bodies. This is very similar in part to the two-aspect doctrine of Śankara. For the personal deity is held to be posterior to the impersonal Absolute lying behind. This expresses in effect two things, first that the blending of mystical and numinous discourse is not perfect (how indeed could it be expected to be?), so that the more anthropomorphic characteristics of the Godhead may be detached, so to speak, and regarded as a separate aspect thereof. And second, it expresses a priority decision, that in substance one kind of spiritual activity is superior to another, that the mystical path is more important than worship. Compare with this the rather different arrangement in the *Bhagavad-Gītā*, where attaining Brahman is coming close to God, but yet remaining apart from him.[37] And indeed it is this priority decision as expressed doctrinally that allows the most extravagantly evangelistic forms of Buddhism, such as the Amida-Buddhism of the Judo sect, to stay within the fold. For even if the *sambhoga-kāya* of Amida Buddha is regarded in certain sects as revealing something essential to the Buddha-nature, yet the idealistic and mystical structure of doctrine remains.

But it needs to be pointed out that the doctrine of an Absolute, as we saw in the Brahman-Atman example, is not a purely mystical one: it is already some of the distance towards a numinous doctrine; and it is by no means fortuitous that the evolution of Buddhist idealism by the Madhyamika and Yogacara Schools coincided with the revulsion of ordinary adherents away from the pure and austerely mystical teachings of the early religion. For it paved the way, through the notion of an eternal, unchangeable, pure, all-pervading, undifferentiated reality, for the appending thereto the concept of personal beings whom one could worship and to whom one might pray – a concept spun forth from the intimations of the numinous among ordinary folk. For the properties ascribed to the *dharma-kāya* are reminiscent of those ascribed to numinous entities: Buddhas also are immortal, unchanging, pure and beyond our immediate range of vision. And there is the further point that the non-dual nature of the mystical experience leads to language such as this: that one becomes Brahman, one is united with God, etc.; so the Buddhas through their Enlightenment become the *Dharma-kāya*. Also, of course, in so becoming they lose their individuality – all Buddhas are in reality but one.[38]

VI

It is, however, clear that though there are grounds for the sort of identity-statements we have been here considering, there remain conflicts nevertheless. For first, differing strands of discourse, having different flavours and different epistemological bases, are being woven together; and each possesses unaccommodated segments. For example, though it is appropriate to worship Christ since it is appropriate to worship the Father, and though Christ too is Creator of the world, not all propositions are such that references to the Father may be indifferently replaced by references to the Son. Thus there is a continual element of paradox in such complex doctrinal schemes. Second, there is a specific spiritual conflict between the numinous and the mystical strand, which can be illustrated as follows: the mystical goal is non-dual – the mystic would wish if allowed to say that he become united with God or Allah or Brahman, since he has been in a state where there is no distinction between subject and object.[39] But on the other hand dualism between God and man is of the very essence of numinous discourse. It is the Other that we worship. God is pure where man is sinful, exalted where he is abased, immortal, invisible. Consequently, the history of mysticism within the theistic religions has not always been happy; and there have been serious conflicts, especially in the Christian Church, between mystics such as Eckhart and the upholders of orthodoxy. Moreover, the immediate vision vouchsafed to the mystic tends to persuade him that he has found the highest truth lying beyond doctrinal formulae and so to ride loosely by the revealed truths that have had conferred upon them some of the sacred immutability of their Author. Third, there is some conflict between the numinous and incarnation strands since it does not seem to everyone in consonance with the terrible majesty of the Supreme Being that any human should be identical with him. It is *prima facie* a great blasphemy.

Finally, there is the general point that the identifications depend upon perceiving certain similarities; but these similarities would not, it seems, be sufficient in another sort of context to justify identity statements. The weaving together of concepts is undoubtedly loose, though sometimes the pattern produced seems to fit nicely. But whether the identifications are allowable or not is a hard question. We may say that certain doctrinal pictures have a good composition and we may back our judgement by pointing to anologies between parts that make them hang together and may appeal to certain spiritual principles here and there. Even so, some may think that doctrinal schemes are over-poetical. Are we to be like those who declare that no bullfinch is purple, let alone in a lilac-tree? Or are we to follow Aristotle in reckoning it to be the mark of an educated man to seek that degree of precision which the subject-matter allows?

4 Numen, Nirvana, and the Definition of Religion

Despite Rudolf Otto's remarkable contributions to the philosophy and comparative study of religion, there is a defect in his treatment of spiritual experience – namely, his relative neglect of, and partial misinterpretation of, Buddhist nirvana.[1] This hinders a fully satisfactory analysis of mysticism and militates against a correct description of the nature of religion. What I wish to show here is, briefly, as follows. Given Otto's analysis of his own illuminating expression 'numinous', nirvana is not, strictly speaking, numinous; but nirvana is the key concept of (at least Lesser Vehicle) Buddhist doctrine and practice; hence it is unsatisfactory to define religion by reference to the numinous or analogous notions. Further, however, by appeal to the idea of 'family resemblance', we can avoid the embarrassment we might feel at not discovering some essence of all religion. Finally I attempt to indicate how a sharp differentiation between agnostic mysticism and theism (together with pantheism and other forms of characteristically numinous religion) can lead to new insights into the structure of religious doctrine and experience.

I

Let us first examine one of Otto's rare and scattered remarks about nirvana: 'It exercises a "fascination" by which its votaries are as much carried away as are the Hindu or the Christian by the corresponding objects of their worship'.[2] It is surely clear that the use of the expression 'votaries' and the implication contained in the phrase 'corresponding objects of worship' accord *nirvana* a status it never possessed in Theravada Buddhism and almost certainly did not explicitly possess in the earliest form of the religion.[3] Gods and god-like entities can have votaries and be objects of worship: but the serenity of *nirvana* is no god, nor is it even the peace of God. It is interesting to note that Otto writes, in his foreward to *Mysticism East and West*, that we must combat the

> erroneous assumption that mysticism is 'one and ever the same'. Only thus is it possible to comprehend such great spiritual phenomena as, for instance, the German Meister Eckhart, the Indian Śankara, the Greek Plotinus, the mystics of the Buddhist Mahayana school, in all their characteristic individuality, instead of allowing them to disappear into the shadowy night of 'general mysticism'. The nature of mysticism only becomes clear in the fullness of its possible manifestations.[4]

The Hinayana is left out, even though it has produced such a striking handbook of mystical meditation as the *Visuddhimagga* and despite the accounts of the Buddha's Enlightenment. Further, Hinayana mysticism exhibits a greater divagation from theistic mysticism than does even the soul-mysticism of Yoga and Jainism.

Before listing rather briefly a few reasons for denying that nirvana, is, in the strict sense, numinous, it is perhaps as well to counter the criticism of unfairness: 'Surely we owe the term "numinous" to Otto, and if he uses it of nirvana, are we not to say that he knows best?' But once a term is introduced it becomes public property: I am not arguing against the use of 'numinous', for Otto's coining has been of great service – it is only that on certain occasions he is loose or inconsistent in his employment of it.

(i) The elements in the numinous discriminated by Otto are, it will be recalled, those of awefulness, overpoweringness, energy, and 'fascination'. Now these certainly depict admirably objects of worship, such as gods and God. To some extent also they define many ghostly and 'spooky' phenomena which Otto uses as examples. But a state such as nirvana hardly possesses all these characteristics: only, perhaps, 'fascination'. Now it may be replied that each of the elements should be regarded rather as a mark; that is to say, each by itself tends to or would establish the numinousness of whatever possesses it. But apart from the undesirable looseness that this interpretation would confer upon the term, Otto analysed the numinous in the way that he did because all the elements are usually or always found in genuine objects of worship.

(ii) Experiences cannot easily be understood in isolation, but are best seen in their whole setting – in the attitude and behaviour which surround them; in particular, religious experience must be viewed in the context of the spiritual practices associated with it or expressing it. Thus characteristically experiences of awe, of an overpowering and energetic presence, are associated with and expressed by such activities as worship and sacrifice. Now altogether it is true that the mystical Path towards some inner realisation as we find it in the Christian setting is integrated with activities such as the worship of and prayer to a personal God, in the Lesser Vehicle there is not merely formal agnosticism, but the religion of sacrifice and worship associated with a divine Being or beings is ignored as being irrelevant to salvation. Moreover, such attention as is paid to numinous entities such as *nats* and *devas* is merely peripheral, springing from non-Buddhist sources; while the veneration of relics such as the Sacred Tooth is moderated severely by the denial of Gotama's divinity.[5]

(iii) Otto, in criticising the subjectivism of Schleiermacher's account of creature-feeling, remarked: 'The numinous . . . is felt as objective and outside the self.'[6] This indeed is a correct description of how a *numen praesens* strikes the religious man; note that not merely is the *numen* in some way 'objective', but there is even a dualism continually being expressed in religious language between the worshipper and the object of awe. But nirvana could hardly be counted a *numen praesens*; and it is only in a rather peculiar sense 'outside the self'. Admittedly we here run into complications, on account both of the fact that in certain spiritual contexts there is the notion of a Self set over against the 'empirical self' and of the peculiarly Buddhist *anattā* (non-self) doctrine. But first, the *numen praesens* is usually thought of as nearby in some spatial or quasi-spatial way. And second, even those who would interpret nirvana as a kind of beatified persistence beyond death[7] not unlike Christian immortality (though without God there) give an account inconsistent with nirvana's being conceived as an object of worship. Also, whatever may be said – and quite a lot can be – in defence of the notion of mystical experience as 'other' than ordinary experience (thus generating the concept of an 'other' Self, etc., realisable through mystical endeavour, as in some of the *Upaniṣads*), quite clearly there is a difference between the sense in which the Atman is 'beyond' the empirical self and that in which God is 'beyond' the visible world and so is that mysterious Other. The difference is indicated by that tension which we find in theistic mysticism and which was well expressed by Rabindranath Tagore when he said: 'What we want is to worship God. But if the worshipper and the Object of Worship are one, how can there be any worship?' Nevertheless, despite the difference, it is the genius of certain religions to fuse together different insights into a single doctrinal scheme – so that, for example, realising the Atman is becoming Brahman and that the cloud of unknowing is the dwelling-place of that God who appeared in a very different sort of cloud to Job: this commingling of strands of religious language, experience, and practice (for the three go together) will be further considered below.

(iv) Nirvana, however, is given certain epithets which might lead one to think of it as something like Ultimate Reality – and this in turn is sometimes an impersonal way of describing God.[8] And hence we get such statements as this: '*Nirvana . . .* is not stated in such a way that it can be identified with God, but it may be said to be feeling after an expression of the same truth'.[9] Thus *nirvana* is called 'death-less' (*amata*), 'unconditioned' (*asankhata*), 'permanent' (*nicca, dhuva*), etc. Now even if these epithets may be held to assimilate nirvana in some degree, though certainly in a loose manner, to God, they reveal themselves upon inspection to be typically applicable to a mystical state in this life just as much as to a genuinely transcendent Being. Thus nirvana is *amata* because it is (to quote another epithet) *akutobhaya*, 'with nothing to fear from anywhere', for in attaining it in this life one loses the fear of death – and not merely because of the doctrine that there will then be no rebirth hereafter,[10] but through the great peacefulness and serenity of it. And also it is *amata* because the mystical experience at its highest level is, in being without perceptions, likewise without time.[11] Again, it is permanent partly at least by contrast with the world of compound things, which are transitory and fleeting: for though early Buddhism denied the soul or *ātman*, the distinction between the spiritual state and the world of ordinary experience is, naturally enough, retained. Similarly with 'unconditioned'.[12] And nirvana transcends the impermanent world by being, so to speak, other-worldly – an otherworldliness defined by the training laid down in the Noble Eightfold Path, and because it is *yogakkhema anuttara*, 'unsurpassed peace', of transcendent value. That is to say, then, the epithets are understandably applicable even to nirvana in this existence,[13] without our bringing in that final nirvana accruing upon death and negatively expressed by saying that there is no rebirth.

(v) Otto elsewhere says: 'The salvation sought in nirvana, like that sought in Yoga, is magical and numinous. It is the utterly supra-rational, of which only silence can speak. It is a blessedness which fascinates. It is only to be achieved by way of negation — the inexpressible wonder.'[14] Here, to put it briefly, Otto's main ground for declaring nirvana to be numinous is that it is utterly non-rational. But that a thing is non-rational does not entail that it is numinous, though the converse may perhaps hold. Otto elsewhere gives an account of what he means by 'non-rational': while on the one hand we may experience deep joy, which on introspection can be 'identified in precise conceptual terms', it is otherwise with religious 'bliss': not even the most concentrated attention can elucidate the object to which it refers – it is purely a felt experience, only to be indicated symbolically.[15] But it is perhaps odd to say that in all non-religious contexts we can if pressed express our feelings 'in precise conceptual terms'. Nevertheless, there are certainly occasions upon which we can say why we are overjoyed, etc., and this clearly has something to do with 'the object to which the state of mind refers'. This under-standing, however, is impossible with regard to a genuine mystical state for a different reason from that which makes it impossible with regard to a feeling of 'bliss' at the fascination of the numinous. For a feeling of supreme exaltation in the context of worship or worship-ping meditation is connected with God: for God is that at which, so to speak, attention is directed; and God is mysterious and overwhelm-ing and so not to be described adequately. On the other hand, in agnostic mysticism (and we find analogies in all mysticism) the state of mind is quite empty and rapt and there is in the nature of the case nothing 'to which the state of mind refers'. A different sort of 'non-rationality' is connected with reaction to the holy from that association with mystical liberation, though the two become fused in religions such as Brahmanism and Christianity. A second and most important point here that there is some danger in overemphasising the 'non-rational' character of such spiritual experiences. This can be illustrated from the fact that Otto, in discussing the difference between agnostic soul-mysticism (such as agnostic Yoga) and the Brahman-mysticism exemplified in Śankara, remarks that the difference be-tween their contents is itself non-rational and only to be com-prehended in mystical experience itself.[16] This despairing statement hardly does justice to Otto's own achievement in discriminating the two types; but it is connected with his belief that religious concepts are merely symbolical. The danger in regarding doctrines and re-ligious terminology as 'only symbols' is that they can easily this way become distorted, by being viewed as somehow pointing to the same Reality. And to say this last thing is to utter at best a half-truth. For we must distinguish between (a) describing one religious view in terms of another, (b) describing it in its own terms, and (c) exhibiting analogies. Now, as for (a), a Christian or a Hindu might wish to say that the two religions are, in certain of their doctrines, pointing to the same truth; but because each would prefer or insist on using one set of symbols rather than another to depict this truth, they would in effect be interpreting the other religion in terms of their own. Similarly we may, as apologists, interpret nirvana in theistic terms, but this is emphatically not what the Buddha said, and to treat nirvana in Hinayana terms we have to retain the agnosticism. As to (c), it is certainly illuminating to trace the respects in which attaining nirvana may be like attaining the unitive life of Western mysticism: it is doubtless on such analogies that an interpretation of nirvana in a loosely theistic sense would have to be based. The differences too are important: but Otto in his extreme emphasis on non-rationality is in difficulty over characterising them.

(vi) Finally, with regard to the interpretation of final nirvana as a transcendent state 'beyond space and time', this indeed is a vexed and complicated subject. But even if we grant that the Buddha's negations leave room for the belief that there is some kind of entity persisting in a non-empirical state after death, the nearest model we have for picturing such a condition is the sheer tranquility of the yogic mystic in his highest self-realisation; and the points that have been made above about the pure mystical state as not necessarily having anything to do with the numinous will hold again in this context.

Briefly, then: although Otto's analysis of the numinous fits very well gods and god-like entities and well describes men's reactions to these in experience – although, that is, it is successful in regard to those beings who are typically addressed in worship and negotiated with in sacrifice – it hardly holds in regard to those states and entities that are encountered along the yogic path. But this point is sometimes obscured because, in the circle of theistic religion (and this is what we are most accustomed to in the West), it is common to associate the beatific nirvana-like state with God; nevertheless, though it may in fact be true that the mystical vision is a vision of the numinous Deity, it is not self-evident, it is not analytically true. We must recognise the possibility of mysticism without worship, just as all along we have recognised the phases of religious history where there is worship, prayer, and sacrifice without any yogic or mystical path; but there is no genuine concept of god or God without worship, and conversely. The importance of nirvana is that it is a purer example of the mystical goal even than the soul-mysticism of

Yoga that Otto studied, for in Buddhism there is not even the *atman*, and it is perhaps a sign of the Buddha's rigid determination to evolve a 'pure' mysticism without any theistic or pantheistic complications that he excluded the concept of an eternal soul, which in being capable of separate existence and in being described substantivally is already too much adaptable to numinous concepts – as both the Vedanta and theistic Yoga demonstrate.

II

The question arises here as to how we are to define 'religion' in such a way that the term will cover not only polytheism and theism (i.e. religions which are suffused with numinousness), together with not too dissimilar pantheistic faiths, but also agnostic and transtheistic Buddhism and Jainism. Of course the problem has exercised many before now, and for this or similar reasons Buddhism has often been regarded as a 'crux' in the comparative study of religion. One way of trying to produce an old-fashioned definition is to point to some 'essence' of religious phenomena; but a result of this is to distort the agnostic faiths by interpreting their negations as a type of theological agnosticism, so as to have an essential content in all religions. Another way is to place heavy emphasis on some essential spirit in all religions, such as their numinosity. In this way religions will have a common form: but again this is to distort, for instance, the numinous aspects of popular Buddhism in the Hinayana which are merely peripheral – it is not *nats* and spirits that make it a living faith, but the call to nirvana. Again, one may try to avoid these pit-falls by escape into empty generality, as with Tillich's definition in terms of 'man's ultimate concern'[17] – to give this content it is necessary to define these terms themselves, which leads back to a definition of the first type; and here we are in even subtler danger of interpreting another faith in terms, albeit vague, of one's own. But all this is unnecessary, once we abandon the old-fashioned notion of definition and throw off the fascination of essences. It is a commonplace in contemporary analytic philosophy that many general words apply to a wide variety of things in virtue, not of some common property, but of 'family resemblance', and so are not capable of an essentialist definition.[18] To give a crude scheme of family resemblance: suppose A has properties a, b, and c; while B has b, c, and d; and C has c, d and e; while D has d, e and f. Although A has nothing in common with D, it is sufficiently like B for them both to have the same name – and likewise with B and C and with C and D. Of course in actual examples the situation is a much richer one, with subtle and overlapping similarities, as with the word 'game' – though patience and hockey have no common item of content, or at least none which would help to define 'game', they are both called games. To call something a game is to place it in a family rather than to ascribe it some complex essence. Similarly, perhaps, with 'religion' – we can place both early Buddhism and early Islam in the same family, even though they have nothing obvious or important in common. Thus appeal to the notion of 'family resemblance' has at least the following two advantages. First, and negatively, it discourages attempts to define 'religion' in an essentialist manner, which leads to misinterpretations accruing upon trying to formulate some common insight in all faiths – there may be different sorts of spiritual insights. Second, and positively, it allows for a sort of disjunctive account of religion: thus, for instance (and crudely), the activities and doctrines associated with worship, sacrifice, *bhakti*, etc., on the one hand, and those associated with the yogic endeavour towards inner enlightenment and with other similar endeavours on the other hand, are two centrally important items in a number of major religions; but we need not insist on the central presence of both or of any particular one of these items for something to count as a religion.

Finally, by reserving the term 'numinous' for describing entities and experiences which inspire worship, awe, dread, etc., as well as those objects, places, etc., intimately associated with these, we can take a new look at mysticism. First, *à propos* of Otto, we avoid a mistaken mode of classification: for because of his conviction that the 'soul' is a numinous entity and that numinousness is central to religion, he was led to say that every higher faith includes in some way a belief in the soul.[19] This means that Buddhism, despite its *anattā* (non-soul) doctrine, has to be subsumed under the heading of 'soul-mysticism'. Second, more importantly, by taking agnostic mysticism as the 'typical' or 'pure' variety, in the sense explained before, one is faced by a number of interesting and fruitful questions. Why should it seem natural to take this kind of experience as intimately connected with the numinous object of worship? And on the doctrinal level, why should concepts seemingly arrived at in different ways (such as Brahman and Atman) be said in some way to coalesce? It is not sufficient to yield to the ever-present temptation in discussing these matters to say that concepts are not important in themselves, but point to something beyond. For it is at least a *prima facie* difficulty that a concept pointing towards a Power beyond, and sustaining, the visible world should be so closely related to one which points towards a mystical 'inner' experience. Nevertheless, we have already observed that there is a loose resemblance – though not so loose that the plasticity of religious language cannot absorb it – between some of the epithets of nirvana and some of those ascribed to God. Thus a theistic interpretation of mysticism is possible, though it is not absolutely forced on one. We may put the point another way, by reference to a classic example, by saying that though it may be a deep insight that Brahman and Atman are one, this is not an analytic or necessary truth, since the concepts are arrived at along different paths and are connected with different sorts of spiritual activity: it is a welding together of initially different insights. The varying weights upon the activities and insights of different sects and faiths, moreover, goes a long way towards explaining doctrinal differences – once the types of doctrine associated with each are discriminated. Otto has done much here in his *Mysticism East and West* and elsewhere; but his somewhat wavering treatment of 'soul-mysticism' and his comparative neglect of nirvana militated against a successful chemistry of mystical, theistic, and mixed doctrines, for one element was not first isolated in its pure form.

5   Myth and Transcendence

My aim in this chapter is to analyse the notion of transcendence, as it occurs in the context of theism. The analysis serves some important purposes.[1]

First, it is relevant to the problem of demythologising. This latter project, which in effect is a way of re-presenting Christianity without the lumber of a prescientific cosmology, presupposes that we are reasonably clear about what it is the myths were 'really' getting at. For example, the three-decker view of the cosmos as found in the Jewish and Christian scriptures does not correspond to how the cosmos literally is; but does this mean that the idea of God's being 'up there' was not pointing to something else? The way we demythologise will be determined by the way we conceive this something else. For Bultmann, there is Heidegger. But the purpose of this paper is to analyse transcendence in such a way that demythologising is possible without prior commitment to a metaphysical system, even if the idea of transcendence is itself in a loose sense a 'metaphysical' one (in that loose sense in which a claim which is incompatible with positivistic empiricism can be dubbed metaphysical). Religious concepts do not have their principal roots in philosophising, so that an analysis of transcendence should not depend on some particular philosophical viewpoint.

Second, it happens that in recent philosophical discussions there have been some supposed analyses of Christian belief (e.g. of R. B. Braithwaite[2] and Paul van Buren[3]) which dispense with the notion of a transcendent being. These analyses concede too much to a this-worldly empiricism to make sense of traditional theistic claims. Because of epistemological difficulties about the verification or falsification of religious statements, it is tempting to reduce the claims of religion. But this distorts analysis. The present investigation may be useful in bringing about something of the nature of traditional ontology. In this sense it is just concerned with analysis. How we know whether there is or is not a transcendent being is a different issue.

Third, a clarification of the idea of transcendence may serve a purpose within Christianity. The existence of divergent religious and theological viewpoints within Christianity may be important, but there is no reason to suppose that there is not an implied substantial agreement about the transcendence of God.

This last point needs expansion. Broadly, the chief theological divergences are epistemological rather than ontological. Roughly, Christian theologians belong to four classes generated by a pair of independent epistemological divergences. They differ about the possibility of natural theology, and they differ about the nature of revelation. Thus we may distinguish first, between those theologians, such as Bultmann, John Robinson and the Neo-Thomists, who in differing ways draw on ideas outside revelation to interpret and defend the Christian faith, and second, Barth and most evangelicals who in differing ways reject such 'liberalism'. The two positions can be conveniently dubbed the 'liberal' and the 'revelationist' respectively. Secondly, religious people are divided over their method of treating the Bible. For some, the truths of Christianity can be deduced from the sentences of the Bible. For others, the latter are a record of revelatory events, but are not themselves revelation. People of widely differing traditions are found in each of these camps. The former school can be dubbed the 'deductivists' and the latter the 'inductivists'.

These two polarities yield the four classes: liberal deductivists (e.g., many Roman Catholic theologians); liberal inductivists (e.g., Robinson and Bultmann); revelationist inductivists (e.g., Barth); and revelationist deductivists (e.g., Conservative Evangelicals). Now no doubt these epistemological divergences often yield different conclusions about particular matters of theology and conduct. No doubt, too, some of these positions are more acceptable to sensitively rational persons than to others. But the divergences will not affect the present analysis of transcendence, for the following reasons. First, I hope to show (briefly) that the Bible implies a doctrine of transcendence, and all the above parties are agreed on the necessary importance of the scriptures. Second, the liberal position may involve the importation of Greek, Existentialist, Whiteheadian or other forms of metaphysics into theology, but the present analysis is not committed to any such system. Third, the analysis does not imply anything essentially controversial about how we arrive at belief in the transcendent. The only points where it touches on epistemology are where epistemological doctrines, such as positivistic empiricism, rule out Christian faith *a priori*.

We need to be realistic about religious belief. If some may find the idea of a transcendent being intellectually unattractive, there is yet no point in watering it down. Religious language is what it is, and there is no need to apologise for it. Apologetics follows after.

A further point before we start. This analysis is concerned with theism, and with Christianity in particular. Other remarks would have to be made about the transcendence of *nirvana*, etc. It is extremely important for philosophical analysis not to confine itself, in a culturally tribalistic way, to the religion of the environment of the practitioners. But there are advantages in delimiting the present enquiry to theism. In any case, religious doctrinal schemes are organic,[4] and a particular notion of transcendence has to be taken in its context, if we are to attain a reasonably rich understanding of it.

Since 'transcends' is a transitive verb, it is as well to consider the important grammatical objects which it takes. As we shall see, one of these, 'the world', is more important than the others, and it is this sort of transcendence that will be my chief concern here. But let us consider the following sentences:

(1) 'God transcends space and time';
(2) 'God transcends the world';
(3) 'God transcends human experience';
(4) 'God transcends thought';
(5) 'God transcends existence'.

The first and second are what principally interest us here, but some brief and fundamental remarks about the others are in order.

(3) If we say that God transcends human experience, in the religious context, we cannot mean that he is beyond all possible human experience. It is axiomatic that the believer thinks that he has or can have some experience of God (in prayer, through revelation, etc.). A God who could never enter into human experience would *a fortiori* have no interpersonal relations with men. This would be flatly contrary both to the Christian revelation and to the beliefs of other theistic faiths.

(4) Similar remarks apply to the notion that God is beyond comprehension or that he transcends thought. There would be a contradiction in saying that he is totally incomprehensible. For the very term 'God' encapsulates a number of assertions that the believer is prepared to make about him. By 'God' the Christian, for instance, means 'the Creator of the world', 'the Father of our

Lord Jesus Christ', and so on. To say that he is totally incomprehensible is to withdraw any basis or sense from these affirmations. An unknowable X has as much to do with atheism as with religion and as much to do with my right foot as with anything else in history.

The remarks of this paragraph might be denied by one who held that religious utterances are never cognitive, except when about 'neat' historical events, such as the execution of Jesus. If 'God is creator of the world' merely expresses joy, awe, and a 'positive' evaluation of nature, then 'God is incomprehensible' might be just a way of saying that the search for descriptive truth about God is useless and vain. The noncognitive analysis of religious utterances can be extremely revealing in showing the performative, expressive and other aspects of religious language. But it does not correspond, in one vital respect, with the intentions of users of religious language: men worship, and would not conceive it to be justified if there were nothing to worship. The activity presupposes something about reality.

(5) 'God transcends existence' — to say this is a way of showing that God is not a finite being, like a star. Yet it is a paradoxical thing to say. What it can scarcely mean is that, by transcending existence, God does not exist. To assert this is to assert the thesis of atheism. Since, notoriously, there are difficulties about treating 'existent' as though it stand for some kind of property, and about treating 'existence' as though it stands for either a property or a substance, it is highly obscure as to how we can decently interpret (5). Suffice it to say that the analysis of transcendence here presented should make it clear that God is not something like a star.[5] Nor is he, for the believer, an entity additional to the furniture of the world: for the believer's universe already includes God.

We may now turn to the more crucial cases.

(1) I shall content myself with God's transcendence of space, and leave the matter of time out of account (for there may be a genuine option as to whether we are to think of God as timeless or not; but he can scarcely, on any account, be properly thought of as a spatial being).

To say that God transcends space can be put in another way (in accordance with the analogy implied by 'trans–'), as follows: 'God is outside or beyond space'. This, of course, is a paradox, for 'outside' and 'beyond' are themselves spatial words. If a rose is outside the kitchen, it occupies a bit of space other than that occupied by the kitchen.

A minimal interpretation of 'outside space' is that God does not take spatial predicates like 'is a thousand feet long' or 'is to the north of Upper Volta'. In this respect God is like numbers. But of course the believer believes that God exists, is powerful and so on; while one would have to be mesmerised by philosophy to think of numbers as existing in such a sense (though, trivially, we do have a use for sentences like 'There is only one prime number between 13 and 19'). This is why it is not enough to interpret God's transcendence as just meaning nonspatiality. We must go further.

But meanwhile it might be objected that God does take spatial predicates, if the scriptures are anything to go by. Was God not on the holy mountain? The Bible seems to be full of such spatial language about God. The reply to this objection has two phases. First, the Bible also speaks of God as creator of the whole world. This implies the existence of God either temporally or logically prior to the existence of spatio-temporal objects. Second, the Bible and some other religious documents certainly speak as though God is specially present or specially active at particular places and times. Without this particularity there would, it seems, be no revelatory events or experiences, and God would be a mere nonspatial First Cause. But the idea of special presence (on the holy mountain or wherever) does not necessarily conflict with that of God's nonspatiality, and does account for the spatial language used of God. We shall return to this point later.

Why do we feel that there is more to God's transcendence than his nonspatiality? One reason may be that we tacitly identify space with the extent of the world. Already we are passing to case (2): 'God transcends the world'.

Here, however, there are ambiguities, which need to be cleared up. 'The world' is an expression of multifarious meanings. Some of these are philosophically rather uninteresting, such as 'the world, the flesh, and the devil'. More exciting is 'the world of Paul Slickey': for it is possible to erect a relational concept of the world, such that a person's world is, roughly, what he is related to in experience. Such a 'world' does not exist before he does, though the past may come to enter into his experience.

But this sense of 'the world' is not, after all, very useful for our purposes. For to say that God is beyond my world, though perhaps true, is to put him in a class that he may not necessarily care to belong to. For Khruschev and Vittorio de Sica are beyond my world, at least in so far as their world is different from mine.

Nor do we want to mean by 'the world' in this context the totality of all entities. For if God were beyond the universe in this sense, he would not exist.

It is much more natural and useful to use the phrase to mean 'the cosmos'. It is in line with traditional usage. Though the Hebrew cosmology may have been primitive and inaccurate, there was the notion of a universe created by God. In this respect, the doctrine of transcendence is not radically altered (or even altered at all) by changes in astronomical knowledge.

We can deduce from the element of nonspatiality, which was detected as being one part of the notion of transcendence, that God does not lie beyond the furthest galaxy or behind the sun. To understand what it means to say that God is 'beyond' or 'behind' the cosmos, we must note the other elements included in, or closely related to, the idea of transcendence.

First, theism, where it is imaginatively and vitally held, implies that God is invisibly present everywhere. He is, as it were, concealed all about us. This recognition of concealment has its converse in the idea of revelation, figured as a kind of unveiling of God by himself.

This element of concealment or 'secret omnipresence', as I shall call it, accounts in part for God's being thought to be 'behind the cosmos' and being (more intimately) behind the things and events which we encounter, and which form part of the fabric of the cosmos. That God is thought of as secret or invisible also implies, in line with his nonspatiality, that just as he is not beyond the furthest galaxy, he is likewise not within things in the way which particles are. He is not smaller than the electron, etc.

The next element to be considered may not strictly be part of the notion of transcendence; but it is impossible to divorce it from transcendence without distorting the meaning of the latter. It is the idea that God is specially present in certain events and experiences, often of an unusual character. In brief, a transcendent God is otiose unless he reveals himself through particular circumstances. This is not to say that God is not in some sense omnipresent. It is not to deny that the continuous practice of the presence of God is possible. But this practice seems logically to depend on the prior recognition of a particular revelation. Consider Dostoievski's seeing of Christ in his fellow convicts in Siberia. The very use of the word 'Christ' presupposes a recognition of Christ, that is, the Christ incarnate in particular circumstances. It might be replied that I am here slipping into mere epistemology: we would not know God anywhere unless we first found him somewhere.

The reply to this is that the concept of special revelation (say in Christ) implies some sort of special activity or relation of God. Thus the Christ in the New Testament stands in some kind of identity relation to the Father. It is not just that Jesus manifests the work of God in a preeminent way – the way an orchid or a saint might, only more so – but rather it is also that Jesus is God. Thus there is an ontological aspect in the idea that God is specially present here rather than there.

Yet it might be further objected that though the notion of special revelation or manifestation may imply an ontological aspect – e.g., God's special causal activity–nevertheless the argument for the importance of such special activity is epistemological. The objection is right in pointing to the danger of dressing up an argument as an analysis. However, the idea of transcendence is everywhere in religion associated with that of a being or state accessible to human experience through particular events or experiences.

The third element, then, is that of special presence. Clearly this element needs further explanation, but for the time being it is convenient to go on to the other main aspects of theistic transcendence. (To recapitulate, we have non-spatiality, secret omnipresence and special presence.)

The notion that God is 'beyond' or 'behind' or 'outside' the cosmos implies or suggests that the cosmos and God are different. This in turn implies that one could exist without the other. Thus we can analyse the God-cosmos difference by enunciating the two propositions: 'Even if the cosmos did not exist, God might exist' and 'Even if God did not exist, the cosmos might exist'. In practice, however, we are not concerned with mere possibilities, but rather with real independence. Thus the notion of transcendence in its theistic context goes with the belief that God is creator. This implies that even if the cosmos did not exist, God would; but it does not imply the converse. On the contrary, the theist believes that if God did not exist, the cosmos would not (would not have). Yet this is a bare and incomplete way of stating the implication of 'beyondness' or 'behindness', for it is compatible with a deistic conception of creation. Rather, the theist would say that the dependence of the world is continuous; or, in other terms, God is continuously the creator and sustainer of the cosmos. This element can be dubbed the 'creativity' element. Thus we have two further aspects of transcendence: creativity and independence.

It may be noted that the thesis that God would exist even if the cosmos did not is compatible with God's logical contingency. It remains conceivable that God might not exist. But I am not here concerned to propound any metaphysical doctrine concerning the necessity or otherwise of God's existence. The formulation given above is neutral in this respect. It might be complained that the contingency of God would make trouble for the Cosmological Argument. This is beside the point here, since I am concerned with analysis or description, rather than with apologetics or metaphysical argument. (Though, incidentally, the contingency of God need not destroy the Cosmological Argument.)[6]

Transcendence then comprises, or is only intelligible by reference to, five elements: non-spatiality, secret omnipresence, special presence, independence and creativity. If God is spatial, science would offer the best key to his understanding, rather than faith. If he is not omnipresent and continuously creative, he becomes the unmysterious deistic being. If he is not independent, either he is a product of the cosmos or identical with it (or with a part of it). If he is not specially present, he cannot be in Christ or speaking through prophets, etc.

But it is not enough to list the elements. We must show that they are compatible and that they hang together.

Regarding incompatibility, it is unfortunate that there is a rather large number of possible contradictions to consider. For the purpose of considering them, let us alphabetise the elements thus: let 'N' stand for non-spatiality, 'O' for secret omnipresence, 'P' for special presence, 'I' for independence and 'C' for creativity. We can generate the following questions:

Is N compatible with O? (More briefly) NO? Then (in the same style): NP? NI? NC? OP? OI? OC? PI? PC? IC?

Let us deal with some of the easier issues first. It seems clear that the notion of creativity on the part of God is not merely compatible with his independence, but actually entails it. Thus the answer to IC? is 'Yes'. It follows that if the answer to OC? is 'Yes' (in brief, OC), then OI.

Further, the notion of God's secret omnipresence can be understood in relation to his continuous activity in events. Hence, we can assert OC, and hence, also OI. Thus, if the answer to NC? is 'Yes', we can assert NI and OI. We may thus single out NC? as one of the key questions.

This leaves NP?, PC? and OP? to be dealt with. Here again we can simplify. From our results so far, we can infer that if PC, then PI and OP. And if NC and PC, then it seems unlikely that there should be incompatibility between nonspatiality and special presence. Consequently, NC? and PC? are the crucial questions.

First, then, is nonspatiality compatible with God's creativity? We could fill out this question by asking whether something analogous to a causal relation can be held to obtain between a state or thing which does not take spatial predicates and one which does. We are certainly aware of a familiar kind of experience where this seems to be so: my memory of a bad thing I have done can enter into the explanation of why I am blushing (or better, of why these cheeks have turned redder). Now it might be replied that my memory depends on spatio-temporal events or objects, and that it only has a proper place as belonging to a spatio-temporal person. But I am only here concerned to show that we already work with concepts where a nonspatial event enters into the account of why spatio-temporal events occur. (There is here no need of advocating dualism, which tends to assimilate the nonspatial to the spatial). Given that we can make use of such modes of explanation, we cannot *a priori* rule out the notion of a nonspatial creator. Thus we have no *a priori* reason to deny NC. Second, the personal analogy is also useful in treating PC? If God is active everywhere, how can he be more active in revelation than elsewhere? It does not seem plausible to think of his making a greater effort here rather than there. Now, however, it is a perfectly intelligible notion that I should be more engaged in one activity rather than another. If I stop digging the vegetable plot to play cricket with my boy, I am more engaged in the latter activity than the former: it reveals more of my interests and concerns. I am not here suggesting that God is bored by his routine creativity: I only wish to show that there can be different degrees of self-revelation or engagement. Hence, it is plausible to argue that PC.

Hence it would seem that there is no special reason to say that the notion of transcendence, as here analysed, is self-contradictory. But are the different elements coherent? Do they have some kind of 'internal' relationship? Do they suggest one another?

Before going on to this, let me make a point about the personal analogy. It hints that God may stand to the world as the mind to the body. Put thus, the idea is full of traps. But there remains an important point to this suggestion, brought out well in the theology of Ramanuja. He explicitly compared the God-world relationship to that of soul to body; but he gave an odd definition of 'body' – as that which is instrumental to the soul.[7] Thus the world is regarded as totally instrumental to God's purposes. This made his doctrine typically theistic. But at the same time Ramanuja had a strong sense of the dynamic unity of the world and God. This is important, because talk of transcendence is sometimes criticised as involving a dualistic world view, as though there are two separate 'worlds'. On the contrary, theists can see the 'two worlds' as a single dynamic complex. Miracles thus are not interventions in a fixed order, for the order consists both of the transcendent world and this world, in the closest possible creative relationship. Thus transcendence need not imply a myth of God as the tinkering mechanic.

Are the elements coherent? We can approach this problem by a consideration of types of religious experience (though other approaches are possible). We can distinguish firstly those experiences which are thought of by the subject as being in some way 'direct' experiences of God; and secondly those where God's presence or activity is seen in things or persons, etc. – as when God may be seen providentially at work in history, or displaying his glory in a sunset or tempest. It is the first type of experience – of a prophet like Isaiah or of a contemplative mystic like St. Teresa – which concerns me specially here; not because the second type is unimportant (it is vital for those who believe in sacraments), but because the first type pinpoints some of the more dramatic instances where God is (supposedly) known by acquaintance.

Now the numinous, prophetic experience of Jeremiah or Isaiah, or indeed of Paul on the road of Damascus, involves a powerful sense of the difference between the individual and God. Out of this, and round this, there comes the awe which is expressed in worship and adoration. Any doctrine of the identity of the soul and God conflicts with this sense of otherness. Thus God's independence fits with this type of experience, which is itself conceived as a form of special presence. In addition the dynamism of the prophetic experience suggests God's powerful creativity. The sense of dependence can easily be projected onto the cosmic environment.

Typically, too, contemplative mysticism involves an experience distinguishable from perception, thinking, remembering, etc. It is void of that content which has its habitat in space. Thus such experiences suggest elements in the doctrine of transcendence. The nonspatiality of God is hinted at too in the prophetic experience, for the latter is like the unveiling of what is hidden by spatio-temporal objects, and lies beyond the symbols and appearances (as with Isaiah in the Temple) by which the sense of the presence of God is expressed. It is not irrelevant that in the sacrament too God is conceived of as present, though unseen.

Thus the notion of special presence ties in with the independence, creativity and nonspatiality of God. Likewise creativity implies independence and suggests omnipresence. It also implies nonspatiality, for otherwise God would be a candidate for being part of the created cosmos.

These are some of the ways in which there is an inner connection between the different elements in the full idea of transcendence. It remains to see whether this idea is in fact found in theistic religion. It is convenient to treat this by reference to a few examples from the Bible, though it would be possible also to use other scriptures and religious writings as evidence.

First, is the God of the Bible really nonspatial? Is not God in heaven, and is not heaven above, in the Hebrew cosmology? But it should be noted that there is great ambiguity about God's location: 'The Lord is in his holy temple, the Lord's throne is in heaven. . .', as Psalms 11:4 says. This does not simply express the crude idea that God is in two different places at once, or that he has left his throne to dwell in the temple. The paradox of such language need not be taken as a contradiction; i.e., it need not be taken literally. Secondly, in the creation narrative in Genesis, God is represented as bringing all things (including heaven) into existence. This implies something about God's 'real' location. Third, where God withdraws his presence and is 'afar off', this signifies alienation, as in Psalms 27:9: 'Hide not thy face from me. Turn not thy servant away in anger'. The points may show, by way of example, that there is no need to think of the God of the Bible as essentially spatial or localisable.

It will need little argument to show that the Old Testament evolved a conception of God's creativity and continued activity. Thus we can infer also that the elements of independence and omnipresence are Biblical. Finally, the element of special presence – God's revelatory operation here and there – is so central a feature of the Biblical narrative that this point needs no labouring. We can conclude, therefore, that the idea of transcendence as here analysed corresponds to what is found in actual religion.

Finally, how does transcendence relate to immanence? If one

treats the latter term simply as special presence, the contrast between transcendence and immanence can be stated as the contrast between N, O, I and C, on the one hand, and P on the other. But equally, we can mean by immanence God's working within all things. In this case the concept becomes identical with that of transcendence, for 'within' is an analogy like 'beyond' – not to be taken literally: who is to say that 'within' and 'beyond' point in different directions? And God's dynamic working within all things is surely equivalent to his continuous, omnipresent creativity. One thus has two choices about immanence: immanence^1 is just P; immanence^2 is just transcendence.

Yet mythologically and psychologically transcendence so often is wrongly thought of as though God is afar off. This is no doubt a disadvantage in using the term. What the theist means can, in terms of the present analysis, be put as follows: 'There is a holy Power working within and behind the cosmos, present to us secretly everywhere, and specially present and active in such-and-such events and/or experiences.

This is what theism means, however its language may be wrapped in myth: but it is a further, and quite different, question as to how we know that the belief in a transcendent and immanent being is true.

6 The Concept of Heaven

There are many concepts of heaven. I want here to explore a number of them and to assess which, if any, are 'viable'.

I

Concepts of heaven have, of course, to be seen in context. There are two features of their religious context which it is especially important to note, for the purposes of this exploration of these concepts. First, schemes of religious belief are organic. By this I mean that it is impossible to understand a given religious utterance or belief without paying attention to the range of utterances or beliefs it goes with, and these in turn have to be understood in the milieu of religious practice, etc. For example, Christianity has traditionally affirmed that Christ is the Son of God. Obviously, this has to be seen in the context of the idea of God as expressed in a whole set of affirmations about the history of Israel and so forth; and equally obviously, the concept of God is the concept of a Being to whom worship is due, and which therefore has to be understood in the milieu of liturgical and other practical religious acts.

The second important point to note is that religious ideas undergo changes, and in particular the mythic or symbolic side of religious ideas is liable to suffer changes as a result of reflection upon them from later cultural standpoints. For instance, it is doubtful whether the question of Adam's being an historical or a symbolic figure (summing up something about mankind's relation to God) could properly be asked in the context in which the Genesis narratives were originally composed. For the mythic way of thinking eschews the distinctions which we are inclined to make. I shall therefore refer to certain ideas of heaven as mythic and others as doctrinal, to signalise the difference between two stages of thinking. For instance, God is mythically represented as dwelling in or beyond the sky, but it would be folly to suppose that this, at the mythic stage, is meant literally, as

61

though God were like a Gagarin. Doctrinally, God is represented as transcendent, in such a way that *now* the language of heaven is treated as symbolic of transcendence.

Perhaps the term 'doctrinal' is a little misleading, and I would utter a warning about it. Some may think that doctrines are simply descriptive, or supposedly descriptive, propositions about the nature of God, the world, etc. But it is worth seeing that doctrines, in their proper milieu, have a strong relevance to forms of piety and religious practice. For instance, the doctrine that God is the continuous creator of the whole cosmos implies that God has a sort of presence everywhere: he is omnipresent, as we might rather barbarously say. But this omnipresence is tied in with the religious life, since it means that God is always here to be addressed in prayer, etc. In brief, I do not want to use 'doctrinal' as though it is an alternative word for 'metaphysical'. Religious affirmations may sometimes have philosophical roots, but their dominant source is religion itself.

I want, then, to insist on the following three preliminary points: first, that a sketch of a given idea of heaven has to take into account the organic milieu in which it has its life; second, that it is convenient to distinguish between mythic and doctrinal concepts of heaven; and third, that doctrinal concepts are as much to be seen in a living religious milieu as mythic ones. But as to the first point, it is not easy in a brief treatment such as we are now undertaking to fill in the organic milieu satisfactorily, so that sometimes I shall be leaving it to you to do so.

The first idea of heaven which I wish to consider is that of heaven conceived as the place of God (or of gods), as in the opening words of the Lord's prayer, 'Our father, which art in heaven . . .'. There are, of course, a number of cultures in which God's place is associated with the sky. Almost inevitably, this mythic idea of God's location comes to be refined into a doctrinal one: this is a way of protecting part of its significance from hard-hearted criticisms of faith – criticisms which persistently reduce the mythic concept in the other direction to a literal one. *Of course* God is not literally in the sky, and yet this is what the mythic concept seems to be saying, once we begin to ask the literal-minded question. Though the substitution of a doctrinal idea of God's place for the mythic one sacrifices some of the poetic flavour of the latter, it is still possible to retain the symbolism by continuing to use the mythology in liturgy. By the 'poetic flavour', I mean that there are suggestions in the idea of God as dwelling in the sky, or beyond it, which are relevant to religious experience and practice, but which are not brought out in such a technical-sounding term as 'transcendence'. For example, the sky shines, it contains the stars above, it is high: it thus hints at God's glory, majesty and supreme holiness. How often do value-predicates connect up with height – 'supreme', 'a high quality of . . .' and so on. A religious tradition is liable to try to retain these suggestions, by continuing to sing hymns about a sky-God, long after it has introduced a severer and apparently more abstract account of God's place. The tension, however, can be so great that liturgy needs to be reshaped.

The doctrinal idea of God's place, – the notion that God is transcendent – can be explained briefly as follows. It ties in with the context of the doctrine of Creation, as commonly interpreted to mean that God continuously creates and sustains the cosmos, which is thus at all points dependent upon him. This belief implies that God and the cosmos are distinct. For this and other reasons, God does not take spatial predicates (except at the mythic level). Thus God is conceived as lying beyond the cosmos – he transcends it – but not in such a way that it makes sense to say that he is a thousand or a million miles further on. There is an analogy in some of the talk we have about human beings: thoughts and feelings are sometimes masked behind my overt behaviour, though it is nonsense to say that they are three inches behind my smile, or wherever. In giving this explanation of the idea of transcendence as applied to God, I am concentrating on the idea that God has, so to say, a transcendent place. There are other ways (sometimes confused ones) of using 'transcend' and its cognates but I do not remark on these here.[1]

So far, we have noted two concepts of heaven, both as being the 'place' of God. One is the mythic concept of heaven up there in or beyond the sky. The other is the doctrinal concept of God as transcendent. But as we have seen, the latter idea can be held side by side with the mythic concept of heaven, except that the latter has now been displaced as the central account of where God is, and is thus treated merely symbolically. When the mythic undergoes this displacement, it is convenient to refer to it as the symbolic concept of heaven. For it has indeed undergone a change – become a new concept, if you like – by virtue of the principle of the organic understanding of religious concepts and utterances described earlier in this essay. Since a given concept has to be understood by reference to its organic milieu, some major change in that milieu in effect, creates a new concept. And this is what happens where the idea of the mythic heaven is no longer taken altogether seriously, but is in essence replaced by a doctrinal concept of heaven, and only retained as a symbolism which points us towards that which is more precisely described by means of the doctrinal concept. This, then, is an argument for distinguishing the original mythic concept of heaven from what we are now calling the symbolic concept.

Before moving to other ideas of heaven, I would like to make one major comment on the notion of transcendence as briefly outlined earlier. If transcendence in this sense means that God is not spatial, and yet is distinct from the cosmos, while sustaining it, so to say, from behind, then there is no strong reason to distinguish this account of transcendence from one main meaning of *immanence*. The belief that God works *within* all things merely uses a different spatial analogy from the belief that he is behind or beyond the cosmos.

So far, then, we may distinguish three forms of the idea of heaven considered as the place of God. Some religions, however, do not involve or do not necessarily involve belief in God, as commonly understood. Buddhism is one of these. Here the central concept is of transcendent nirvana, a state realisable through treading the Eight-fold Path. It is true that Buddhism does not abandon the concept of heaven, but the heavenly state is inferior to nirvana: it belongs to the realm of the impermanent, while nirvana is the permanent abode. There is a certain ambiguity in the Pali Canon as to the status of heavens, just as there is an ambiguity about the gods. Sometimes the heavens are matched with meditational states, and it leads one to wonder whether they are not in the last resort simply symbols of psychological, contemplative stages. But it is unwise to insist too strictly on treating them as symbolic. What seems to have happened is that Buddhism consciously retained the mythic concept of heaven, but placed it firmly below nirvana in order of priority. The gods who are in heavens themselves are much inferior in insight to the Buddhas and indeed to anyone who has gained nirvana in his life. The Buddhist way by-passes the gods, even the great god Brahma. For this reason, it is not the case that, in the Theravadin tradition at least, the mythic concept of heaven comes to be treated as symbolic of nirvana. We see a different pattern from the development in theistic faiths, and this is not surprising since in many respects the whole structure of Buddhism is so different.

With these points in mind, it nevertheless is not too misleading to say that there is an analogy between the doctrinal concept of heaven as God's place and the doctrinal concept of nirvana as a transcendent state, beyond the impermanent world. But nirvana is neither the locus of God nor of souls: it is rather the transcendent place of liberation (though one should not ask what is *contained* in that place). We can thus distinguish a fourth idea of what loosely can come under the head of heaven, namely the idea of a transcendent place of liberation.

This brings us to a further notion: for in some religions (though not in Buddhism) there has been a theory of souls. It thus becomes possible to treat heaven as the place whither at least some souls are translated upon death. Not surprisingly, something depends upon the nature of beliefs about souls and persons. Thus it is possible to have a rather ill-defined belief in the persistence of personhood beyond the grave – a mythic picture of post-mortem existence; and this fits in with the mythic concept of heaven as the place of God (or the gods). People who go to God's presence thus can enjoy a mythic position close to him. But it is tempting, especially when there has been elaborated a doctrinal idea of God's transcendence, to have a doctrine of souls, constituting the eternal, non-spatial aspect of the person, which can in this way plausibly make the transition from the cosmos to the state lying beyond it. This concept of heaven can be summed up as the idea of a place of liberated souls.

It is worth commenting that there are schemes of belief which retain a form of soul-theory without entailing that there are many souls: thus notably for Śankara, in his exposition of Advaita Vedanta, there is only one atman, and this is identical with the one divine Being. Thus liberation does not involve translation of an individual soul to a heavenly state, but simply the shedding of those factors which obscure the self's true identity. There is thus an analogy with Buddhist nirvana, at least in the sense that there is a state of liberation, but no individual being who enjoys it.

One reason in theistic systems for the idea of a plurality of souls to be attractive is that theism implies a gap between the focus of worship and the worshipper. It would indeed be blasphemous and absurd, from this point of view, to identify the individual soul with God. There are, of course, other reasons why a plural soul-theory has entered into the Christian and other traditions.

It seems then that we have at least the following ideas of heaven to consider: heaven as the mythic place of God; heaven as the mythic place of liberation; heaven as the doctrinal place of God; heaven as the doctrinal place of liberated souls; heaven simply as the doctrinal place of liberation; heaven as the symbolic place of God; and by analogy heaven as the symbolic place of liberation.

Ideas of the so-called future life or last things are not exhausted by the forms mentioned above. For there is the faith in the resurrection of the dead. This has its own form of ambiguity. The more natural interpretation of it in the Christian tradition, for instance, is that it occurs upon earth, in this world – it is a consummation of human history. It is thus not other-wordly in its emphasis, as many ideas of heaven are. But it does not take much shift for the mythic concept of the general resurrection, etc., to slide into the symbolic idea of heaven. Thus some writers have treated the idea of a resurrection body as an unimaginable vehicle for personhood in the next world. On the other hand, doctrinal elaboration of the hope of the last things can replace the expectation of risings from the dead as a consummation of human history, in which the hope of heaven in a transcendent sphere is essentially absent. The doctrine becomes a way of expressing hope about the divine guidance of human history, etc. Though resurrection of the body rather than immortality of the soul is probably the dominant motif in New Testament hope, I shall not comment further upon it, since it lies outside the discussion of the concept of heaven, except in so far as it sometimes is collapsed into the symbolic idea of heaven.

Finally, in this rapid account of beliefs about heaven, it is worth mentioning a common form of ordinary hope, namely that people survive death in some higher realm, but not necessarily oriented towards God or concern for salvation or liberation. Ordinary folk want to meet their loved ones in the beyond, even if they are not specially concerned with religion, worship, piety or contemplation. There is indeed often a tension between religion and ordinary hopes: ordinary hopes may be pointed towards simple continuation of life in company, but not particularly the company of God. Since traditional Christianity sometimes pictures heaven, the place of liberated souls, as containing the realisation of the summit of the contemplative life (the beatific vision of God in heaven only has its foretastes in the mystical life here on earth), there is a gap between ordinary concerns and those encouraged by religion. The contemplative life tends to be for the few rather than for the many. What men do not do here on earth they may not feel called to do in heaven! There is then, a popular concept of heaven as being simply the place of survival among loved ones.

Though the ideas we have considered have a rather other-worldly flavour, it should be recalled that in the living milieu of religion they can have a strong this-worldly significance. The transcendent state of nirvana can be 'seen' by the saint here and now. Eternal life can be possessed on earth, just as God can be encountered on earth, though his 'place' lies beyond it.

It is now time to comment on some of the various ideas of heaven, to see whether they are consistent and meaningful.

II

I shall argue in this section of the essay that a crucial, but peculiar, place is held by the doctrinal concept of heaven as God's place. But I shall not argue directly that this concept is free from contradiction, nor that it is necessary to the expression of theistic faith. This lack of directness here is partly due to the fact that I have elsewhere tried to show that the idea is free from contradiction.

But first, let us consider the mythic idea of heaven, as God's place. I think it is largely the case, in the major religions, that it has become deeply eroded by the very fact that the major religions have evolved theologies or schemes of doctrine which effectively reduce it to symbolic status. But in any event, it is almost inevitable that we should here treat the mythic idea as dead: for the very question as to its consistency requires us to ask such questions as whether it is possible to locate God in the sky, and such questions belong to a different cultural and intellectual milieu from that in which such a mythic idea had its genesis. I am far from saying that myths are unimportant: but we are not here concerned with the vital and underdeveloped project of gaining a deep insight into the nature of myths. As we shall see, there may be a way of consistently using the mythic idea of heaven, even within the framework of modern cosmology, etc., but only by using it in a parabolic way, which almost amounts to giving it symbolic status.

The symbolic idea of heaven, as such, need not detain us, in that when the mythology of heaven is reinterpreted in a doctrinal way, the symbolic concept of heaven merely serves to point to the transcendence of which the doctrine of the beyond speaks. By the same token, the idea of heaven as the symbolic place of liberation or salvation can be left for the moment on one side.

What can be said about heaven as the doctrinal place of souls? It will be recalled that a principal motive of this idea is that the soul is in theory non-spatial, though somehow connected with the spatial organism, which constitutes or, more mildly, at least expresses human personhood. The non-spatiality of the soul helps us to understand how it can be that there is a transition from this world to the world of transcendence. For indeed it makes little sense to ascribe my thought or feelings to a place a few inches to the left of my right ear (a point canvassed in Gilbert Ryle's *The Concept of Mind* and elsewhere). One can be grateful for the thesis that spatial predicates have a limited purview, even within the realms of space: electrons and minds behave oddly. But the gratitude is only for this – that it rids us of a too-standard view of the concepts we use. It does not warrant us in inferring that because spatial predicates do not typically apply to mental processes, therefore the mind or soul can make an easy transition to the hereafter. The reason why this remark is in order is that it is quite feasible to treat predicates about the mind as applying essentially to the whole organism. Though Ryle's treatment of the topic was in some ways rather crude, it remains quite possible to take over the basis of his analysis. This in itself is not a criticism of the crucial notion of God's transcendence, which also trades on the possibility of non-spatiality, since it is open to us to treat the cosmos as God's body – a doctrine which we find in Ramanuja's writings and which has the attraction of militating against a strongly two-worlds view. It is obvious, of course, that the cosmos does not *look like* the bodily manifestation of an organism. Ramanuja indeed produced a whole series of telling arguments against the Teleological Argument and of the argument from the likeness of the cosmos to an organic body (an argument only partially treated in Hume's famous *Dialogues*, written a few centuries later). But one must distinguish between the grounds of a belief and its conceptual viability. The conflation between the two can cause much trouble. In essence the recent tendency to condemn religious utterances as meaningless turned on the lack of ordinary sorts of grounds for them: in short, on the view that because groundless (i.e. according to some preconceived straitjacket of epistemology) they are meaningless or without conceptual viability. Hence, even if the cosmos may not look like the body (to use only one analogy) of God it does not at all follow either that the idea is absurd or that it is false. Needless to say, the concept of a body here undergoes some change: but it is natural in religious discourse as elsewhere to use analogical terms.

However, the possibility of a consistent notion of heaven as the place of God does not guarantee the possibility of a consistent idea of the disembodied existence of the soul in the next world. It might be that the idea of transcendence is a necessary condition of the acceptability of belief in the existence of souls in a liberated state. But the latter idea, especially in the context of belief in God, has some notorious difficulties. First, it is an important sentiment within the context of worship that God and the worshipper are distinct (unlike the non-dualistic Hindu view to which we made reference). The notion of distinct, but non-spatial, entities is difficult, since there would be problems of how to identify separately such beings. That is, our present criteria of identity of persons are heavily bound up with bodily positions. It could be objected, from a Christian point of view, that the Trinity doctrine does indeed imply distinct (though also united) persons within the Godhead. But it would be reasonable to hold that identification here is through the different modes under which God manifests himself in salvation-history. As to the inner constitution of the Trinity, it is hard to know what can be said. By analogy, it might be argued that people could be identified here and now in the way in which we normally identify them, and this would somehow guarantee their separateness in a heavenly existence.

The second difficulty arises out of this, namely that the notion of an independent 'something' which can link an embodied person to a non-spatial existence does not, partly because of the thinness of the life which it might have, provide what is often required of people in immortality. That is, it is doubtful whether we could talk of the immortality of a *person*. It is true that some Indian schemes of religious belief would not find a difficulty here, in that liberation is conceived as a state where the person as an individual is transcended. As has been pointed out by some Buddhist writers in the Indian tradition, the Buddhist 'agnostic' belief in a liberated state constitutes as rich an account of liberation as such soul-theories, which effectively divorce the soul from the normal psychological and physiological aspects of the individual. It would therefore seem that the best that one could do in the way of a concept of liberation in a transcendent place would be to adopt an 'agnostic' view, that is one where no specific description of such a state can be given in terms of a soul theory.

However, the thinness of this account does not agree with the richer picture which is given, for instance, in the Christian tradition. Is it possible to use the mythic idea of heaven not just symbolically, which would imply that the picture described in images could be described *otherwise doctrinally*, but parabolically? By this I mean (in line with suggestions made by I. C. Crombie, T. R. Miles and others) that the picture of heaven would tell us something about the nature of heaven, but there would be no one-to-one correspondence between the details of the picture and the state which it depicts. In this way, the idea of heaven could be retained within the whole scheme of Christian belief and practice, but it would not be possible to spell out what it meant doctrinally. There are, however, difficulties about a *totally* parabolic account of a scheme of belief, since that which parables refer to becomes in essence indescribable; one ends up with the silence qualified by parables canvassed by T. R. Miles. There must be a richer doctrinal account of the object of reference so that it is possible to make sense of the notion that there is something for the parables to refer to. I would therefore conclude that one might accept a parabolic account of heaven, provided there was not also a totally parabolic account of God. This seems to be a further way in which the idea of heaven as a transcendent place of God is in its way crucial to a continued acceptance of the idea of heaven as a place of salvation.

Another way to avoid the difficulties of understanding any transition to a future life is to make the mythic idea symbolic of what happens here and now. I recall reading an account of a British visitor to a Tibetan home whose host invited some lamas to meet him. When they arrived they were laughing, as at some joke, and the visitor enquired what was so funny. The lamas replied that they had been discussing the question of whether heaven is a place or a state of mind. Certainly there are treatments of the conquest of death which imply that this is something to be attained here and now through facing it in some way (the way is sometimes treated opaquely, by existentialists). Is a kind of serenity and authenticity in the face of death what the idea of heaven refers to? There is something in this approach, by the very fact that eternal life, as we have said earlier, is, in religion, thought to be available to us now. However, this view also by implication denies the belief in a future life, and for this reason might be criticised as failing to take account of the predicament of those who die without having conquered death. This criticism can perhaps be bypassed by treating it simply as another aspect of the problem of evil; it is doubtful whether one should believe in heaven simply to redress the wrongs of the present world. This 'existentialist' solution to the problem of heaven is a possible one, but again it could hardly work as an account of religious belief if the concept of God is to be treated in the same manner, for then the focus of religious aspiration itself evaporates. That is, the 'existentialist' account has an analogy to the parabolic one, namely that its viability depends upon the retention of the idea of transcendence – unless, that is, one wishes to make a radical break with the traditional meaning of Christian faith. Putting it crudely, a sort of 'Christian', atheism is consistent, but it scarcely connects with the hitherto established sense of Christian language.

It is for these reasons that the notion of the transcendent place of God holds a crucial position. I have not here argued that this notion is consistent. But it may be useful to reflect briefly upon a non-philosophical objection which might be brought against it, namely that it implies a kind of split into two worlds, so that religion, by focusing on God or heaven, becomes other-worldly at the expense of the concerns of this world. It is not surprising if sometimes ideas of heaven have generated this attitude. However, there is no necessity about it. The idea of transcendence can be treated so that it is indistinguishable from the idea of immanence, that is, that God is working in everything. The world also can be looked upon as the self-expression of the Creator, so that there is no need to undervalue it or to flee from it (any more than one would wish to scrape away a person's smile or frown in the hope of penetrating to his true personality).

7 The Philosophy of Worldviews: The Philosophy of Religion Transformed

The philosophy of religion has greatly concerned itself with some old questions, about God and immortality, about miracles and evil; and in the last three decades much too with the question of the rumoured vacuousness of religious utterance. Speech about God by some has been tied to pictures and parables and forms of life. But basically the agenda has been Western theism: this is what above all has exercised Wisdom, Flew, Hick, Hepburn, Phillips and others. The tradition remains dominated, from the rear, by the idea of natural theology; or by something called theism; or more particularly Christian (sometimes Jewish) theism. But whose theism? From two directions the philosophy of religion has been too much cut off from some significant realities.

In one direction the notable split between Christian theology (especially) and analytic philosophy of religion arises from their differing intellectual roots. Overwhelmingly the former's (in modern times) lie in the German-speaking world – think of Barth, Bultmann, Bonhoeffer, Pannenberg, Rahner; while the latter's lie in the Anglophone – as witness my list above, not to mention such masters in the background as James, Peirce and Russell. Often the philosopher of religion deals, at the intellectual level, with a system of ideas much simplified in comparison with the complexities of modern systematic interpretations of Christianity (or Judaism).

In the other direction there has been a tendency for the philosophy of religion to ignore practice – or to put it another way to ignore the history of religions. Maybe 'forms of life' come nearer, but the fact is that Christianity is living sacrament as well as theism, symbolism acted out as well as philosophy of life, ikon as well as argument. A more intimate bond between the philosophy of religion and the study of living religious practices would have been welcome.

The danger thus has been that philosophers deal in a somewhat denatured theism, or perhaps it would be better to say a somewhat bony one – the anatomy is there but not much of the physiology. Also, on looking so much to Western theism, the challenge to it of other perspectives, notably Buddhist and Hindu, has been less considered than it should have been.

The fabled Martian arriving on the planet and inspecting among other things our intellectual resources might also be struck by a strange thing. Journals he would note, devoted to the philosophy of religion. The more advanced essays therein might discuss the question of truth as between religions. But over Cambodia he would not look down to perceive Christians struggling spiritually with Buddhists: he would find Marxist rural anarchosyndicalism destroying temples and monks. In Tibet he would see the clash of ancient religion and Maoism. In Romania he would note subversive Baptists. In Sweden he would see Christianity softly overwhelmed by social democracy. In brief, he would think that as far as rivalry goes (and this is an index of competing truth-claims, perhaps) religions and ideologies were tugging against each other, and that really from a practical point of view it was odd that such a struggle was rarely depicted in the journals of the philosophers of religion. The logical scientism of Flew would be but one of the many, sometimes much more powerful than it, challenges to theism, itself a pattern of only one main kind of worldview.

He might be further puzzled at how blithely men could come to put religion in a sort of ghetto, considering so many professed not to be able clearly to define it. But even accepting a certain consensus that one can use the word sensibly of certain mainly traditional systems of belief as distinguished from secular ideologies including liberal atheism, it must surely remain a question as to whether worldviews of the differing kinds do not, despite their contrasts, share some fundamental properties in common.

Let me name a few. My list represents overlaps. I am saying 'Importantly some religions and some ideologies are thus', not 'All and all'. So: closely relating theory and practice; not being straightforwardly verifiable or falsifiable; calling for dedicated commitment; possessing an account of human history; implying ethical principles; possessing a doctrine of human nature; being capable of intellectual and practical development; having an eschatological orientation;

possessing a cosmology; and having a theory about the genesis of religion. Let me simplify: religions and ideologies both guide men regarding the meaning of life. Moreover, since theology is very often the product of struggle at the interface between a religious tradition and secular ideologies; and since the history of religions reveals remarkable contrasts between religions in both belief and practice: it would seem that the opening out of the philosophy of religion to theologies and religions itself pushes us onward in the direction of an even more plural range – the range of both religions and ideologies, the range of *existential worldviews* as they might jointly be called.

In parenthesis: it is a great shame that there is no simple word for such *Weltanschauungen* – *sasanas, darsānas, margas* are suggested by India, and other cultures could supply other terms. The briefest, least bad English word seems to me to be 'worldview'. But it is far from the feel of praxis and of faith, or the smack of sacrament or angst. Nor is there an easy way out by neologism – something which Hellenizes perhaps that mix of theory and value, of belief and feel, of faith and rite which the systems in question incorporate. In the fashioning of such newly minted Graecisms it was when I got to *biodoxy* that I gave up (but I still welcome suggestions).

In brief, it is perhaps rather sad that so little of the philosophy of religion has been aimed at a wider range. What I am now proposing is that it would be better called something like 'the philosophy of worldviews'. Of course, this represents a somewhat radical suggestion in that it implies something too about religious studies. But I will not here pursue my suggestion in its longer ramifications.

Now a desideratum of such a philosophy of worldviews, if it is to be realistically tied to worldviews as they actually exist in the world, is analysis of the structure and history of such systems. There is a close analogy with the philosophy of science, which in recent decades has so much benefited from a close relationship with the history of science. From history of course we can learn various lessons: that, for instance, it is not easy to pin down certain religions to an essence – consider the great fluidity of Christianity and in its differing way Buddhism; that nevertheless at differing times variant doctrines may fulfil much the same existential function; that many aspects of religion and ideology have to be considered as dynamic – ready for development; and so on. From history and from the comparative study of religions we can begin to piece together the so-to-say logical structure of systems – how the differing dimensions of religion such as doctrine, myth, ritual and experience are bound to one another in relations of implication and suggestion, of expression and definition; also, too, how within the range of doctrines in a system they are mutually related and organically influence one another. Let me illustrate very briefly with just one example of such structural interconnections.

'In the beginning was the word . . .' Think of how in this amazing passage a new perspective is opened up on the old doctrine of creation, now interpreted anew in relation to the Incarnation. The meaning of the doctrine now has changed. It is no longer Creation-of-the-world-to-the-power-history-of-Israel but now Creation-of-the-world-to-the-power-history-of-Israel-to-the-power-Incarnation. If you have a red stripe and a white stripe and add a blue stripe, lo there is the French flag; a green stripe and lo, there is the Italian flag. The reds and the whites change their meaning according to their companionship. One might say that doctrines, in *St. John*, are organically related; more, they come to tie in with what may be described as a historical myth, the passage of Christ from Galilee to his meaningful and tragic end in Jerusalem, and to his overcoming of the tragic in his resurrection.

Moreover, for most Christians the meaning of Incarnation is not just to be gleaned from the good book and from the expositions of doctrine; it is also to be understood more intimately in experience, and in the Eucharistic sacrament. Thus if the Word described in *St. John* is the Christ of faith as well as the Jesus of history his identity is understood transactionally, and not only is there a bond between doctrine and myth, but also between doctrine and sacrament, myth and experience and so forth.

Structurally, therefore, the analysis of a religious system points to a suggestive web of interconnections. The relations are rarely ones of significant kinds of mutual dependence. Systems are *organic* systems, to put the matter briefly, and in their lives can grow or shrink. Often a religious or political question is: How much in the way of limbs can an organism lose and still live?

So there is a vital task of structural analysis and comparison to be undertaken by the philosophy of religion or at least *for* it. For obviously a main question, 'What are the kinds of evidences for and against the truth of a religious claim?', will vary in its impact and answer according to the actual organic version of a religious faith under inquiry.

There is a kind of dialogue which informally involves itself in such organic analysis: the Christian, say a Catholic, who engages in serious conversations with a Marxist is probing to see how far there are collisions and tensions between the two systems. More formally, one aspect of the task was undertaken in William Christian's *Oppositions of Religious Doctrines*. What is needed is a sort of comparative systematics. But of course it is not just doctrines and to some extent myth and ethics, such as are the typical pastures of systematic theology, that such analysis must be kept to, for it must also relate, as we have seen, to sacred and other practice and experience.

It is at this point, though, necessary to propound a *caveat* and make a distinction. Sometimes systematic theology is not is not so much descriptive as constructive: it is the fashioning of a new Christian (or Jewish, etc.) system of belief: a new worldview. Likewise in dialogue often the mutual exploration leads beyond existing positions to new ones, on both sides. Excellent such explorations and new articulations of a worldview are; but they should not be confused with descriptions of existing systems. Doing theology is not the same as analysing theologies. One should be clear about this, not only for the sake of truth but also clarity as to what stage one is at. So far I am saying: let the philosophy of religion take seriously the comparative structural (or better one should say: organic) analysis of worldviews. The analysis, with the aid of history, can be diachronic as well as synchronic.

I am not saying that such a concern for realism of analysis is absent in modern philosophy of religion. It is not however very prominent. It incidentally represents a way in which philosophical concerns are to be integrated very closely into those of the history of religions. But in accord with my plea for a broader range than traditional religious systems for us to work on, the history of religions must go beyond religions. We are caught up in worldview history and worldview analysis: *Weltanschauungswissenschaft*, one might say.

So far I have been talking in the plural. Religions, not religion; ideologies not ideology; worldviews not worldview (note by the way the incongruity of this last). But does not the history of religions offer more than histories and comparisons of systems? Of course, and especially if we look towards the influential Chicago school. For one thing it offers an account of key structures and elements within the world of myth and experience. We can look at it as a kind of organ comparison: just as the hearts and livers and tongues of differing animals can be much alike, so there are elements within the organisms which comparative worldview analysis explores which are markedly similar. To take a heterogeneous list: symbolisms of height, attitudes to the earth, fertility cults, shamanistic rites, mystical experiences, techniques of contemplation, the numinous experience, rites of passage . . .'

The exploration of religious symbolism, including acted symbolism, can begin perhaps to shape a kind of grammar of religion, and indeed much else besides. The interest shown among anthropologists, such as Clifford Geertz, Mary Douglas and Victor Turner, in the symbolic structures of religion and 'ordinary life', points towards ultimately the creation of a science of symbolic behaviour, which would also include that found within the ambit of secular ideologies.

Unfortunately again we are in some quandary because of available language. Terms such as 'symbol' and 'symbolic' have unfortunately drifted in the direction of the 'mere' or the unreal. Speaking of something as a *mere* symbol denigrates it, and often so-called symbolic gestures are substitutes for the real thing – the rude sign instead of the physical assault. Consider, to take a modern 'secular' example of a Chinese guide telling visitors the statistics of pig production in a particular commune. He does so, we suppose, proudly, and with more than a hint of revolutionary fervour. Evidently the pigs are meaningful: they are charged with special value. They are pigs with haloes, we may say. Why? Because they symbolise something. They are part of making the better life for the ordinary peasant. Producing pork is a small part, but a vital part, of the process of clothing the peasants in dignity. They are also symbols of joint enterprise, and of the change wrought by the Liberation and all that that has subsequently meant. Are they just symbolic? Are they 'substitutes for the real thing'. Not at all: plastic models of pigs would not do (like straw surrogates for human sacrifices). Pictures of pigs, it is true, can have symbolic impact, but only because the pigs are real or represented as such. Throw away the pigs and keep the pictures – this does not serve. So in many cases X is symbolic because it is a real X. Perhaps therefore we ought to use differing language to talk about such cases, which after all permeate our very daily existence: clothes, gestures, smiles, furniture, spires, skyscrapers – they all talk, wordlessly, but deeply.

There is, then, a continuum between the formality of much religious ritual through to the rites and expressive acts of daily life. If it is reasonable to extend the philosophy of religion so that it more explicitly becomes the philosophy of worldviews, then the history of religions has a more general destiny; namely, the enquiry into the grammar of gesture and symbolism. That there is no such continuum is in my opinion part of an ideology which seeks to partition off religion, either defensively so it can have its own norms and be *sui generis*, or aggressively so that 'serious' men can neglect it as being traditional and cut off from the vital concerns of secular living.

Moreover the grammar of symbolic action is an ingredient in our understanding the structure of worldview. To take a simple example: Why should the heliocentric theory have been resisted? Partly because of its damaging the symbolic value expressed in the notion of man's being at the centre. Consider the emotional impact of such notions as *revolution, class warfare, progress, growth, people, national identity* and many others of the common coins of current political and economic discourse. There is a major task of analysis to unravel the modes whereby things and acts are specially charged with existential meaning; for it is such symbolic meaning which provides the bridge between pure cosmology and a world-picture, between pure history and a philosophy or theory of history, between scientific and value-free descriptions and expressions of the symbolic substance of things. Even a kind of agnostic nihilism has to reject meaningful patterns: it does not simply fail to affirm them.

No doubt such remarks are obvious enough: but we sometimes in the field of religion do not take their implication seriously enough. For if they are correct then the field of religion includes a field beyond religion (in the conventional sense). Perhaps we could say that the domain of the study of religion should be seen as that of the spiritual in general: the way we respond more deeply to our world – that is part of what Tillich had in mind in talking of men's concern (though the *ultimate* bit was hardly, even loosely, quantifiable, and may just be hyperbole).

However, it is more from the lateral pluralism of worldviews that the main task of the philosophy of religion seems to me to emerge. I shall first put that briefly, and then go on to an inventory of considerations and topics that seem to arise. The task, then, briefly is to clarify the criteria for determining the truth as between worldviews. I am assuming that worldviews are not totally compatible, and there is a sense in which the view that they are compatible (such as neo-Vedanta) is itself an additional worldview. Naturally therefore a prior task is the comparative analysis of the structure of worldviews: this is the very heart of the comparative study of religion plus of course a consideration of atheistic and anti- or non-religious systems of belief. An immense task? Naturally; but there are many workers in the field, and the subject is as yet rather young.

The question of criteria is a high-order one, though admittedly this claim has to be modified somewhat when we recognise that a theology (for instance) may have a philosophical component, a view about how one tells what the truth is. Still, broadly the distinction of levels can I think be maintained, perhaps more as a kind of heuristic device or as a mode of orientation. Also one needs to notice that it is not just a question of criteria of truth, but of truth wedded to practice, and so a matter of criteria of correctness or appropriateness. Since also action is mediated by symbolism and feeling we have to pay attention to the living or vibrant quality of a system or tradition.

So then let me outline an inventory of considerations relative to the truth of worldviews.

First there is of course consistency. But *applied* consistency does not typically involve straight contradictions. Whereas that God is one and God is three on the surface is a contradiction, already we note something peculiar: it does not say 'There are three Gods'; and when we come to consider how the tension is resolved in the idea of the three Persons, we no longer can point to contradiction clearly established, though there remains tension. So one might ask: How much internal tension does a worldview contain? Other things being equal, the less tension the better – though it has to be said that a rich system, covering different facets of human experience is liable to have some strong tension.

Internal tension itself may encourage formulae designed to stabilise it, but the stability of the formulae themselves may be in question: this is very much the history of Christian orthodoxies and heresies. Fix up the tension in the God-man idea in one direction, and some such divergence as Nestorianism may emerge.

Tension may be also related to the interface between the received beliefs and values of contemporary society. Consider the tension concerning evolutionary theory and conservative interpretations of the Bible; or the tension between Stalinist Marxism and modern biology. More obviously in regards to values, but the same applies also to truth-claims, it may turn out that the tension is a consequence of the falsity of contemporary views. Thus there is a clash between most liberal and women's liberation views on abortion and Catholic views – but it might be that the latter's views are the correct ones. Again, the Confessing Church experienced more tension with the values of German society in the thirties than did the German Christians. Since values are typically debatable – open to intuitive decision often – tension itself has a debatable disvalue. Similarly it may turn out that a traditional religious view is right about some matter of science; for instance, traditional Buddhism believed in many world systems, or as we might now say, galaxies. This is a point in favour of that tradition, when one comes to see it over against the tiny little cosmological cage in which the Jewish and Christian imaginations were long confined.

Both in regard to beliefs and values there is also what may be described as an epistomological tension, or so it may appear. Science does not appeal to revelation or the experience of enlightenment. There are of course some well known debates on this score, and ways of abolishing the tension: for instance, religion is to do with personal existence not the objective world; or revelation and natural knowledge are in harmony, but since knowledge changes so our worldview is constantly in need of revision (on the latter view, the adaptability of a worldview becomes a sign of truth or acceptability).

There is a special valuational side to such tensions and resolutions of tension. It is not just that some range of data has to be seen in conjunction with some other range: it is also that one is existentially more significant than another, seen from within the perspective of the worldview which is making sense of the data. Thus Jewish theology has to make sense of the Holocaust; but, sympathetic as the Buddhist may be, he is less concerned with the traumatic or other passages of history.

In fact there is a whole area of priority decisions where it is hard to know how to judge. Thus Christianity may claim to be historical, its revelation woven into the fabric of history; but how much *weight* should be attached to historicity and the historical? Again, Buddhism has contemplative experience at its heart: generally its *bhakti* or devotionalism is subsidiary to that. But for much of Christianity, such a weight placed upon the contemplative side is regarded as excessive – among Calvinists for example. Looked at from the angle of religious experience the history of religion is a ballet of different kinds: prophetic, mystical, shamanistic, psychedelic, conversional. How much weight to place upon each of the varieties? Both epistemologically and spiritually – that is, both as regards authority and applications to one's own life – the answers will be important, since the differing experiences tend to lead in differing directions, of calm, fervour, dualism, monism, fullness, emptiness, worship, meditation, ethical resolve, quietism and so forth. It may be that a criterion is comprehensiveness. For instance, can both devotional fervour and contemplative calm be held within the fabric of one faith? (It is indeed hard to resist the application of this test, which makes certain forms of Christianity, Islam, Hinduism and Buddhism, for instance, superior to others.)

Not only is there a possible tension between religions in regard to the weighting of types of religious experience – for instance Theravada Buddhism does not take seriously prophetic utterances expressive of relationship to a personal God, while the non-theistic contemplative style of the Theravada often is not taken seriously by more prophetically-oriented believers, such as Wahhabis and many conservative evangelicals; but there is also the question of the seriousness with which *any* such experience should be taken. Are they valid and are they desirable? The Marxist might doubt that they are.

It is here that there is a criterion of the persuasiveness of a given metaphysical or quasi-metaphysical framework for worldview-commitment. Thus though Marxist materialism has its symbolic side as we have noted, it also does express a certain ontology. The denial of the transcendent represents a challenge to most, though not all, religious worldviews. But the resolution of the challenge is itself a strange matter, in that it will in great measure depend on the weighting of experience and the weighting of data. Let me put things another way. Without entertaining the possibility of the transcendent one rules out religious experience as a valid avenue to the truth; but the possibility of the transcendent is taken seriously because religious experience is.

Since ethical insights are partially independent of worldview, another criterion of truth relates to the ethical, or more generally social, fruits of differing systems, both positively and negatively. Of course, fruits vary, and are shaped by their trees: preferences therefore will again figure in the weighting of fruits – how does a dozen avocadoes compare with a crate of oranges, or a gallery of saints with a procession of *arahants*?

At this point two objections, long simmering, might be raised. First, since religion is often seen as a matter of revelation, of being chosen rather than choosing, this elaborate parade of criteria is beside the point. Second, maybe a religion in any case is not universal, but really for a particular group. To take the second point first, let us consider two cases – the religion of an ethnic group, such as the Gikuyu or the Toraja: is it not just for Gikuyu or Toraja folk? The Torajas do not want to sell their faith to mankind at large; they just want to keep it in the face of outside pressures. But of course those very pressures are universalist, and to combat those forces a modification of tribal religion is needed: a kind of universalist modification to the effect 'Our religion is true too and reflects the Truth in a way peculiarly suited to our history and temperament.' Another noted case is that of Judaism, which some could interpret as the religion of a particular group: even so it is a *world* religion in a pregnant sense, for it contains within it a view of world history relevant to all men, and exhibiting the special place of the Jewish tradition within that divinely controlled pattern.

As for the point about revelation: so be it. One criterion of the truth of a worldview is its capacity to exhibit a sensitive epistemology. It may well be that if there is a God then by revelation the heart of his truth must come to men: revealed authority is epistemologically appropriate, what one might expect. Still, the fact is that there are rival revelations. It is at this point that the criteria I have already pointed to will come into play. Let met illustrate by a parable. I do not create Scotland or Canada or Italy, but supposing I am choosing which country to live in, do I not balance up the various good and bad points, the arguments for and against? We have not merely to do this, but to blend our results and make a choice. So with revelations or more generally worldviews. For we are indeed in the modern world faced with a rich and daunting range of choice. To this I shall return. Meanwhile, let me add a further point about psychology which is tangential to our previous discussion of religious experience but vitally important for all that, for it links up with the question of fruits.

Worldviews include beliefs and feelings about the nature of human beings: about whether we are intrinsically good or bad, whether our troubles originate from sin or ignorance or both, where we stand in the universe – as naked apes or what: such anthropologies gibe or fail to gibe with experience and with ordinary life, and so have the profoundest effect upon our ordinary behaviour in relation to religion and values. The testing of the plausibility of diagnoses of our condition is of course extraordinary complex: partly a matter of science (usually rather speculative, e.g. concerning the evolutionary origins of certain human traits, such as the prevalence of war and violence); partly a matter of individual experience; partly a matter of metaphysical perspective. And since religious traditions incorporate ritual elements, such as worship, sacraments, etc., then the logic of the ritual dimension has to make sense in regard to anthropology (in this sense of the term: again, a new expression is needed, for so to say one's manview, as element in a worldview–one's *anthropism*, perhaps). In other words, there is probably a highly vital link between the symbolic grammar to which I referred before and the application of ritual elements in secular worldviews.

My discussion of criteria hitherto implies a kind of interplay, even rivalry, of worldviews. For instance, the whole discussion of religious experience is vital to the claims of all the major religions, and the question of validity, with attendant questions about the status of Freudian and other psychological accounts of such experience, is clearly relevant to the secular ideologies. This of course introduces the following factor: That every tradition in a planetary world needs to have a theory about the others (even maybe the negative theory that they are blasphemous delusions). This itself generates a criterion – namely the test of the degree of plausibility of such theories (very often they break down on the facts). This need for some 'theory of the others' is part of a more general demand: that in these latter planetary days, in particular, when histories have flowed together in the estuary of world or planetary history, a worldview needs to have a theory of its place in planetary history. A universal destiny implies something of a universal accountancy. It is true that a religion like Jainism may think itself to be in an age of great decline as predicted by its own scriptures – that is itself a theory of history (though how far old Indian ideas of *kalpas* and *yugas* can stand up to modern scientific knowledge of the wide reaches of the geological and biological past is open to doubt). Again the degree of tension involved in maintaining, say, a Christian theory of history will be relevant to the truth of Christian belief.

From the foregoing it will be clear that the criteria do not dictate, for the most part, sharp decisions. The questions of truth as between worldviews are fluid, malleable. Even if biology refutes Lysenko, this does not by itself refute Stalin, and even if Stalin be in disgrace this does not refute Soviet Marxism. Even if historians refute some of the Gospel claims, this does not destroy the Gospel. This does not of course mean that *decisions* cannot be sharp: joining a monastery, being twice born, leaving the Party – these are crisp enough decisions or events, when they come, but their basis, epistemologically, is bound to be impressionistic. Epistemologically we are not of course forced into a kind of relativism, which in any case is self-defeating; but I think we are impelled towards a certain toleration, seeing that there can in religion rarely be proofs.

The philosophy of worldviews, by exploring the criteria, itself of course from its higher level has an effect on the lower. Undoubtedly some uniquenesses vanish in a comparative world; but more importantly that world in dictating criteria provides an altered agenda for Christian or other theology, Buddhology, Marxist philosophy, etc. This makes systematic theology more difficult, but richer, of course.

And incidentally, since it is faiths which men live by, part of their lives, the philosophy of worldviews must have a crucial place in general philosophy. We are of course still very far from understanding how beliefs influence actions, so there is much to explore in the relationship between the philosophy of worldviews and ethics.

Personally, I believe that what I have here sketched as the task of the philosophy of religion and more broadly the philosophy of worldviews is of extraordinary importance at the present time in world history. Maybe I can expatiate a little on why this is so, for important though it is in this kind of philosophising to preserve a kind of higher-order neutrality and an even-handed empathy, it in no way follows that the results of one's thus calmer cerebrations do not have some important, disturbing and exhilarating implications. In what follows I sketch such consequences as I perceive them.

The first consequence is that our intellectual enterprises, in so far as they reflect on the nature and destiny of human beings, need to be consciously planetary. The remarkable histories of Chinese, Indian and other thought, the achievements of varied cultures – these can all now be tributaries towards the fashioning of a worldview. The element of toleration liable to arise from a recognition of the softness of criteria naturally tends towards a kind of federal and to some extent eclectic approach to worldviews. Indeed, though there are oppositions of religious doctrines and imperatives, there are areas of noncontradiction – for religious systems being organic are not clusters of entailments, not geometries of the spirit; by consequence there are always insights which can be woven into one's own tradition or movement. It is true that some worldviews are not very tolerant or open, but again it does not follow that the perceptions behind them cannot be learned from. So I do not see all religions and ideologies merging in a fuzzy haze – this is neither logically appropriate nor humanly likely; but there is a strong argument for a federalism of persons of good will.

Second, the philosophy of worldviews forcibly suggests that since ongoing religions and ideologies need to 'place' themselves in world history, to contemplate, that is, their planetary destiny, so there is humanistic need to revive concern for this kind of history-making.

Third, the philosophy of worldviews reminds one how much the practical and the theoretical are interwoven in men's systems of belief, in a way which leads to a gap between epistemology and commitment: that is between the softness of evidence and the deep meaning of movement or tradition. Certitude combines with impressionistic grounds – as with a man 'certain' a given horse is going to win. This in turn means that the philosophy of worldviews is also about communities, nations, parties, groups. It is not just about beliefs or about propositions which an individual as an individual can adopt or reject. Thus a kind of liberal atomism of belief is not a good conclusion out of the pluralism of men's worldviews. There needs to be a federalism of groups as well.

Furthermore, as philosophy of worldviews wrestles with the analysis of myth and of that charged facticity which somehow bridges the gap between object and feeling, it will increasingly remind us of the symbolic character of so much human belief and action. Herein lies, in my view, the clue to a new approach to politics as well as to ethics. Maximising human dignity, which is the best we can strive for in these spheres, implies considering not just what material things, bureaucratic institutions, work conditions, etc., *do* for people, but what they *mean* to people. The student of religion has an important function in extending our understanding of the symbolic phenomenology of everyday life.

I hope I have argued clearly enough that the philosophy of religion should be extended to be the philosophy of worldviews, and that it should be the upper storey of a building which has as its middle floor the comparative and historical analysis of religions and ideologies, and as a ground floor the phenomenology not just of religious experience and action but of the symbolic life of a man as a whole.

Part II
The Comparative Study of Religion

8 Living Liberation: Jivanmukti and Nirvana

Too often the understanding of the early Buddhist idea of nirvana has been hampered by the failure to note the two aspects of liberation. Or to put matters another way, nirvana has not been looked at sufficiently as a case of *jīvanmukti* or 'living liberation'. Such a conception has, of course, proved highly influential in the Indian tradition; and perhaps its most natural milieu has been that of a yogic tradition. That is to say, it implies the overcoming of those forces impelling the individual to further involvement in the round of *saṃsāra*, in such a way that the individual has only to finish off the remains of his current life; then there will be no more rebirth. Typically, the means of achieving this state of *jīvanmukti* are yogic meditation and austerity. Different schools and movements have differing emphases.

Let us consider, by way of illustration, the situation in Sañkhya-Yoga, as this dual school came to formulate itself. Here innumerable *puruṣa*s are implicated in rebirth; but more generally they are implicated in *prakṛti*, that is, nature. The material, natural world is one great system breathing in and out, so to speak, as the cosmos forms out of chaos through the interplay of the *guṇas*, and then relapses at the end of an enormous cycle into grey equipoise once more, waiting secretly for the next evolutionary process to begin. In this great system are dotted an infinity of transmigrating souls, experiencing *duḥkha* or illfare, moving perhaps towards release. Release means, of course, the freeing of the *puruṣa* from the psycho-physical organism to which it has been wedded hitherto forever. Imagine, therefore, what strain and self-control, what knowledge and meditative skill, are required to achieve assurance of release – to achieve assurance through actuality, and to be released here and now.

However, we would be a little anachronistic in comparing directly this Sañkhya-Yoga system with that of early Buddhism. Yet undoubtedly the *general* form of such a belief in rebirth, yoga, souls and

89

mukti was present in the Buddha's environment. And we also have to look towards the pattern of Jaina belief and practice, not at all dissimilar; stressing, however, *tapas* and *ahimsā*.

Yet it was more than in practice that early Buddhism trod a middle path. In theory also it steered between souls and materialism, rejecting the former but asserting rebirth. This mediation meant an entirely original perspective upon rebirth and salvation. For whereas other movements – Ajivakas and Jainas, for example – postulated souls and so something which could, *post mortem*, achieve 'final liberation', Buddhism could not treat its *jīvanmukti* in this mode at all. And that, as is well known indeed, was bound to lead to the question as to what becomes of the Buddha or saint (*arhant*) after death. That nirvana can, however, looked on profitably as a form of *jīvanmukti* should not on that account be doubted, and Louis Finot was right to insist upon the point.[1] Yet what is at first sight puzzling is that in the case of Buddhism there is nothing to be liberated, or rather (to put it more particularly) there is no soul (*puruṣa*, *jīva* or *ātman*) to be liberated.

Nevertheless it is unwise to be *too* puzzled by this. For consider the situation in our previous 'model', namely Saṅkhya-Yoga. The *puruṣa* there is only in one sense individual. It is individual in the sense, first that it is not numerically identical with any other *puruṣa*, and, second, it is uniquely co-ordinated to a given psycho-physical organism (and its predecessors in the transmigratory sequence). For the sake of clarity I shall refer to the individual in a given (e.g. the current) life as 'individual' and to the sequence as the 'macro-individual' – so that John Jones is an individual but the sequence up to and including him (and stretching into the future, unless he is a *jīvanmukta*) is the macro-individual.[2] To recapitulate, the *puruṣa*, in the Saṁkhya-Yoga system, is uniquely correlated to a particular macro-individual. Similarly, the *jīva* in the Jaina system is so correlated. However, though the *puruṣa* is uniquely correlated to a macro-individual, the characteristics and elements which make up the latter do not belong to the soul. To put it more concretely, what makes up the individual Surasena and his predecessors in the sequence is not carried over into the *post mortem* liberated sense. Thus it is characteristic of systems of salvation of the relevant sort – mainly śramanic – not to consider final *mukti* as belonging strictly to the psychophysical individual. All this can be put another way: the soul is *beyond* the mental constituents of the individual. The soul-organism distinction is not all to be equated with the mind-body distinction. So the Western question 'Can there be disembodied existence after death?' is not strictly relevant to the Indian case.

This is brought out at the cosmological level also. As is well known – and it is a striking aspect of Buddhist cosmology in particular – many Indian systems of belief do not equate *post mortem* liberation with heavenly existence. Nirvana lies beyond heaven. One can have a glorious disembodied existence in one of the heavens, say as one of the Brahmas. But this is still impermanent and in principle shot through with *dukkha*. Thus imaginatively the line between unsatisfactory existence and liberation is drawn in a different place and in a different way from its analogues in the traditions of the West and the Middle East.

This match between the cosmic and the individual levels may in part help us to understand why the question of the infinity (endlessness) of the *loka* as to space and time was also undetermined, as well as the question of the survival of the 'thus gone' person after death. A.K. Warder writes:

> These extracts would seem to confirm that the notions of 'soul' and 'universe' are very closely associated, belong to the same realm of ideas, from the standpoint of the Buddha. If we are right in concluding that for the Buddha there was no such thing as the 'universe', then we must conclude that for him the question of its being finite or infinite in space and time is meaningless instead of being beyond our knowledge.[3]

However, something more than this needs to be said.

First, the question of the survival of the *Tathāgata* after death seems to be meaningless in a deep sense, as K. N. Jayatilleke pointed out; the parallel with Wittgenstein's doctrine of certain utterances as being meaningless is plausible.[4] Perhaps one can put the point by the following example. It is not the case that the present king of France is bald; nor is he not bald – and the reason is that there is no king of France. And the survival of the *Tathāgata* cannot be affirmed or denied, in that there is no soul to 'carry over'. But whereas it merely *happens* to be the case that there are no kings of France these days, the non-existence of the *atman* is not thus contingent. It is part of 'the nature of things' as revealed by Buddhist analysis and experience.

It might be replied that this interpretation of meaningless depends heavily on the passage about the fire going out (whither does it go when it goes out? – a wrongly-posed question);[5] whereas there is also a pragmatic interpretation, implied by the simile of the arrow: work out your salvation without bothering yourself with the distractions of metaphysical speculation. But of course the two accounts are up to a point compatible. Theory and practice go solidly together in the teaching of the Buddha. There might be incompatibility in so far as the pragmatic interpretation can easily be taken to mean that one *can* answer the question about the *Tathāgata*, that there are possible theories here. And this is in conflict with the notion that the question is wrongly put and so unanswerable. Incidentally, it is of the utmost importance to notice that in early Buddhism, and in the later Theravada, it is only a certain set of questions that is held to be unanswerable. There is no necessity for the inference that *all* metaphysical views were excluded; for instance, the analysis of the *skandhas*, the doctrine of dependent origination, more generally the account of causation – these and many other aspects of Buddhist teaching are in an important sense metaphysical. (The Madhyamika, of course, was bold enough to generalise the fourfold negation; but this is only one interpretation of the Buddha's meaning, not shared by most other schools.)

In brief, then, one needs first to note that a partial pragmatic account is not inconsistent with the 'Wittgensteinian' interpretation; and second to bear in mind that particular questions are undetermined – and this means that we need to see in particular why this is so. In the case of the survival of the *Tathāgata*, part of the reason is the non-existence of the *atman*, the *necessary* non-existence of it, on Buddhist analysis. It is only part of the explanation, in that we have to consider positively why there is a nirvāna without substrate (*anupādisesa*). But in the meantime let us apply the present account to the question of the everlastingness of the universe, etc. As we have seen, Warder considers that the Buddha essentially rejected the very idea of the *loka*, just as he rejected the *atman*. But is this correct? Certainly there are plenty of uses of the term in the Pali canon, yet this is a very indecisive argument, for the term *attā* is also used in a conventional (*vyāvahārika*) way.

First, note a parallel between the question about the *Tathāgata* and the question about the *loka*. In the former the question is about continued existence, but there is no question about the existence of the *Tathāgata* here and now (so to speak) – this is assumed. So is it not more proper to look on the question of the *loka* as about its continued existence, but without any implication that there is no such thing as the *loka*? In the discussion preceding the conclusion which I have quoted above, Warder rightly draws attention to the connection between ideas of continued existence (of the *loka*) and survival (i.e. of the macro-individual). But it would be more apposite to conclude that the reason for the *loka*'s neither being nor not being endless in space and time has to do precisely with the question of 'how you come to the end of the *loka*', that is, with the question of nirvana.

Let us look at this from the temporal aspect. Virtually Buddhism treats rebirth as endless – so that the macro-individual always was and always will be unless he attains nirvana, in which case rebirth ceases and there is a state of ultimate liberation, but of whom we cannot properly inquire. All this implies that in some important sense the *loka* or cosmos always was and in principle always will be. True, it cannot be treated as a timeless entity, it is made up of events – of impermanencies. Still looking at the *loka* existentially – that is, from the point of view of experience, or from the point of view of the indissoluble wedding between theory and practice which so charac-terises the Buddhist approach – it has a sort of end. The question, however, is wrongly put if it is asked simply about what is 'out there', for the spiritual relevance of the question necessarily connects with the possibility of our 'making an end'. There is a sort of end of the cosmos as we disappear 'into' nirvana and there is no rebirth any more for the particular macro-individual. On the other hand, the disappearance of one macro-individual from *saṃsāra* does not entail the disappearance of others. *Saṃsāra* still goes on. If the question 'Is there an end to the *loka*?' is asked simply from an autobiographical point of view, then the answer is that there is a possible end to the macro-individual, but it is not a spatial limit, so to speak. From the autobiographical point of view, where the existential question has to do with liberation, the question about the endlessness of the world in space is wrongly put, i.e. irrelevant.

However, if there is an end of the macro-individual through the onset of *nibbāna*, surely there is a temporal end to the cosmos, for *me*? But here the question becomes virtually identical with the question about whether the saint exists after death. Further, there is a question about whether the *nibbāna* element is to be counted as part of the *loka* or not. We must remember the very fine gradations of existence which are to be found in the Buddhist cosmology. The matching of differing types of existence to the range of *jhānas*, right up to the sphere of neither-perception-nor-non-perception,[6] indicates a partly psychological approach to cosmology, one which could perhaps be characterised as 'existential' in the modern sense. How-

ever, the fineness of the gradations means that at the most elevated
level of consciousness and existence one is getting to what in other
system of belief could be regarded as liberation. Nirvana lies beyond, of course; but the Buddhist mood is not one of a sharp line to
be drawn between the *loka* with all its invisible and divine realms and
the state of ultimate liberation. The Buddha, as a liberated one,
could come to be regarded as transcendental or *lokottara*; and there
is an important sense in which nirvana is transcendent. But the
distinction between the highest spheres of the *loka* and nirvana is a
delicate one. It turns, of course, essentially on the idea of permanence, to which I shall return in a moment.

As to the distinction between transcendental nirvana and the *loka*,
another point is worth seeing – namely that it is (roughly speaking)
the same distinction as that between *anupādisesa* and *saupādisesa*
nibbāna.[7] Nirvana with substrate is a dispositional state of an identifiable individual, one which accrues upon a form of *gnosis*, or existential knowledge of the truth of things accompanied by complete
serenity. It is a dispositional state in the sense that the person who is
nibbuta is no longer in the grip of craving and ignorance, and this
shows through in his actions, words, gestures and so on. On the
orthodox line, it is an unbreakable disposition – the *arhat* cannot fall
away. (If he appears to do so, it only goes to show that he was not
nibutta in the first place.). Since, however, nirvana without substrate
involves, as we have seen, the disappearance of the macro-individual,
we cannot speak of anything or anybody as now identifiable, so that
the dispositional analysis of nirvana cannot any more apply. And in
so far as the saint in this life can be said to have 'seen' or 'tasted'
nirvana and to have, as it were, crossed to the other shore, we can
also quite legitimately think of *anupādisesa nibbāna* as being, as it
were, a transcendent state already present to the saint. Or, to put this
another way, the nirvāna with and without substrate coexist as well as
succeed one another in time, in relation to a given macro-individual.
Empirical nirvana (nirvana with substrate) involves 'seeing' transcendent nirvana. The saint sees and is in contact with the changeless.

Here we need to turn to the question of permanence. The whole
way of analysing the world from a Buddhist point of view turns on the
distinction between that which is impermanent and that which is
permanent. It may not be the whole of the doctrine of *dukkha* that
what is impermanent is therefore unsatisfactory and painful. But yet
there is some plausibility in seeing the other two marks of existence
(*anattā* and *dukkha*) as flowing from the impermanence of things

(*anicca*). The impermanence of individuals entails that they do not consist partly in changeless souls. Likewise the *loka* has no eternal changeless heart (so to speak), even if it may in effect be everlasting, continually in flux. It is no great exaggeration to say that the whole Buddhist metaphysical and existential analysis depends on where the line is drawn between the changing and the changeless. (More generally, it is this distinction which is vital in most Indian systems of salvation; thus, for example, Saṁkara's doctrine of *māyā* boils down essentially to the notion that the world is changeable and impermanent and so does not bring the higher satisfaction, the realisation of one's destiny into the eternal Brahma.)

But whereas Saṁkara, for example, could be said to draw a dualism between substance and substance – between Brahman and the visible universe, etc. – which has some analogues at least between the God–world distinction in the Western tradition, the Theravadin distinction between the temporal and the changeless is more a state-state dualism (or an element-element dualism). That is, in the one case the distinction is between a permanent entity and a congeries of impermanent entities; in the other the division is between the eternal state of nirvaṇa and the impermanent state or events of the empirical world (including the various heavens and purgatories).

Since Saṁkara was a bit influenced by the Mahayana and in particular by the Madhyamika school, it is interesting to bring into the comparison the idea of *śūnya*, the Void, also called *tathatā*. These words are used fleetingly to refer to 'ultimate reality'. And yet *śūnyatā* suggests a phantasmagorical ultimate *unreality*. The 'higher truth' of the Void confronts the 'empirical truth' of ordinary experience. It goes without saying, in the Buddhist context, that the Void has a reference in meditational experience. However, the atmosphere (if I can put the matter so vaguely) of the Madhyamika is more that of substance-substance dualism than of state-state dualism.[8] This connects, perhaps paradoxically, with the nirvana-*saṁsāra* identification, which looks like a kind of monism. The identification can without too much strain, but alas with a certain crudity, be explicated in the following way. Liberation means the attainment of Buddhahood. The essence of the latter is the *dharma* (or the *dharmakāya*), which is what the teaching refers to. This is the Void, which has two aspects, one experiential and the other metaphysical. (These two aspects, indeed, correspond loosely to the two aspects of the Buddhist doctrine of the *loka* – both metaphysical or analytic and at the same time practical and experiential.) The experiential aspect is that the perception of the higher truth (in brief, enlightenment) is non-dual and uncharacterised, therefore, by the distinctions of everyday existence. From the latter point of view it is empty, and it is in fact devoid (or one should, no doubt, say *void*) of the distinctions and distractions of discursive thought and ordinary emotions, etc. On the metaphysical front, the world of everyday entities is empty, for nothing has real substance, and every theory of reality contains contradictions. The tangible and the real – these turn out to have no real permanence and no 'inner stuff'. Their real nature is the void. It follows that *saṁsāra* has the Void as its inner reality. But the Void is the true nature of the Buddha. So the essence of Buddhahood, which is also nirvana, is the essence of the phenomenal world. Therefore nirvana and *saṁsāra* are the same! A meaningful and intelligible paradox.

The identity signifies a kind of monism; but there remains the dualism, for there are two levels of reality or truth to notice. The main difference between this idea and the main distinction of the Theravada is that the void is 'the true nature of things' while also being the essence of liberation, while in the Theravada liberation is not the 'true nature of things' (the latter is dealt with rather separately through the idea of the three marks of conditioned existence) but a distinct state. It is possible to evolve a theory of why the Mahayana went for what I have referred to as a 'monistic' account, and I have tried to give some sort of an explanation elsewhere.[9]

It might further be remarked that the Mahayana dualism is marked, more positively than in the Pali tradition, by a doctrine of two levels of truth. Though the distinction exists in the Theravada, it is there treated (if I may put it so) 'less ontologically'. And being less systematically applied, it turns out to mean that the analysis of reality is hampered by the conventional acceptance of words: once analysis umasks reality, however, it is entirely legitimate to carry on talking 'conventionally' (even if the illusions of language have now been dissipated, so that ordinary language suffers a sort of a sea change).

Perhaps we can now return, after these excursions, to the idea of *nibbāna* or liberation as it is to be found in the Pali canon. Although the analysis of the world in terms of the three characteristics of existence is itself a means of liberation and so to be interpreted up to a point as 'existential', the analysis leans towards the realistic (just as by contrast the Mahayana analysis leans towards the subjective and the ideal). The fact that the Theravadin analysis is of this kind is no coincidence. The equation between nirvana and saṁsāra implied that knowledge was the key – for the adept had only to realise that there was no difference in order to be liberated: the realisation of the non-difference makes the difference. This doctrine (whatever its other merits and defects) was one which was favourable to laymen. They were, so to speak, already there, if only they could realise the truth; and the lack of distinction between the 'beyond' and 'here' was also reflected in increasingly strong feelings that the laymen would here and now attain conversion and release. By contrast the state-state dualism of the Theravada did not encourage lay optimism, and there was and is a very powerful insistence on methods of meditation as the key to the way upward and ultimately to nirvana. This emphasis is, of course, not absent from the Mahayana. But the Theravada retains an emphasis on the effort of the individual as the key to liberation.

It is a strong, strong effort, because of the way in which lives previously led and previously conceived to have generated a lot of *karma* may strongly jeopardise the vocation of the monk. The whole pattern of belief in rebirth and *jīvanmukti* implies strenuous self-training, as also in the Jaina tradition. Further, the pursuit of liberation as it is represented in the Pali canon does not imply anything about reliance upon divinity.[10] On the other hand, the celestial Buddhas and Bodhisattvas of the Mahayana provide a means towards liberation where individual effort is stressed much less.

At all events, the realism of Theravada metaphysics and the dualism of impermanent states and permanent state fits in with the ethics of energetic striving after liberation. At the same time I have in this analysis been concerned also to stress the 'existential' aspects of Theravadin cosmology, and it is partly because of these that the questions about survival after death and the everlastingness of the cosmos are undetermined. I have attempted to indicate how it is that both the Wittgensteinian and the pragmatic accounts are relevant to the understanding of the Buddha's teaching on these matters. It is difficult to solve the historical question of what early Buddhism said without trying to penetrate to what it meant.

9 Interpretation and Mystical Experience

Unfortunately the term 'mysticism' and its relations ('mystical', etc.) are used by different people in different senses. For the purposes of this article I shall treat mysticism as primarily consisting in an interior or introvertive quest, culminating in certain interior experiences which are not described in terms of sense-experience or of mental images. But such an account needs supplementation in two directions: first, examples of people who typify the mystical life should be given, and second, mysticism should be distinguished from that which is *not* (on this usage) mysticism.

First, then, I would propose that the following persons typify the mystical life: St. John of the Cross, Tauler, Eckhart, Al-Hallaj, Shankara, the Buddha, Lao-Tzu (if he existed!), and many yogis.

Secondly, mysticism is *not* prophetism, and can be distinguished from devotionalism or *bhakti* religion (though mysticism often intermingles with these forms of religious life and experience). I would propose that the following are *not* mystics in the relevant sense in which the Buddha and the others *are* mystics: Isaiah, Jeremiah, Muhammad, Ramanuja, Nichiren and Calvin.

Needless, perhaps, to say, such expressions as the 'mystical body of Christ' have no necessary connection with mysticism in the proposed sense. It is unfortunate that a word which etymologically means sacramentalism has come to be used in a different sense. Since, however, 'mysticism' now is most often used to refer to the mode of life and experience typified by men like St. John of the Cross and Shankara, I shall use the term, though 'contemplation' and 'contemplative' can be less misleading.

Thus 'mysticism' will here be used to refer to the contemplative life and experience, as distinguished from prophetism, devotionalism and sacramentalism (though we must keep in mind the fact mentioned

98

above – that prophetic and sacramental religion are often interwoven with that of mysticism).

II

In a number of works, Professor Zaehner has distinguished between three categories of mystical experience:

(1) Panenhenic or nature mysticism (as exemplified by Rimbaud, Jefferies and others).
(2) Monistic mysticism (as found, for example, in Advaita, Samkhya-Yoga).
(3) Theistic mysticism (as in the Christian tradition or the *Gītā*).

His distinction between the first and the other two is correct and valuable. The sense of rapport with nature often comes to people in a striking and intimate way; but it is to be contrasted with the interior experience in which, as it were, a man plumbs the depths of his own soul. It is probable that Zen *satori* is to be equated with panenhenic experience, though Zen also makes use of the general pattern of Buddhist yoga which elsewhere culminates in an interior rather than a panenhenic type of experience.

But is Zaehner's distinction between monistic and theistic mysticism a valid one? He criticises those who believe that mysticism is everywhere the same – a belief sometimes held in conjunction with the neo-Vedantin thesis that behind the various forms of religion there is a higher truth realisable in contemplative experience and best expressed through the doctrine of a universal Self (or Atman). On Zaehner's view, monistic mysticism is 'realising the eternal oneness of one's own soul' as contrasted with the 'mysticism of the love of God'.[1] The latter attainment is typical of Christian, Muslim and other theistic contemplation.

Zaehner believes in an eternal soul, as well as in God, and is thus able to claim that there is a real entity which the monistic mystic experiences, even if it is not the highest entity (which is God). In addition, he holds, or has held, that monistic mysticism can be explained through the doctrine of the Fall. Thus he is not merely concerned to analyse mysticism, but also to explain it through a (theological) theory. He writes as follows:

Assuming, as we are still encouraged to do, that man developed physically from the higher apes, we must interpret the creation of Adam as an original infusion of the divine essence into what had previously been an anthropoid ape. Adam, then, would represent the union of the orders of nature and grace, the order of coming to be and passing away which is created from nothing by God, and the infused spirit of God. Adam, after he sinned, brought bodily death into the world, but did not and could not destroy his soul, because the soul was infused into him from God and therefore was itself divine. Though Adam may have repented, he was no longer able to take the supreme step of offering himself back completely and entirely to God, because he had lost contact with his source and could no longer find it again. Thus, tradition has it, at death his soul departed to Limbo, where, like all disinterested Yogins who have sought to separate their immortal souls from all that is transient and ungodlike, yet who cannot acknowledge God, it enjoyed the highest natural bliss, the soul's contemplation of itself as it issued from the hand of God and of all created things as they are in the sight of God. . . . The proof, it seems to me, that I am not talking pure nonsense is the complete difference of approach which separates the theistic from the monistic mystic. The latter achieves liberation entirely by his own efforts since there is no God apart from himself to help him or with whom he can be united. In the case of the theistic mystic, on the other hand, it is always God who takes the first step, and it is God who works in the soul and makes it fit for union.[2]

Thus Zaehner not only distinguishes types of mysticism: he links his distinction to a theology of the Fall. Though it is not the main concern of this article to consider this theological theory, it may be useful to go into certain criticisms which can be levelled at it, since some of them are relevant to Zaehner's doctrine of types of mysticism.

III

In linking his analysis of mysticism to a theory about the special creation of Adam and his Fall, Zaehner weakens his position, since his interpretation of the Adam story may be radically questioned. The doubts and objects which arise are, briefly, as follows:

(a) The Biblical narrative, which is the principal basis for people's belief in the existence of Adam, says nothing about anthropoid apes and nothing about an eternal soul as such. Still less does it make Adam out to be like a Yogin.

(b) Adam cannot have brought bodily death into the world, since the apes are not immortal. But let us assume that Adam was different, and was initially immortal, because of the divine essence infused into him. How does this imply that there was no bodily death for him? Does it mean that God did something to the bodily side of Adam, making the flesh and bones which Adam inherited from the apes into something mysteriously imperishable? It is not a likely story.

(c) Not all Christians would accept the theory of a substantial eternal soul. But in any case, it does not follow that this is what the monistic mystic realises in his inner contemplative experience. The Advaitin would believe that he has realised the oneness of the Atman with the divine being; while the adherent of Yoga would not. This is a big difference of interpretation, and if we were to take it at its face value we might be inclined to say that the Advaitin and the Yogin have attained different states. But do we have to take their claims at their face value? This raises important methodological issues.

Does the Advaitin make his claim simply on the basis of an inner contemplative experience? It is not so. The concept of Brahman as a divine Reality ultimately derives from an extension of the idea of the sacred Power implicit in pre-Upanishadic sacrificial ritual. The famous identification of Atman with Brahman involves bringing together different strands of religious thought and life. It is not something yielded by contemplative experience alone, even though the latter is highly relevant to it.

Likewise, the theistic mystic, in thinking that he has attained a kind of union with God, must already have the concept of God – as a personal Being, creator of the world, author of revelation, etc. His description of his experience, where this includes mention of God, is thus not derived *simply* from the nature of that experience. The mystic does not know that God is creator from a mere inspection of an interior state: rather he relates that inner state to beliefs which he already has.

Zaehner's theory, too, obviously includes data derived from sources other than those contained in mystical literature. In interpreting what happens to the Yogin he draws on certain elements in the Christian tradition. It therefore seems that the truth of his theory depends partly on the truth of Christianity (at least, negatively: if Christianity were false, Zaehner's theory would be false, though the falsity of his theory is compatible with the truth of Christianity, since the latter is not necessarily committed to beliefs about anthropoid apes and the like).

These points indicate that we must examine in more detail the methodology of the evaluation and interpretation of mystical experience.

IV

That some distinction must be made between experience and interpretation is clear. For it is generally recognised, and certainly by Zaehner, that there are types of mystical experience cutting across different religions and theologies. That is to say, it is recognised that a mystic of one religion and some mystic of another faith can have what is substantially a similar experience. Thus as we have noted, both Christian and Muslim mystics come under Zaehner's category of theistic mysticism; while, for him, Advaitin and Yogin mysticism belong to the monistic category. But the interpretations within a type differ. We have seen a large doctrinal distinction between Advaita and Yoga. The latter believes in a plurality of eternal *purushas*, not in a single Atman. Consequently its account of liberation, and therefore of contemplative experience, differs from that of Advaita. Thus on Zaehner's own thesis it becomes very necessary to distinguish between experience and interpretation, when two experiences belong to the same class but have rather different modes of interpretation.

Nevertheless, the distinction between experience and interpretation is not clear-cut. The reason for this is that the concepts used in describing and explaining an experience vary in their degree of ramification. That is to say, where a concept occurs as part of a doctrinal scheme it gains its meaning in part from a range of doctrinal statements taken to be true. For example, the term 'God' in the Christian context gains part at least of its characteristic meaning from such doctrinal statements as 'God created the universe', 'Jesus Christ is God', 'God has acted in history'.

Thus when Suso writes 'In this merging of itself in God the spirit passes away', he is describing a contemplative experience by means of the highly ramified concept *God*, the less ramified concept *spirit* and the still less ramified concept *pass away*. In order to understand the statement it is necessary to bear in mind the doctrinal ramifications contained in it. Thus it follows, for Suso as a Christian, that in this merging of itself in the Creator of the universe, the spirit passes away; and so on.

By contrast, some descriptions of mystical experience do not involve such wide ramifications. For instance 'When the spirit by the loss of its self-consciousness has in very truth established its abode in this glorious and dazzling obscurity' – here something of the nature of the experience is conveyed without any doctrine's being presupposed as true (except in so far as the concept *spirit* may involve some belief in an eternal element within man). This, then, is a relatively unramified description. Thus description of mystical experience range from the highly ramified to those which have a very low degree of ramification.[3]

It is to be noted that ramifications may enter into the descriptions either because of the intentional nature of the experience or through reflection upon it. Thus a person brought up in a Christian environment and strenuously practising the Christian life may have a contemplative experience which he sees *as* a union with God. The whole spirit of his interior quest will affect the way he sees his experience; or, to put it another way, the whole spirit of his quest will enter into the experience. On the other hand, a person might only come to see the experience in this way after the event, as it were: upon reflection he interprets his experience in theological categories.

In all descriptions of mystical experience, then, we ought to be on the lookout for ramifications. Their degree can be crudely estimated by asking: How many propositions are presupposed as true by the description in question?

It would also seem to follow, if we bear in mind the notion of degrees of ramification, that the higher the degree of ramification, the less is the description guaranteed by the experience itself. For where there is a high degree of ramification, some statements will be presupposed which have to be verified in other ways than by immediate mystical experience. Thus a mystic who claims to become united with Christ presupposes that the historical Jesus is the Christ; and the historicity of Jesus is guaranteed by the written records, not by an interior experience. Again, where contemplation is regarded as a means of liberation from rebirth, the description of the mystical experience may involve reference to this doctrine (thus the concept nirvana presupposes the truth of the rebirth doctrine). To say that someone has in this life attained the peace and insight of nirvana is also to claim that he will not be reborn. But the truth of rebirth is not discovered through mystical experience as such. It is true that the

Buddhist yogin may claim super-normal knowledge of previous lives: but this is in the nature of memory, if anything, and is to be distinguished from the formless, imageless inner experience which accrues upon the practice of *jhāna*. Also, Buddhists appeal to other empirical and philosophical evidence in support of the claim that the rebirth doctrine is true.[4]

The idea of degrees of ramification may help to clarify the distinction between experience and interpretation. But a further methodological point is also important. Descriptions, etc., of religious experience may be made from various points of view. There is the description given by the man himself, in terms of his own tradition. There is the description which others of his own tradition may give. Also, men of another tradition may describe his experience in terms of *their* tradition or standpoint. Thus if a Christian says that the Buddha's Enlightenment-experience involved some kind of interior vision of God, he is describing the experience from his own point of view and not from that of the Buddha. We crucially, then, should distinguish between a mystic's interpretation of his own experience and the interpretation which may be placed upon it from a different point of view. In other words, we must distinguish between what may be called *auto*-interpretation and *hetero*-interpretation.[5]

The difference between the auto-interpretation of an experience and the hetero-interpretation of it will depend on, first, the degree of ramification involved and, secondly, the difference between the presupposed truths incorporated in the ramification. For example, the Christian evaluation of the Buddha's Enlightenment-experience posited above uses the concept *God* in the Christian sense. The Buddhist description on the other hand does not. Thus the Christian hetero-interpretation presupposes such propositions as that God created the world, God was in Christ, among others, and these propositions are not accepted in the Buddhist auto-interpretation. By contrast the Jewish and Christian interpretations of Isaiah's experience in the Temple overlap in great measure. This is because the beliefs presupposed coincide over a reasonably wide range.

These methodological observations, though rather obvious, need stating because they are too commonly neglected.

We may conclude so far, then, that a description of a mystical experience can fall under one of the following heads:

(a) Low auto-interpretation: auto-interpretation with a low degree of ramification.

(b) Low hetero-interpretation: hetero-interpretation with a low degree of ramification.
(c) High auto-interpretation: auto-interpretation with a high degree of ramification.
(d) High hetero-interpretation: hetero-interpretation with a high degree of ramification.

We may note that a high hetero-interpretation of experience (E) will usually imply the falsity or inadequacy of a high auto-interpretation of (E), and conversely. It would therefore seem to be a sound principle to try to seek a low hetero-interpretation coinciding well with a low auto-interpretation. In this way an agreed phenomenological account of (E) will be arrived at, and this will facilitate the attempt to distinguish experience from interpretation. But since (E) will often be affected by its high auto-interpretation, it is also important to understand this high auto-interpretation, without obscuring it by means of a high hetero-interpretation.

I shall argue that Zaehner's distinction between monistic and theistic mysticism partly depends on his own high hetero-interpretation, and partly on his not distinguishing between high and low auto-interpretation.

V

A difficulty about Zaehner's classification arises once we examine Buddhism. It is undoubtedly the case that Buddhism – and very clearly in Theravada Buddhism – centres on mystical experience. The Eightfold Path incorporates and culminates in a form of yoga which may bring the peace and insight of nirvana to the saint. Crucial in this yoga is the practice of the *jhānas* or stages of meditation. It is thus necessary for any account of mysticism to take Buddhist experience and tradition seriously. But regrettably (from Zaehner's point of view) Buddhism denies the soul or eternal self. Zaehner, in order to fit Buddhism into the monistic pigeon-hole, denies this denial, and ascribes an *ātman* doctrine to the Buddha.

This will not do, for a number of reasons.[6] First, even if (incredibly) the Buddha did teach an *ātman* doctrine, we still have to reckon with the Buddhists. The phenomenon of Buddhist mysticism, not involving an *ātman*-type auto-interpretation, remains; and it is both widespread and important in the fabric of man's religious experience.

Secondly, it is asking too much to make us believe that a doctrine which has been eschewed by nearly all Buddhists (with the possible exception of the *pudgalavādins*, who significantly did not dare to use the term *ātman*, even though their Buddhist opponents castigated them for wanting to introduce the idea) was explicitly taught by the Buddha. The *anattā* teaching is about the strongest bit of the earliest tradition which we possess.

Thirdly, it is easy enough to play around with the texts by translating *atta* with a capital, as 'Self'. Thus Zaehner translates *attagarahi*[7] as 'that the Self would blame', and so on. He refers us to *Dhammapada* 165 to show that evil is done by the empirical ego; so that in vs. 157, when we are enjoined to treat the self as dear, it must be the eternal Self which is being referred to. But consider the former passage. It reads: 'By oneself is evil done; one is defiled by one-self . . . by oneself one is made pure; the pure and the impure stand and fall by themselves; no one can purify another.' Does one really want to translate: 'By oneself is evil done; . . . by one's Self is one made pure'? The point could have been expressed more clearly if the author had wanted to say *this*. The whole purport of such passages is that one should be self-reliant and responsible (and I do not mean Self-reliant!). The fact is that the word *atta* is very common, and has an ordinary usage. It is a gross strain on the texts to read in the meaning ascribed to them by Zaehner.

Fourth, Zaehner thinks his case is confirmed by the passages 'illustrating what the Self is not'[8] – it is not the body, feelings, dispositions, etc. But these passages in no way help Zaehner. Their import is clearly explained in the famous passage of the *Milinda-pañha* (40–45), where the Humean analysis of the individual is given. The Buddha himself, furthermore, is reported as having asserted that though it is wrong to identify the self with the body, it is better for the uninstructed man to make this mistake than to commit the opposite error of believing in an eternal soul.[9]

For these and other reasons, Zaehner's interpretation cannot seriously be defended. But embarrassing consequences flow from this conclusion. It means that a main form of mysticism does not involve a monistic auto-interpretation.

Nevertheless, Zaehner could still argue as follows. Admittedly a monistic auto-interpretation is not present among Buddhist con-templatives: but it is still reasonable to 'hetero-interpret' their attain-ment in a monistic fashion. We can still say (can we not?) that what the Buddhist *really* achieves in and through contemplation is the isolation of his eternal soul.

Such a defence, however, implies that there can be a misunderstanding on the part of a mystic as to what it is he is attaining. It implies that auto-interpretations can be widely mistaken, in so far as they are ramified.

Likewise, since Zaehner classifies both Yoga and Advaita together as monistic, and since their doctrinal auto-interpretations differ very widely, within the Hindu context it has to be admitted that wrong auto-interpretation can occur.

Let us bring this out more explicitly. According to Zaehner, Buddhist, Yoga and Advaitin mystics belong together, and fit in the same monistic category, and yet the following three doctrines of liberation are propounded by them:

(1) That there are no eternal selves, but only impermanent individuals who are, however, capable of liberation, through attaining nirvana in this life, in which case they will no more be reborn.
(2) That there is an infinite number of eternal selves, who through Yoga can attain isolation or liberation, a state in which the soul exists by itself, no longer implicated in nature and in the round of rebirth.
(3) That there is but one Self, which individuals can realise, and which is identical with Brahman as the ground of being (which at a lower level of truth manifests itself as a personal Lord and Creator) – such a realisation bringing about a cessation of the otherwise continuously reborn individual.

Now these are obviously very different doctrines. Why should the crucial difference lie between them and theism? Is not the difference between (2) and (3) equally striking? If the monistic category includes heterogeneous high auto-interpretations, there is no guarantee that we should not place *all* mystics, including theists, in the same category; and explain their difference not in terms of radically different experiences, but in terms of varied auto-interpretation. The gaps within the monistic category are big enough for it not to seem implausible to count the gap between monism and theism as no wider.

Admit that high auto-interpretation can be mistaken, and there is no great reason to isolate theistic mysticism as belonging to a separate category.

If I am right in proposing this on methodological grounds, we can go on to explain the difference between Yoga (say) and theism by reference to what goes on outside the context of the mystical life. The devotional and prophetic experiences of a personal God – prophetism and *bhakti* religion – these help to explain why the theist sees his contemplative experience in a special way. He already considers that there is evidence of a personal Lord and Creator: in the silent brightness of inner contemplative ecstasy it is natural (or supernatural) to identify what is found within with the Lord who is worshipped without.[10] A *priori*, then, there is no special call to assign theistic mysticism to a special pigeon-hole. Of course, there are theological motives for trying to do this. It avoids some ticklish questions, and it suggests that there is something very special about theistic mysticism. It is a covert means of preaching theism. Now doubtless theism should be preached; but *fairly*. Methodologically, the assignment of theism to a special pigeon-hole is suspect. The arguments are more complex and difficult than we think.

But it may be replied to all this that the discussion has been largely *a priori*. Do we not have to look at the actual words of theistic mystics? Of course. I shall, however, content myself with examining some passages which Zaehner quotes in favour of his own position.

VI

An important part of Zaehner's argument rests on a couple of passages from Ruysbroeck. I quote from these.

> Now observe that whenever man is empty and undistracted in his senses by images, and free and unoccupied in his highest powers, he attains rest by purely natural means. And all men can find and possess this rest in themselves by their mere nature, without the grace of God, if they are able to empty themselves of sensual images and of all action.[11]

Zaehner comments that Ruysbroeck here has in effect described (Advaita) Vedantin mysticism. Talking of men who have attained this 'natural rest', Ruysbroeck goes on:

> Through the natural rest, which they feel and have in themselves in emptiness, they maintain that they are free, and united with God without mean, and that they are advanced beyond all the exercises of the Holy Church, and beyond the commandments of God, and beyond the law, and beyond all the virtuous works which one can in any way practise.[12]

Now it will be noted that Ruysbroeck's criticism chiefly rests on moral grounds. He condemns quietists of arrogance, complacency and ethical sterility. They do not properly connect their inner experience with the God taught by the Church, who makes demands upon men, and who wishes that they may love him. But the ordinances and teachings of the Church do not spring from mystical experience: they have other sources. And moral insights are not simply derived from contemplation. In other words, the criteria for judging mystical experience are partly exterior to the contemplative life. Thus, even given that Ruysbroeck is a good guide in these matters (and this need not be so), we might still say: the trouble with 'monistic' quietists is a failure in their auto-interpretation of their experience. They do not really see the God of the Bible and of the Church there. But this does not at all entail that, given a low interpretation (i.e. a relatively unramified account) of their experiences, these experiences differ radically in character from those of theistic mystics. In short, these Ruysbroeck passages are quite compatible with my thesis, and thus do not strongly support the Zaehner analysis.

Quietists, for Ruysbroeck, are not sufficiently aware of the working of God's grace. But the doctrine of grace (and by contrast, nature) is a theological account of God's activity. A person could have a genuine mystical experience, but be wrong in not ascribing it to God's grace. Ruysbroeck's high hetero-interpretation of monistic quietism conflicts with the latter's high auto-interpretation. But the experiences for all that could belong to the same type.

Zaehner also makes use of a very interesting passage from al-Ghazali, part of which reads as follows:

The mystics, after their ascent to the heavens of Reality, agree that they saw nothing in existence except God the One. Some of them attained this state through discursive reasoning, others reached it by savouring and experiencing it. From these all plurality entirely fell away. They were drowned in pure solitude: their reason was lost in it, and they became as if dazed in it. They no longer had the capacity to recollect aught but God, nor could they in any wise remember themselves. Nothing was left to them but God. They became drunk with drunkenness in which their reason collapsed. One of them said, 'I am God (the Truth)'. Another said, 'Glory be to me. How great is my glory', while another said, 'Within my robe is naught but God'. But the words of lovers when in a state of drunkenness must be hidden away and not broadcast. However,

when their drunkenness abates and the sovereignty of their reason
is restored, – and reason is God's scale upon earth, – they know
that this was not actual identity . . . For it is not impossible that a
man should be confronted by a mirror and should look into it, and
not see the mirror at all, and that he should think that the form he
saw in the mirror was the form of the mirror itself and identical
with it . . .[13]

What Ghazali is saying here – to translate into my own jargon – is
that the mystic's auto-interpretation of his experience as involving
actual identity with God is mistaken, and that the correct interpretation must say that there is some distinction between the soul and
God. In the passage quoted he goes on to explain how the mystic, in
his 'self-naughting', is not conscious of himself (or even of his own
unconsciousness of himself), and this is a main reason for the language of identity.

This seems to me a clear indication that the monistic and theistic
experiences are essentially similar; and that it is the correct *interpretation* of them which is at issue. The theist must maintain, in order to
make sense of worship and devotion, that there is a distinction
between the human individual and God. The non-theist, not being so
much concerned with devotion (though he may allow a place for it at
the popular level), can more happily speak of identity with ultimate
Reality, or can even dispense (as in Yoga and Theravada Buddhism)
with such a concept of the Absolute. Thus the question of what is the
best hetero- and auto-interpretation of mystical experience turns on
whether devotion and worship are important. Or more generally: the
question of interpretation is the same as the question of God. One
cannot answer this by reference to auto-interpretations of mystical
experience alone; for these auto-interpretations conflict, and they
have ramifications extending far beyond the sphere of such experience itself.

This is why my thesis, that maybe there is no essential distinction
between what Zaehner has called monistic and theistic mysticism,
does not at all entail that proponents of neo-Vedantin views of a
'perennial philosophy', involving a doctrine of the Absolute Self,[14]
are right. The thesis 'All introvertive mysticism is, as experience,
essentially the same' does not entail any doctrine. Truth of doctrine
depends on evidence other than mysticism, and this is true even of
the doctrine of the Absolute Self.

I have tried to argue that the interpretation of mystical experience depends, at least in part, on evidence not given in the experience itself; and that therefore there is always a question about the degree to which non-experimental data are incorporated into ramified descriptions of mystical experience. I can best illustrate this, finally, with a passage written by Zaehner himself:

> We have already said that when the mystic claims attributes that are necessarily divine and demonstrably not human, – such as omnipotence and omniscience, – it is fairly clear that he is not enjoying union with God, but rather some sort of natural mystical experience. Apart from this important consideration it would seem that the mystic who is genuinely inspired by the divine love, will show this to the world by holiness of his life and by an abiding humility in face of the immense favours bestowed which he always will see to be God's doing, not his own. Only such criteria can enable us to distinguish between the genuine state of union with God and the 'natural' or rather 'praeternatural' phenomena we have been discussing.[15]

The two criteria here mentioned can be called respectively the theological and the moral. The theological criterion shows, or is claimed to show, that the mystic cannot have enjoyed real union with God because he makes false theological claims (e.g. omniscience) on his own behalf. The moral criterion can show that a mystic has not enjoyed real union with God because his life is not holy, or not humble. Some comments are in order.

First, *both criteria are indirect.* If they are, as Zaehner here says, the *only* criteria that distinguish genuine union with God from something else, then *one cannot establish this latter discrimination on the basis of a phenomenological account of the experience itself,* but rather on the basis of the verbal and other behaviour of the contemplative. This supports my thesis that phenomenologically there is no need to distinguish between monistic and theistic mystical experience (auto-interpretation apart).

Secondly, the first criterion depends on the truth of theism. This is why the interpretation and evaluation of mystical experience from a doctrinal point of view cannot be separated from the general question of the truth of theism. The theological criterion could not work for a Vedantin.

Thirdly, to some extent the same is true of the moral criterion. For humility is a virtue for the theist, who sees the wonder and holiness of the divine Being; but need not be a virtue for the non-theist. In so far as moral ideas depend on theology (and they do in part), one cannot really separate the moral from the theological criterion.

VII

The above arguments by themselves do not establish the truth of my thesis that monistic and theistic contemplative experiences are (except in so far as they are affected by auto-interpretations) essentially the same: but I hope that they are sufficient to cast doubt on the Zaehner analysis.

Mysticism is not the same as prophetism and *bhakti* religion; but it may gain its auto-interpretations from these latter types of religion. But there is no need to take all interpretations as phenomenological descriptions; and this is the main point of this paper. To put the possibility which I am canvassing in a simple form, it can be reduced to the following theses:

(1) Phenomenologically, mysticism is everywhere the same.
(2) Different flavours, however, accrue to the experiences of mystics because of their ways of life and modes of auto-interpretation.
(3) The truth of interpretation depends in large measure on factors extrinsic to the mystical experience itself.

Thus, the question of whether mysticism is a valid means of knowledge concerning the Transcendent is only part of a much wider set of theological questions.

Finally, let me express my debt to Zaehner's learning and fertility of ideas. If I have criticised a main thesis of his, it is because it is itself an important contribution to the discussion of mysticism. In my view, his analysis is wrong; but interestingly false propositions are worth far more than a whole lot of boringly true ones.

10 Problems of the Application of Western Terminology to Theravada Buddhism, with Special Reference to the Relationship between the Buddha and the Gods

It is natural in the days when evolutionary theories of religion were more popular than they are today for scholars to attempt rather general comparisons of religious systems, so that they could be fitted into such categories as animism, polytheism, monotheism, etc. There is still some advantage in reflecting upon such general categories; and the purpose of the present paper is to consider how far traditional Western categories can be made to fit Theravada Buddhism. I shall concentrate primarily on the Theravada Buddhism of the Pali canon: some of my remarks may not apply so precisely to various contemporary forms of Buddhism in Theravadin countries.[1]

The puzzlement sometimes occasioned to Western scholars in the treatment of the Theravada in part arises from the fact that though gods and spirits are not at all infrequent in the scriptures, they have an ambiguous and even peripheral place in the structure of Buddhist doctrine and practice. It is not plausible to look upon Theravada Buddhism as basically polytheistic; nor on the other hand is it monotheistic; nor is it pantheistic or monistic. Its highest value and goal is not, in any plain sense, divine. The favourite Western categories fail to get a grip upon it. It is therefore worth examining the actual role of the gods and their relation to the Buddha.

First, it is to be noted that the *devas* are not, from the Theravadin point of view, properly the objects of a cultus. That is, worship of the gods, making sacrifices to them, etc., is of no use in the pursuance of the holy life. But clearly among the gods of the Pali canon are those who were recipients of a cultus – for instance Sakka[2] (indeed the use of this name rather than 'Indra' arises from its employment in the *upahavya* rite,[3] and may have been the name under which he was best known in popular religion in the Gangetic region). But while in some measure accepting the existence of such gods, the Pali canon does not endorse their cults. Thus the status of the *devas* is ambiguous in so far as the typical characteristic of gods in their being objects of cults (unless promoted to being *dei otiosi*). Why then did Buddhism retain these beings amid its cosmological furniture? The diagnosis of this matter may be similar to the conclusion reached by Prof T. O. Ling in his study of Mara[4] – that they represent a bridge to popular religion. The Buddha, so to say, did not launch a direct assault upon current beliefs; but retained something of their outer form, while sucking away their inner substance. To this process I shall come in a moment.

It is perhaps significant that Brahma Sahampati should visit the Buddha after his enlightenment to encourage him to preach the *dhamma*.[5] In a way, the trouble about the *dhamma* at first sight is that it moves against the stream of people's worldly goals, towards the attainment of which the *devas* and *devatās* can often assist them. This conflict between the requirements of the holy life and the sentiments of people may lie behind the concept of *paccekabuddhas*.[6] It is not unreasonable to see these as a reflection of a contemporary or pre-existent ascetic movement eschewing the creation of a genuine religious frontier with 'lay' belief. By contrast the Buddha, or early Buddhism at least, did this, partly by accepting some of the gods (and creating new ones, via the idea of rebirth in one of the heavens).[7] This acceptance, however, was essentially upon Buddhist conditions. These conditions can be described as follows.

First, the life of the gods is impermanent (though the gods may not realise this, owing to their longevity, such as Brahmā wrongly supposes himself to be creator).[8] It is thus just as much to be transcended in *nirodha* as earthly existence.

Second, worship of the gods does not conduce to liberation.[9]

Third, it is the normal condition of liberation that a god has to be reborn as a human being.[10]

Fourth, the Pali canon strongly suggests that *perception* of the gods is confined to *arahants*, and numerous passages indicate that the gods visit or appear to the Buddha and other liberated followers when they are in *samādhi* or other higher states of consciousness.[11] Hence, partly, the criticism of Brahmanical claims for the authority of the three Vedas (in the *Tevijjasutta*): the force of the question as to whether brahmins have *seen* the gods and so possess their knowledge at first hand is that the liberated person, notably the Buddha, *has* so seen the gods, and in effect seen through them.

Fifth, the Buddha himself transcends the gods. Put from the side of popular religion, he is *devātideva*,[12] or 'god above gods'. But strictly he is not a god (for gods are impermanent, and after his nirvana he is indefinable, and not, so to say, 'there' to be prayed to, etc.). Moreover, there are many occasions on which the gods are represented as coming to the Buddha for clarification of points of doctrine, etc.[13] – a mythic mode of affirming the superiority of the salvific effectiveness of the *dhamma* over anything the gods can do.

Sixth, the Pali canon testifies to the 'existence' of gods who appear to be essentially Buddhist creations (such a being, for instance, as Anathapindika),[14] wherein the doctrine of rebirth is used to elevate notable Buddhists to a divine position in subsequent lives.

Seventh, the state of liberation (*nibbāna*) is superior to even the most refined states of *jhāna* and by the same token even the most refined forms of supramundane existence (such as the *arūpadhātu*). It is interesting in this connection that the *jhānas* are so explicitly co-ordinated to supramundane realms of existence – this is, as it were, the psychologising of the heavens.[15] It may not be entirely amiss to see in the Buddha's cryptic answer to the question of whether there are gods,[16] an indication that the texts understood the gods, and Mara for that matter, as data of experience in the higher ranges of spiritual attainment.

For all these reasons, it is clear that the divinities and spirits of popular and Brahmanical religion were partially accepted, but in the process emasculated. Here is one mode in which the *dhamma* could be co-ordinated with existing beliefs, but on conditions which safeguarded the central values of the *dhamma*. It is the Theravadin mode of *upayakauśalya*. The gods and Maras are the interface along which the central message of Buddhism is adapted to features of existing religion. It is perhaps in the same light that we can see the establishment of a Buddhist cult of *cetiyas*,[17] issuing in the more florid and well-developed cult of *stūpas*.

It is thus misleading to dub the Theravada Buddhism of the Pali canon polytheistic. If you like it transcends polytheism, and so can be called 'transpolytheistic'[18] (Zimmer used the world 'transtheistic,[19] but my locution seems more apt). But even to say this may be to concentrate overmuch on the periphery – like categorizing Roman Catholicism as a good example of non-Nestorianism.

The typical categories which have been used for characterising religious viewpoints proceed largely by trying to pinpoint the main focus or foci of religious activities. If we were to ask ourselves what the primary focus of Theravadin activities are, as described in the Pali canon, it would undoubtedly be liberation – for the analysis of reality, the teachings of the Buddha, the various practices of meditation all have to do with the attainment of higher peace and insight, which brings cessation from rebirth and *nibbāna*. It scarcely needs saying that *nibbāna* is not an object of worship, nor is it a kind of ground of existence, such as the Advaitin Brahman.

It can, however, be characterised as transcendent, differing in kind from 'empirical' existence. But even here it is necessary to be cautious in applying Western terminology. The early Buddhist cosmology is, as we have seen, somewhat psychologised, through the co-ordination of various levels of the cosmos with levels of spiritual attainment. The essential break occurs not between this world and the heavenly realm, which in some religions has come to be symbolic of God's transcendent place, but rather between the impermanent and the permanent.

A further reason for the difference of style as between theistic transcendence and that of the Theravadin canon is that God's otherness connects up with, and in a degree reflects, the worship, etc., directed at him. In the case of the Theravadin canon the whole emphasis, from a practical point of view, is on self-mastery and meditation. That is, it is essentially a path of *contemplation* which leads to *nibbāna* (ethical values being subordinate to the contemplative life). Precisely because of this, it differs also from Christian or Sufi mysticism, where the goal of contemplation, namely God, is already given as the supreme focus of worship. There is no Creator to be united with. In this respect it is more important to characterise Theravada Buddhism in terms of the type of religious practice central to it than in terms of the major focus. (There remains too the question, which I do not now go into, of the possible categorisation of other religions in terms of the main interest of Theravadin Buddhism – for surely it is no accident that Western terminology has proceeded from an interest in whether a given religion approximates, or does not do so, to monotheism: value judgements have lurked secretly or explicitly precisely because scholars are liable to begin with a norm of religion.)

Yet there are aspects of the matter that remain unresolved by the above account. It is clear that many marvels occur in the Pali canon, like the occurrence of earthquakes at suitable times, as described in the *Mahāparinibbāna Suttanta*.[20] More generally, the world and the gods respond to the crucial events of the Buddha's career. His birth was not without such marvels. This mythic milieu and acceptance of the fabulous world of *asuras*, *yakkhas*, *gandhabbas*, and so forth, not to mention the *parittas* produced as ritual substitutes for the *yaksa-mantras*[21] and the like, are all suggestive in the Pali canon of a far from 'rationalistic' approach to popular religion. Is there not in all this a congruence with the typical world of the gods, and is the Buddha to be exempted from the category of a numinous Lord?

It is too facile to suppose that the original teachings of the Buddha have just been overlaid by myth. It is so, for two well-canvassed reasons. First, it is hard to penetrate to the original teachings, and this must always have a strong subjective element influenced by modern presuppositions. Second, there is as much difficulty in detecting original doctrinal elements in Buddhism as in detecting mythological ones. There are, too, evidences of early quasi-cults in Buddhism (I use the barbarous term 'quasi-cults' advisedly, for reasons which emerge).

An explanation of the two-faced situation of Theravada Buddhism as found in the Pali canon is that it *is* Janus-faced. On the one hand, there is the pursuit of the contemplative path, the institution of an Order to facilitate this, the elaboration of an analysis of reality (*annica, anattā, dukkha* and so forth). On the other hand, there is the frequent reference to marvels, *devas*, *Brahmās*, *Māras*, spirits of various kinds, heavens, purgatories, the myth of the Buddha himself, the cult of *cetiyas*. The Janus-faced character of the religion can be represented by a simile. It is like people looking at a stained-glass window from two sides. Those looking from within towards the sunlight can see marvellous things, yet through them the light of the Enlightened One and his liberated disciples can be seen, as more glorious than the marvels. Those on the outside can see the window, but dully: it has no charm or fascination. Or to put the matter less extravagantly, the social and religious situation allowed a movement of mendicants to establish a prestige greater than local and Brahmanical cults, and to present their doctrines and final goal as being the supreme truth, in a manner not riding roughshod over the population of whom, in the last resort, the Sangha lived.

So a great man and his Enlightenment and the other great events of his life could find an echo in nature. What could be the privilege of the gods was a reverberation in nature, testifying to the transcendence of the Buddha over the numinosities of current religion. Yet secretly the religion was being changed. It is partly for this reason that any evaluation of the Pali canon must accept its *double-entendre*. If one *must* categorise it by relation to the traditional concerns of such classifications, it is a trans-polytheistic, non-theistic religion of contemplation.

11 Nirvana and Timelessness

The teachings of the Buddhist canon are extremely complex and subtle. They are often highly unexpected. And yet there is a certain simplicity about them. Nowhere is this more apparent, strange to say, than in the doctrine of nirvana.

What, after all, is nirvana? It is a cooling off, a quenching of the fire of *taṇhā*: but above all it is liberation. It is the *jīvanmukti* and *mokṣa* of Buddhist tradition. But with regard to liberation we must ask: From what and to what? On the latter point, the 'to what', the Theravada can be said to be embarrassingly silent, till we grasp the point: to that I shall come a little later. But as to the 'from what' there is an embarrassment of riches of description. Consider the whole notion of *dukkha*, the theory of impermanence, the grand panorama of rebirth, the psychology of Buddhism, and so on. Still all that can be from one angle reduced to a single thought: impermanence. So we have the polarity or dialectic – impermanent existence and (on the other hand) liberation. I believe that the analysis of impermanence is the essentially brilliant contribution of the message of the Buddha. For what does it mean in depth?

First, it explodes substances, as commonly understood. Solid trees and lively women dissolve into swarms of events, themselves utterly short-lived. The world is a moving, evanescent *pointillisme* – Seurat gone cinematic. So the outer world of solidity begins to melt and to go hazy, dancing in a new metaphysical perspective. So the inward. My solid self, such as it is, likewise dissolves in Humean speckles of experience, perceptions, impressions. Impressionism thereby becomes alarmingly inward. It is the *pointillisme* of the soul.

Or do I make it all sound too attractive? The impressionists, the masters of the evanescent, made it lovely in its way: but we should not forget that Buddhism emphasises how we get entangled in what we see and handle. Suffering and dissatisfaction accrue from grasping the glories of the world, even when seen theoretically as being evanescent. Still, the essence is to do with the evanescence, so let us pursue the theme of impermanence, from which (permanently) we may be liberated (in nirvana).

The doctrine of impermanence raises, as we have seen, problems about ordinary common sense. Things are not what they seem to be. Further, it suggests – a strong Buddhist theme – that conventional language is misleading: it talks of solid tables rather than swarms of micro-tables. Being misleading, it distracts from liberation. So we are led to convergence from metaphysics and language towards a common goal.

In its most developed form the concept of impermanence involved a theory of virtually instantaneous atomic events, a remarkably sophisticated account of the physical world amazingly congruent with modern science. But here we are stepping over the bounds of the canon itself. However, certainly the seeds of that conception were contained in the earlier teachings. And it indicates two main aspects of impermanence as seen in Buddhist perspective. These are respectively the ideas that things are compounded and that entities are short-lived. On the first point: Buddhism offers a method of analysis – a way of breaking things up into their constituent parts. This serves, among other things, as an aid to meditation, for it allows us to 'see through' the gross world about us and indeed within us. By contrast therefore liberation is uncompounded, simple. On the second point, everything turns out in effect to be made up of events. An event is localisable, and it carried a temporal marker. It has a where and a when. By contrast therefore liberation is nowhere and timeless.

Of course, to say it is nowhere is to say, in Western jargon, that it transcends the spatio-temporal cosmos, even the highest and most refined heavens of the Buddhist cosmological imagination. Nirvana is not nowhere in the sense in which unicorns are nowhere. Yet here we come to a problem about the timelessness of nirvana and perchance also about its being nowhere. For apart from the fact that nirvana is liberation from impermanence, it seems to be the liberation of *someone*. For example, the *Mahāparinibbāna Sutta* describes the last days of the Buddha in relation to his decease and so 'final' nirvana. Here, let us pause for a moment to remind ourselves of an important distinction concerning nirvana. It is the distinction between nirvana 'with substrate' and 'without substrate'. Substrate is in effect psychological organism. Thus nirvana with substrate is when the individual realises in his own experience his liberation. Let us say that it takes place at the age of thirty and he lives on till he is eighty. This is, so to say, the period of nirvana with substrate. Then at his decease we have nirvana without substrate.

Now nirvana with substrate seems to be somewhere and some-when. It appears to be located in an individual and to be achieved at a certain time. This raises the uneasy question as to who, if anyone, is liberated. In one sense no one is – there is no self, no person, to be liberated. Still, in plain and conventional language a nameable, locatable person is the one who has gained nirvana, as is evident from some of the poems of the *Theragāthā*. So one can ask, 'In what circumstances, and when, did you attain nirvana?' So mysteriously nirvana can be both timeless and given a date. Is this not a contradiction? Perhaps, but there is a sort of solution to the paradox – a solution which itself may serve to throw light on why it is that we so often feel unconsciously impelled to hypostatise nirvana, to make it into a kind of *thing*, albeit a transcendent one. The solution comes from reflecting on impermanence and its contrast. Impermanence boils down the solidities, the fats of the world so to speak, into the fluid events, and the stream of consciousness. The world is a vast compound of events: we likewise are complexes of events.

Now just as doctrines of transcendence (and for that matter creation) which conceive of the world as an arrangement of substances conceive of the Transcendent as a sort of super-substance, so a doctrine which sees the world as events will see nirvana as a transcendent Event. It is a timeless Event. This may be thought to be *obscurum per obscurius*. But at least it brings out that nirvana is not a *thing*, but more like a state of affairs. That is why nirvana cannot be personal, creative, etc. To say that it is transcendent is to say that it does not belong to the cosmos within which entities are impermanent, soulless, unsatisfactory. Yet because it is permanent it does not follow that it cannot be perceived. Indeed it is quite common in the Pali writings to hear of nirvana being 'seen', 'touched' and so forth. Obviously this is not ordinary seeing. It is a kind of gnosis.

But this gives us an impulse to think of it as a thing out there, admittedly in the transcendent nowhere. Its being a permanent Event, something not sharing the imperfections of the events in which we are immersed or indeed form a sub-current, can fool us into making it substantial. But the attack on substances of all kinds is at the heart of the Buddhist metaphysical analysis. Even when the Mahayana, through the doctrine of *śūnyatā*, comes close to postulating an underlying, pervasive something, it turns out to be a nothing, a Void. It is ultimate unreality. So the temptation to hypostatise nirvana, must be resisted. Yet there is a manner in which nirvana, though no thing, is 'there' to be perceived.

So it is that the grasping of nirvana can be dated, even if nirvana itself is timeless. The situation of the saint is reminiscent of Vaughan's line 'I saw Eternity the other night'.

I have said that the seeing is a kind of gnosis. Not for nothing does that Greek term relate to Pali *ñāṇa* and Sanskrit *jñāna*. There is an analogy to intellectual discovery in the attainment of nirvana. It involves seeing through the world as hitherto received, and so seeing into its amazing fluid structures undreamed of in the ordinary transactions of life. Still, typically (though not quite universally in the literature), nirvana's attainment is not just gnosis. It is also a consequence of meditation, and in particular the *jhānas*. The 'seeing' of the *amatam padam*, the immortal place under which nirvana's nature is figured, is a sort of mysticism. It is a contemplative vision, the eye being as it were turned inward. This is very evident in the detailed descriptions of the *jhānas*. Let us not, incidentally, fail to see their centrality in Buddhist meditational experience, for at the very point of death the Buddha himself went through them, so the *Mahāparinibbāna Sutta* tells us. (Could any one have known what went through the Buddha's mind at any time let alone at this last speechless time of his earthly existence? Never mind. The presumption that his mind was so to say leaping nimbly among the subtle stages of meditation is a tribute to the vital character, the loaded significance, of the *jhānas*.)

And what does the observation that mystical contemplation is central to nirvana add to our understanding of Buddhist liberation? One frequently repeated motif in the description of the cloud of unknowing, the dazzling obscurity and bright void of the interior vision, is that the vision is not like eyesight, where subject and object are entrenched in the experience. The duality of ordinary perception seems to disappear. This is one reason why theistic mystics can encounter trouble: they for sincere but perhaps not too reflective reasons abolish the gulf between awesome God and puny devotee. They even seem to claim unity with the divine and so a blasphemous divinity. It is unfortunate that persecutions, as with al-Hallaj, have sometimes resulted. Mysticism could be seen as dangerous. Be that as it may, the contemplative failed, in his inner brightness and gnostic vision, to see the subject-object distinction. Atman was one with Brahman. Yet such an interpretation could scarcely fit the Buddhist case: there was no Thing for the non-soul to be one with. All this implies that the *arhat* or saint in 'seeing' nirvana becomes it. Or not he, nor his soul, for these are in flux, and compounded, disappearing entities. Still, sticking to conventional speech, the saint identifies with nirvana. That liberation is timeless. At one level the saint does not experience time (how could he when the experience is undifferentiated, not complex, not outer?). At another level, what he experiences is transcendent and so outside space and time.

The analysis of impermanence and of its opposite, the permanent Event, together with the recognition of the quality of contemplative experience, leads to the following conclusion – that the saint who gains final nirvana replaces a set of impermanent states, stretching back indefinitely into the past, over a virtual infinity of lives, with a permanent Event. And what of the period when there is substrate? In a way it is like the permanent and impermanent coexisting in his consciousness in parallel. In another way it is doubtless like what Catholic tradition has referred to as the 'foretaste of the beatific vision'.

Can all this be affirmed without contradiction? Some people have had difficulty with the idea of the attainment of liberation when there is no permanent self to attain it. But not for nothing has the Buddhist tradition itself affirmed that there is no one treading the way. There is of course, as we have seen, a conventional sense in which the saint who attains nirvana can be named and identified. But the radical application of the whole conception of the insubtantiality of things means that the self is eliminated – both metaphysically and (hopefully) existentially: for the destruction of the ego is, so to say, the beginning of wisdom. That there should be no one who reaches nirvana is not a contradiction. For the idea represents a radical reappraisal of attitudes and concepts. Let me illustrate it with an analogy.

Suppose we believe that trees have selves, and are purposive entities. Then I might say that the eucalyptus tree in my garden has reached beyond the neighbouring rhododendron. It does not destroy language or thought if I revise my whole attitude, abandon any previous theory of trees, and affirm 'No being has reached beyond the rhododendron, but the eucalyptus is taller than the rhododendron.'

Nor is it contradictory to conceive of nirvana, though 'achieved', as timeless, any more than it would be to treat God, though creative, as outside space.

There is at least one further question. If being beyond time is valuable, why is impermanence such a disadvantage? In a way it is cheering, for I can have today's good and tomorrow's and so on – without impermanence, such repetition could not occur. Is timelessness a symbol of something supreme? It is hard to offer opinions on these matters, beyond making the following, perhaps elementary, observations.

First, what we have we wish to hold. Permanent satisfaction is an ideal. The evanescence of achievements, possessions, relationships, pleasures – such evanescence has much to do with *dukkha*, dissatisfaction, illfare. So the permanent Event is liberating from such illfare. Second, timelessness is a symbol of immortality. Nirvana means no more death: its condition is no more birth. (Here of course we have a problem, as to the causative influence of timeless transcendent nirvana on the world – but the question is wrongly put: you have to kill the forces of rebirth and redeath before you can see nirvana.) Third, the mystical perception of the timeless is like reaching a mountain-peak: from there the landscape below – ordinary life in effect – can be viewed with aplomb and equanimity, not to mention breadth of vision. The timeless illuminates the temporal.

It might be argued that the Theravadin teaching about nirvana would only make sense if we believe in rebirth. Perhaps so. Yet most of my previous attempt to unravel the Buddhist experience of liberation and timelessness has not depended upon the presupposition of rebirth. I mention the matter only because the Westerner's crisis about God is being echoed by the Eastern crisis concerning reincarnation. That is why arguments and evidences about reincarnation are unusually frequent in these latter days. Myself, I would adopt rebirth as a heuristic device, perchance, as it helps to contextualise Buddhist nirvana. But here I go beyond analysis to constructive dialogue. If my analysis has been simplistic, I hope it also has been simplifying.

12   Precept and Theory in Sri Lanka

Richard F. Gombrich's *Precept and Practice: Traditional Buddhism in the Rural Highlands of Ceylon* (London: Clarendon Press, 1971) on traditional Buddhism in rural Ceylon (now Sri Lanka) is very important, both for the study of Theravada Buddhism, and for the study of religion in general. The book combines history and contemporary anthropological observation, theoretical discussion with rich description, and a sensitive awareness of the varying relationships between doctrine and behaviour (precept and practice). In terms of existing allegedly separate disciplines it is 'polymethodic'. My discussion here will start with a summary of the book followed by critical comment.

I

The book studies religious change, and uses comparisons between current Sinhalese Buddhism and that portrayed in the Pali canon and later historical accounts. The desire of Gombrich to study change to some extent dictated his choice – the historical and linguistic continuity between early Buddhism and Sinhalese Buddhism. In order to give concentration and depth to his enquiry Gombrich selected a particular village, Migala, in the Kandyan highlands, to live and work in; but he draws on information and experience of a much wider area. It is indeed intended as a study of traditional Buddhism not as a monograph on religion in a Sinhalese village. The problem of change within this tradition is initially set in a Popperian framework: the 'rationality principle', that is, you assume that people behave in their own interests. However, Gombrich is somewhat influenced by Weber and others. The approach turns out in practice to be rather subtler than the theory of it.

As well as some account of the methodology there is an excellent introduction to the relevant general features of Ceylon. In chapter one, there is a brief discussion of the problem of whether Buddhism in Ceylon is syncretistic, Gombrich concluding that it is not, for both conceptual and empirical reasons. But there are distinctions – between great and little (i.e. relatively local) traditions or sub-traditions and between traditional and modern forms of Buddhism in Ceylon.

Chapter two consists of an exposition of the basic vocabulary of Buddhism. One of the more important sections of this deals with the problems of terminology, notably that of worship, belief, etc. Thus (p. 61) Gombrich writes: 'That Jesus is God also makes it possible to say "I believe in him". No one will say "I believe in Julius Caesar": he lived, is dead, and that is that. The Buddha is in the same state as Julius Caesar. We shall see that affectively he is a dead man.' Also he comments on the Sinhala word *vandinavā* misleadingly translated 'worship': as he points out 'revere' is probably best, though Gombrich later mostly neglects this suggestion.

In chapter three, Gombrich investigates the status of the Buddha, and relates the doctrinal position to the practice of *pūjā* and the like in the temples. There is a good account of the attitudes towards Buddha-relics, the usual reverences towards Buddha-images and a full treatment of the *nētra pinkama* or 'eye festival' in which somewhat esoterically the painting in of the eyes of the image occurs. Gombrich interprets this as a convergence with the Hindu concept of the god's statue as 'living' or expressing the presence of the divinity. He also stresses (p. 140) a well-known Pali couplet directly addressing the Tathagata as a real presence. In general Gombrich treats the Buddha as cognitively dead but affectively a kind of god.

In chapter four there is a full and remarkably rich account of the universe as seen from Migala, which includes a highly perceptive account of the ideal and actual gods who do or do not interact with the people – especially important is the description of changes bringing about the great importance affectively and otherwise of Kataragama – the bus has played its part. Also of considerable importance is the account of the rôles of the *devales* (shrines to gods), 'magic' and astrology, etc., in Ceylon society; and the ways in which the Buddhist institutions are continuous with the so-called popular religion. As Gombrich rightly points out there is no sharp division between an élitist 'pure' Buddhism and the religion(s) of the masses. This conception is due to *a-prioristic* European grids being imposed on the material. Further, Gombrich sees an essential solidarity between the modern situation and the earliest records of the Pali tradition. Where changes have occurred it is more in relation to concepts like that of liberation. In the following chapter Dr Gombrich explores material of *karma* and responsibility, concluding that though cognitively the full rigour of the doctrine remains, there are in fact modifications of it affectively. Chapter six deals with ethical attitudes and the gaps between orthodoxy and practice. A lot of this material is of considerable interest. A major point made is that of the Christian triad of faith, hope and charity only the last is really reflected in Ceylonese Buddhist attitudes (in Sinhala there is no word for 'hope' – though there is of course an eschatology). In chapter seven, Gombrich deals with the monastic system; while in chapter eight, he looks at the practice of caste in the Sangha, contrasting theory and practice.

The general conclusion is worth quoting in the witty ending (pp. 326–7):

> Early Theravada was an uncompromising doctrine. It is continually difficult to be responsible for your fate. 'For emotional mass religiosity [Gombrich here quotes Max Weber] there have been and are but two possible types of religiosity: magic or a saviour.' Sinhalese 'mass religiosity' has accepted indeed, though not in a word, a modicum of both. . . . These acceptances are as old as the commentaries, some of them far older. The words are hardly changed at all. If this is popular Buddhism could it be that *vox populi vox Buddhae*?

II

The 'rationality principle' is too narrowly stated, as it does not make much sense of altruism. Later on Gombrich tentatively gives an explanation of certain celebrations of suffering as due to masochism – again, the Popperian principle needs such heavy interpretation that it becomes somewhat empty. However, it has the merit of drawing attention to the need to look at people's conceptions of aims and means. It is in this way phenomenologically heuristic; and an admirable feature throughout the book is the way Gombrich attempts to see the world of the Sinhalese Buddhists through their own eyes.

The judgement about syncretism seems a sound one and Gombrich rightly sees the world of gods and spirits as something which is already there in the Buddhist cosmos from the earliest times to which we can penetrate through the texts. Unfortunately rationalistic West-ern suppositions have been brought to bear too often on the Pali material. On the other hand it is legitimate to look upon variations of local practices as belonging to a set of 'little traditions' – here some use is made of Redfield. However, a better theoretical framework might be the idea of a Buddhist matrix, which includes gods, ele-ments of the magical and so forth; but which in differing times and places may incorporate varying elements – consider the spectacular advance in recent times of the cult of Kataragama. Gombrich rightly points to the difference between traditional Buddhism and Buddhist modernism, the latter being more rationalistic and influenced by Western appraisals of 'pure' Buddhism. It tends to be this modernist Buddhism which takes root for the West, for various obvious reasons.

One of the crucial points of the interpretation of Theravada Bud-dhism is the status accorded to the Buddha. I am not sure if Gom-brich in claiming that the Buddha is in the same state as Julius Caesar – a dead man and that is that – is altogether correct, in that the status of the Tathāgata after death is one of the *avyakatāni* or undetermined questions. I am not of course wishing straightly to deny Gombrich's assertions, for that would have to be incorrect too. However, the ambiguity of the Buddha's status *even at the doctrinal level*, though it in no way implies that the Buddha is accessible as an object of worship, may throw light on some of the problems raised by the evolution of the cult of the Buddha-image. What is clear is that from a relatively (or even absolutely) early time there was a cult of the Buddha's relics and those of *arhats*. As Gombrich, partly following Obeyasekere, observes (p. 105), the term *dhātu* has a meaning hinting at the 'essence', so that a relic (*dhātu*) in this sense conveys the essence of whatever it is a relic of. But here ambiguities arise. The relics are of Gautama (how could a bone be transcendental?); but on the other hand Gautama cannot be said to persist (or not to, etc.). In brief the relic spans the personal, and now dead, Gautama and the unspeakable transcendental world to which his life pointed (and *dhātu* is not a personal concept). I think we can have no doubt of a sacred potency in Buddha relics as generally understood in Sinhalese culture. But this does not at all entail actual worship of the Buddha. Here a more personal conception is called for: and in a personal sense the Buddha is gone. Thus it is not enough to pose the dicho-tomy between cognitive and affective attitudes to the Buddha. I do not at all deny Gombrich's admirable insistence upon the difference between the doctrinal interpretations of the monks and literati (and more generally of those puzzled or *en garde* about apparent changes between original texts and doctrines and current practice) and those of the layman and so on. It is of course important to stress the gap between the reconstruction (often by Western scholars) of ideal and 'original' Buddhism and actuality. I am inclined to accept the hint of Gombrich that contemporary Sinhala Buddhism may in fact be closer to the original in the Gangetic plain than Western 'rationalistic' accounts. However, it is still insufficient to look at the cult of the Buddha as though he is affectively a god, or God. Little evidence is adduced beyond relics and the ceremonies of *nanumura mangalya* and *netra pinkama* (pp. 134–141). In the first the Buddha is treated as a king or super-monk. Why not? He is both according to the tradition. I am not here denying that the ceremonial may owe something to Hindu and Mahayana practices – these can be taken for read, in a corner so to speak, of the dominant Theravadin tradition. The second item, which suggests taking the statue as alive when its eyes are painted in, is important in a way – but how far does it affect ordinary practice? There are (however) some questions to be unravelled here – whether, for example, the idea of painted eyes as signs of numinous life is also Greek/Romano-Greek in provenance, etc., and the relationship to Mahayana practices. But significant as the ceremony of *nētra pinkama* may be, Gombrich is right to stick to a minimum supernaturalism in his interpretation of the cult of the Buddha – but this scarcely squares with the rather simple cognitive/ affective contrast. There is also bound to be doubt in his tendency in practice to translate *vandinavā* as worship in this connection, despite his own earlier judgement on the matter. How far one should take the couplet also cited as seriously as Gombrich implicitly suggests, I do not know. These are delicate and difficult areas. But I do not see the cognitive/affective contrast so clearly as Gombrich. However, I think it is right to stress the numinous aspects of the Theravada, even though they are not of the essence.

Still, if one is to look at Sinhala Buddhism as a system the increasing power of Kataragama cannot be overlooked. Yet the distinction, as Gombrich rightly points out, between 'wordly' and 'spiritual' goals is maintained. I recently made some inquiries of mainly middle class Buddhist people, going to Kataragama – and certainly the ideology was maintained. Yet in the spirit of Gombrich, one should ask how far theory and practice coincide. One companion on the trip to Kataragama was monk – he has been (I hear) rewarded. But here we are reaching, some would maintain, the limits of tolerance in the Buddhist traditions: a hermeneutic problem exists. However, the practice cannot be very far from the India of Buddhism's origin. The gap between doctrine and modification in interpretation is quite wide; so one can appreciate the pressures for change – although Gombrich is right I suspect in minimising it. In an ironic way traditional Buddhism in the Kandyan highlands – far removed from the Gangetic plain – reflects in principle Indian Buddhism of an earlier period, once it had made the transition from mendicancy to monachism.

The observation about hope is, as a comparative judgement, original and as often with new ideas entirely obvious (but alas hope is in short supply in most contemporary thought about Christianity! – as in other, in principle, eschatological faiths; hence no doubt the veneration of Teilhard de Chardin).

In general this book is a delight to the Buddhologue, a refreshing and dense contribution to the study of religion – going beyond history and social anthropology – and a herald of new standards in the study of religion.

13 Beyond Eliade: The Future of Theory in Religion

The appearance of a study of Eliade[1] is a good occasion to estimate his place in the future of theory in religion. I use this phrase because of a degree of confusion which still reigns in the field of religious studies about what may be meant by 'history of religions'. This is brought out by Dudley in relation to the disputes which animated scholars attending the 10th Congress of the International Association of the History of Religions in Marburg in 1960. The attempt was there made to separate the history of religions from theology and certain kinds of philosophy of religion, and a platform was devised which had among its signatories Eliade, Joseph Kitagawa and Charles Long. I think the simplest way to avoid confusion in these matters is to spell out the following distinctions.

First, there are, of course, various religious traditions and sub-traditions and one form of exploration is to study particular aspects of the life of a tradition. These may be called *particular* studies, and in the context of the history of religions aim to be value-free. But the methods can vary according to circumstances: they may involve philology, conventional history, sociological and anthropological approaches, of which the use of participant observation and, at one level, human dialogue is an important ingredient. Second, particular studies in differing traditions may invite comparisons. That is, aspects of separate histories may show resemblances. Naturally I am not thinking of those comparisons which are understandably regarded as odious: comparison in the scientific context is not judgemental. Third, theories about religion may be developed – and then can arise from various directions, out of the East of anthropology, the South-East of sociology, the South of psychology, the West of *Religionswissenschaft* or the North of history. Now it may be that some scholars believe that no general theory can stand up to the particular evidences, and some might even more extremely eschew all comparisons, even the harmless, not the odious, kind. But whether theories stand up is itself partly an empirical issue. But only partly, since some theories and perchance all fruitful theories use key categories as types or patterns rather than as ingredients of universal law-like statements. I shall return to this matter, since it bears upon Dudley's discussion of the relation between Eliade and empiricism.

That some degree of theory is unavoidable in the study of religion is fairly plain if we attend to the following points: first, the use of general categories (such as the terms *numinous, sacrifice, god* and so forth) faces us with decisions of classification, which even if it is only at the theoretical level of butterfly-collecting, to use Lord Rutherford's dismissive analogy, still has some theoretical component; second, historical explanations involve some theoretical elements (such as views about patterns of human motivation, the likely effects of certain kinds of experience and so forth); and third, there is a laudable, but admittedly sometimes rash, nisus to see whether cross-cultural and other resemblances in the field of religions can be explained.

So the question which may be asked about Eliade, since he undoubtedly wields a theory, is how fruitful that theory is. Before turning thither, however, I would like to make the following observations. It is unfortunate that in certain areas schools take over subjects. A school can be seen as a movement within a field which defines methods against the background of a theory which itself should be open to scrutiny by independent methods. One thinks of Skinnerian behaviourism, Freudian analysis, functionalist sociology and so on. Thus whatever else we may think about Eliade's theory (and I for one find it fruitful, impressive and eccentric), there is no question of identifying history of religions with the Chicago school. But this is not at all to deny the great and encouraging influence which Eliade and his friends have had on the study of religion in a period when that influence and weight was needed.

A theory may bear different fruits. It may, for instance, suggest ways of further research, and this is probably more important than the question of whether it conforms to some methodological model, such as the empiricist theory of induction. This is, roughly, the line taken by Dudley, drawing somewhat on the work of Imre Lakatos, who of course owed much to the stimulus of Popper's philosophy of science. Dudley writes:

Recent methodological proposals in the sciences actually point in a very promising direction. Historians of religion can argue that comprehensive theories, or research programmes, are as indispensable for the advance of understanding in their field as they are in the natural sciences. They can take Lakatos' proposal seriously and apply it fruitfully to methodological formulations in *Religionswissenschaft*. The field desperately needs to commit itself to a research programme. It needs a core theory that can be pursued until its potentialities have been explored. Eliade is one of the very few modern historians of religion who has proposed a comprehensive theory of man's religious behaviour and thought. The core of his system is the postulates of the archaic ontology and the trans-conscious, the dynamics of hierophanies, symbols and archetypes, and the cosmicization of space and time. The protective belt of auxiliary hypotheses that can be adjusted or rejected are concepts such as the *axis mundi*, the Cosmic Tree, the *hieros gamos*, the analogies between human birth and the creation of the world in myth and ritual, festival time, the sexualization of the world, ritual androgynization, the New Year as cosmogony, orgy and re-integration, sacred stones as epiphanies, the coherence of all lunar symbolism the hidden sky (*Deus Otiosus*), the solarization of supreme beings, and many others.[2]

Now it may be that Dudley's concept of a protective belt is itself too powerful a protective belt – a chastity belt that, so to say, prevents fruitfulness. For he remarks that Leach's criticisms of Eliade belong to that level, and Eliade can afford to make concessions and adjustments at that level. This is close to saying that Eliade's theory would stand whatever the empirical evidence as to the details of his scheme. And such an unfalsifiable theory could scarcely be the basis for a research programme with any cutting edge. However, let us first ask what a theory, such as Eliade's, might be expected to do.

It might, for one thing, supply a grammar of religious and other symbolism. I say *and other* here for a good reason little discussed either by Eliade or by his critics. It is a somewhat arbitrary matter how we divide up worldviews, and it is partly a matter of convention that we tend to assign the study of (say) Marxism to political scientists and the study of (say) Buddhism to religionists. It may of course be argued that the sense of transcendence and of the sacred marks off religious worldviews from others; but this by itself should not imply the separation of studies (any more than the male-female differences should imply a differentiation into male and female biology). It is unfortunate that there is no simple expression in English covering practical and existential worldviews, whether religious or secular. I shall stick with *worldview* for want of a better term, but certainly the right expression might have broken down a tendency we have to neglect the mythic and symbolic aspects of secular behaviour, or alternatively to treat them, as to some extent Eliade does, as fragmentary reflections of a more full-blooded symbolic life to be found in traditional religions. It might of course be part of a theory of symbolic behaviour that it appears 'natural' to the actors – that the recognition of the symbolism is unconscious. Symbols that surface change their style. If so, it would be an easy fallacy for secular men to think that the symbolic life perishes with religion, and to identify the mythic with an archaic, not a modern, way of looking at the world. (But modernity is part of the myth of modern men.) So then, I would propose that a theory, such as Eliade's, ought to supply a grammar of symbolic behaviour, whether that falls under the rubric of traditional religion or not.

Now this immediately brings us up against the fact that the key polarity in Eliade's account of religious symbolism is that between the sacred and the profane. As Dudley notes, however, Eliade quotes with approval a remark by Roger Gaillois, that 'the only helpful thing one can say of the sacred is contained in the very definition of the term: that it is the opposite of the profane'. But this makes one wonder whether the religious polarity is not an instance of a more inclusive one – that is the polarity between that which has a positive emotional charge and that which does not. Men's symbolic thinking is related to feelings, for a worldview 'makes sense' of the cosmos and of men's place in it because it helps somehow to exhibit patterns of meaning, and meaning has to do with a sense of worth, and this is a matter of feeling. Consider, negatively, the idea that some activity appears meaningless to a person. Thus for most Americans and for many other folk the playing of cricket is meaningless – and not just because the rules do not seem transparent but because one requires some form of initiation to make the activity seem beautiful, exciting, and an end in itself. It therefore seems reasonable to make use of some such concept as the power possessed by things, persons, etc.: that is the power to effect changes inside people – to alter their feelings. Here I lean towards the approach of van der Leeuw, though expanding the scope of his enquiry to range beyond religious worldviews. In brief I would suggest that we do not need to begin with the *sacred-profane* polarity as the starting point of a systematic phenomenology, or grammar as I shall call it, of religion. Further there are some more particular features of Eliade's treatment of the sacred which may attract some questions. However, let me make my general claim a little more perspicuous by outlining very briefly the substance of the grammar of religion which might prove to be more inclusive than Eliade's.

A person or thing endowed with an emotional charge, which I shall call substance, may be in contact with another – and this in turn may be thought of in the widest way as a ritual or, to use J. L. Austin's term, *performative* contact. This contact can be conceived as either positive or negative, that is as a blessing or threat. If I were introduced to some great hero like Pele, the handshake and all would convey a kind of blessing: my substance would increase with even a minor infusion of that of the hero. Consequently the Latin word *hostis* meant both stranger and enemy. The approach of the stranger might be a threat: hospitality was a ritual means of establishing a positive relation with the stranger, and thus gaining something positive rather than negative from his presence. If for whatever reason you are yourself very strong, there may be emotional advantage in diminishing the other person's substance, by such rituals as insult, arrogance or (more extremely) torture.

Substance comes in forms of layers. Thus my own substance is built up most obviously of such layers as national identity (I participate ritually in the substance of Scotland). Then I participate in the profession of professing, and religion and philosophy in particular – so part of my substance is drawn from the worth of the job. Partly it is drawn from my place in the profession, that is from reputation, etc., which provides a kind of ordering of people's substance. One might see human behaviour from this point of view as involved in preserving or expanding individual substances.

Since communication of substance is essentially a ritual matter, the grammar of ritual itself becomes vital – the way, for example, in which the substances of the past and future are made available, and the substances also which exist in other portions of space, not to mention those which transcend space and time.

A further aspect of a general theory would have to do with the relation between categories through which substances are differentiated. The more the emotional charge the more important boundaries round a concept may be, since proper ritual response is necessary for the charge to be communicated in a benign manner. Similarly where an entity goes through a re-categorisation clarity of ritual becomes important, hence rites of passage. Since communication of substance is a matter of created affinity, much ritual implies getting into a condition of affinity with what one is confronted with. Hence the drawing of performative boundaries in relation to what is powerful, and in particular the sacred. So it may be that we do not need to begin with the sacred-profane polarity as an ultimate but see it in a wider theory of emotional charges and their ritual accompaniments. I might add that it seems to me that whatever some modern science may say about the momentariness of events and the insubstantiality of things, where feelings are involved men operate according to notions of what Lévy-Bruhl's translators called mystical participation. Or to put it in another way: perhaps Plato through this theory of Forms reflected the way we think emotionally, though not how we ought to think in regard to scientific exploration. And perhaps we should even eschew substance-thinking in regard to what moves us in feeling and ritual – it could be that Buddhism's attack on substance is a correct attack too upon men's 'natural' emotional life.

Now of course Eliade's fixing on the sacred-profane polarity as ultimate involves various other limbs of theory. For the sacred is conceived by him ontologically: what is perceived as sacred in a hierophany reflects an archetype attests to the primordial ontology, which Eliade characterises as Parmenidean (the real is timeless and inexhaustible), Platonic (archetypal) and Indian (temporal experience is illusory). Attitudes to time, of course, permeate Eliade's whole theory of myth and history.

Now Eliade's theory is in its own way philosophical and speculative. There is, of course, nothing wrong in this, and indeed one sometimes wishes more historians of religion were bolder in theory. But there are theories and theories, and intentions behind them. It seems to me that we have a problem where a theory in effect is an expression of a worldview, which is then brought to bear upon worldviews. For instance in the past there have been those who have pursued the comparative study of religion from a Christian-theological angle – consider such works as Farquhar's *The Crown of Hinduism*, Zaehner's *At Sundry Times*, Kraemer's *The Christian Message in a Non-Christian World*; and there have been others who have started from some other religious point of view – consider the works of Radhakrishnan and other products of modern Hindu thinking in which Christianity and other faiths are interpreted from a Hindu, and in particular a Vedantin, angle. But of course such essentially theological presentations are the subject matter of the history of religions, not exercises in it. Does this mean that all interpretative theories have to be eschewed? How do we draw the line between the pursuit of theology and the pursuit of Eliadean philosophy?

It is partly a matter of evidences, and partly a matter of intention. Revealed and authoritative spiritual messages are not accepted as part of the evidence brought to bear in their capacity as being normative for the investigator, for they have no such capacity. But of course in other respects a theory is to be tested by evidences: here Dudley comments, not altogether favourably, on Eliade's handling of evidence, for instance, from the New Testament and Zuni mythology. It was of course an aspect of Edmund Leach's fierce attack on Eliade in *The New York Review of Books* that Eliade failed a number of evidential tests (doing bad history, bad ethnology and bad psychology, it was alleged). I do not think Eliade is altogether to be exempted from the charge that he sometimes is highly selective in his use of sources. But on the other hand he has undoubtedly brought together some highly suggestive symbolic complexes, especially in his major works on Yoga and shamanism.

It is worth adding that Guilford Dudley brings out well Eliade's normative thrust and his apologetics for a soteriology which will free people from 'the terror of history': here Eliade is seen as guru. However, looking at Eliade's theory from the point of view of the study of religion, and more generally from within the ambit of the human sciences, it is important to note whether he yields fruitful accounts of some of the key notions which the religionist needs to wield. And here I think he is open to criticism, and I shall illustrate this in relation to his analysis of myth and famous accounts of *illud tempus*. Here it is useful to reproduce a passage discussed by Dudley:

The mere recital of a myth causes an interruption of the sacred no matter what the narrative might be:
It is the irruption of the sacred into the world, an irruption narrated in the myths, that *establishes* the world as reality . . . To tell how things came into existence is to explain them and at the same time indirectly to answer another question:
Why did they come into existence? The why is always implied in the how – for the simple reason that to tell *how* a thing was born is to reveal an irruption of the sacred into the world, and the sacred is the cause of all real existence.[3]

Certain things are clear. First, telling a myth is a kind of ritual act. Indeed one of the ways in which the literature of the history of religions can be misleading on myths is where the story (in print, paradigmatically, and thus reified) is divorced from the ritual telling. You cannot divorce the nature of a myth from its use (hence the same story can be a fairy story or a legend). And Eliade is right in seeing a myth as ritually channelling some sort of power. But two questions arise: First, is he right in seeing the mythtelling as making available *illud tempus*? A subsidiary issue here is whether he is correct in polarising so sharply the distinction between mythic and historical time. Second, is he right in assimilating all myths to a cosmogonic pattern?

Now much unclarity has been generated in these matters, even if (I admit) time tends to bafflement. Dudley, expounding Eliade, writes thus: 'Rituals not only regenerate individuals, but they also regenerate time itself. New Year rituals imply a return to *illud tempus*, where the cosmogonic act can be enacted.'[4]

What one can say about ritual enactment is that it may make available to us what occurred at a previous time. Let us consider the logic of this, and to make it easier I shall take the familiar instance of Easter. The simplest version of the Easter story as reenacted at the festival is: 'Jesus Christ is risen today'. What occurred at one date is present at another date. It could also be said that what occurred at another place is available here at this place. Now the fact that a place can be represented in no way implies that the primary space is itself not literally space. The fact is that many people operate with the following spaces – their own area, then layers of more indefinite space beyond their area, and some kind of unknowable limit of the world: and vertically there is the sky (or layers thereof), culminating in heaven, a sort of para-space. Simplifying we may talk about: definite space, indefinite space and transcendental space. For certain purposes a charged line may be drawn between this-worldly space and transcendental space. One might wish to make a similar division of time. Again it does not follow that because one event is re-presented at a later date the first time is not literally a time, with a date. It may just be that some dates are more charged than others. Was Archbishop Ussher profoundly misguided, obtuse one might say, to place the date of creation at 4004 BC? The problem arose because of the fact that the creation was represented as having happened before various pre-historical and historical happenings, and 'before' implies a date. Or at least it implies belonging to an indefinite stretch of time which locates it very roughly. So far I see no special reason to differentiate out very sharply *illud tempus* from later dateable time. And still less is there reason to exclude from the realm of myth or sacred story those stories which refer to dated events (such as the siege of Troy or the resurrection of Jesus). If, *functionally*, a story is narrated in a ritual context to re-present the substance of the original event, then that story should, in my view, be counted a myth. And the Easter story belongs to that category.

But of course cosmogonies speak of origins, beginnings. Why are origins important? Here perhaps we touch on an important part of Eliade's view of the archetypal significance of the creation myth set in *illud tempus*. Any 'first' involving what is a highly charged transition from one level or category to another is seen as a prototype (thus: the first man to fly, the first man on the moon, the first motor car, etc.), and in ritually re-presenting such a first, one is celebrating the type of thing in question. But also from a ritual point of view, if B is caused by A it partakes somewhat of A's power. But creation involves a dialectical process. Thus if God creates man (say), then two truths have to obtain: first, man is like God in some measure because he derives his substance from God; but he is unlike God because, among other things, he is created as *man*, as having his own proper and peculiar substance and definition. So creatures in general are a mixture of good substance derived from the Creator and their own natures. Consequently, a feature of celebrations of Creation is their re-presenting the pristine essences of the world. But it does not follow that all myths are archetypally cosmogonic. What does follow only is that myths which celebrate new transitions have an analogy to creation myths.

Since those new transitions, existentially charged events and so on, can occur in the sphere of the dateable, there can be no ultimate contrast between archaic views of the world, as expressed in cosmogonic myths, and those which incorporate a strong sense of linear history. Here there is in any case a confusion between two notions of repetition in time. In one application of the idea types of events repeat themselves cosmically, as in the Hindu theory of *kalpas*. In the other application, a single event is replicated ritually. In the Christian tradition, for instance, an unrepeated linear series of events is replicated liturgically.

In his discussion Dudley relates Eliade to Foucault, in that both authors, he claims, perceive the mythic nature of modern man's historical consciousness. This, on the side of Eliade, seems a back-handed way of expressing his account of history. Some distinctions, in any case, are necessary. At one level, doing history is a rather technical research enterprise. At another level, though, it is a means of expanding a culture's consciousness of its past and that of the planet. As such it pushes back the temporal field of vision. But as Foucault perceives, modern preoccupation with history tends to take a further character, namely it tends towards patterning the past: and here I think we can genuinely begin to discern a mythic view of history, for the events and movements of this historical process now carry with them an air of existential significance. They 'mean' something to us. Notable are the dialectical views of history found in Hegel and Marxism, but even Tolstoy's appreciation and expression of the messy and tangential ways history works bear its own mythic character. Of course, both Hegel and Marx wield great abstractions, rather than seeing events created and moved by divine heroes and the like, as befits the mythological genre. But Marxist history one might say stands to certain metaphysical accounts of creation as salvation history stands to *Genesis*. In the latter pair we have a myth of redemption figuring divine persons and conscious acts, as compared with a myth of creation likewise figuring the divine person and his acts. In the former pair, we have a metaphysical history – a sort of ballet of abstractions, but moving in time – as compared with the dialectic unfolding of the One (for example) as depicted by Plotinus.

It is incidentally surprising that, almost naively, Eliade regards historicism as a typical product of those nations 'for which history has never been a continuous terror. These thinkers would perhaps have adopted another viewpoint had they belonged to nations marked by the "fatality of history" ' (quoted by Dudley, p. 71, from *Cosmos and History*, p. 152). Here we note Eliade's Romanian roots. A word on this may be in order. Eliade can be considered under one aspect as a Romanian narodnik. His philosophy, underpinning his work in history of religions, has some existentialist roots (his attitude to time owes something to Heidegger), while his theory of the transconcious and his theory of archetypal symbols have Jungian affinities. But behind these stands the forbidden forest – archaic Romania. And Romanian experience has been peculiar: a Latin-speaking nation, compounded of Dacians and Roman colonists, which virtually vanished from recorded history for a millenium, then reemerged, Latin still, Orthodox in rite, and destined to maintain its identity through the peasant's loyalty to the Liturgy, through long periods of foreign oppression. Identity means a continuous return to the history-less past. Eliade's remarkable visit to India as a young man took him in the opposite direction from so much that pulled the Romanian intelligentsia, which owed much to its links with France, and which had too a somewhat dangerous (in the interwar period) liaison with German ideas. In differing ways the intelligentsia and the workers were attracted to central European historicism: for the workers Marxism was to prove less than liberating, for the Romanian Communist Party was forced to make accommodations with the Soviets. For Eliade, perhaps, the peasant spirit of the Romanians, so evident in the continuing fervours of religious beliefs, remains the salvific factor. So Eliade's own theory has a way of functioning as a myth which 'makes sense' of the Romanian experience.

Eliade's approach, via archetypes, not only incorporates a view about time which devalues the historical consciousness. It is also somewhat ahistorical. Guilford Dudley refers to him as the 'antihistorian of religions' (p. 148). But there are diachronic processes which, according to Eliade, one can attend to: the tendency of the local symbol to approximate to its archetype constitutes the law-like principle through which the historian of religions can show how religions develop. This seems a rather constricted appreciation of what can be done.

First, there is historical investigation into the messy particularity of the histories of religions, etc. Second, there is the discernment not just of synchronic types, but diachronic ones too. Thus there is the fruitful field of considering the various kinds of moves which one culture makes when brought into contact massively with another – as happens along what may be called the White Frontier, i.e. the interface between Western culture and technology on the one hand and the various traditional cultures of the 'third world'. There are discernible types or patterns of reaction. This goes beyond the tendency to universality referred to above. Third, there is the construction of a grammar of religion, where the interplay between the various types of symbols is articulated, and a general theory constructed. Further, if religious history is to be undertaken effectively there must be some way of discerning what counts as the religious factors in a given situation (this is a bit like the discernment of economic factors when one is doing economic history). Then one must see those in relation to other factors. Putting it crudely, sometimes religion is a dominant force, and sometimes it is moulded by non-religious factors. Some estimate of this helps to clarify the notion that religion plays a significant part in influencing human history. It seems to me a defect of Eliade's approach that he tends to ignore anthropological, sociological and economic estimates of religion, partly because he looks on the scientific enterprise as essentially reductionist. Now it is true that forms of reductionism and (its brother) projectionism have played a leading role in 19th and 20th century analyses of religion on the part of social scientists in particular; but logically the scientific student of religion should be methodologically agnostic, as I have called it elsewhere.[5] That is, he should treat the objects of religious experience and beliefs as factors independently of whether they exist/are true.

We do not need to decide whether Allah actually revealed anything to Muhammad to see that Allah impinged on Muhammad's consciousness and thereby changed the course of human history. A neutralist approach to the so-called social sciences is thus possible, and is something which also embraces the phenomenological history of religions.

Thus the religionist is at least partly in the business of explanations, for the very attempt to distinguish between internal and external factors (that is, internal or external to the religious factor or more generally to the factors inherent in the symbolic life) implies the possibility of showing how the two sides are in interplay, and how one can explain historical developments in these terms. This after all was the procedure, roughly speaking, of Max Weber. And here a certain aggressiveness may be needed – it is a strange world where economic life (itself suffused so heavily with symbols) is seen so widely as a subject of serious scientific enquiry, and where the exploration of religious and other forms of symbolic behaviour is thought of so frequently as just a private affair. From the angle of the social sciences, religion is one of the most important subjects studied in academe. Thus though I have much admiration both for Eliade's work and the way he has given stature to the history of religions, my regret is that his creative hermeneutic is in the end restricted – the vehicle of a certain worldview, and a means of giving life to much of man's archaic religious symbolism, and yet somehow cut off from the wider explanatory task which religion can and should perform.

In brief, it may be that Guilford Dudley, in proposing Eliade's core theory as a research program, is not bold enough in the step which has to be taken *beyond* Eliade.

14 Religion, Myth and Nationalism

Professor Zeman remarks, in his account of *The Twilight of the Hapsburgs*,[1] 'Like the Hungarians, the Czechs had had a long history behind them before they came under the rule of the Hapsburgs . . .' This shows us something about the concept of a people's history. For from one point of view everyone has as many ancestors, roughly speaking, as anyone else. What is implied in this passage is that Czechs as a collectivity had had quite a long time together; and presumably they were in some general way aware of that time. A number of notions are entwined here: the sense of belonging to a group, the awareness of the past of the group, identification with that past. And of course in regard to the rise of Czech and other nationalisms – a large part of Zeman's theme in the book – the group not merely acknowledges its collectivity, but desires to establish a nation state, to achieve (in other words) self-determination. Crudely: a nation wishes to possess its own territory and to administer itself, undominated by others.

These notions I wish to explore, for they are relevant to questions of identity and myth which are to be encountered in the field of religion. But first, let me say something briefly about modern nationalism. It is, of course, a very powerful force – the most powerful perhaps in politics. It is at heart the theory that each nation should have its state, but more existentially it becomes the sentiment that our people should have our State. Renan said that a nation is a daily plebiscite; but we could go behind this to say that the creation of a national consciousness is a necessary feature of true nationalism, and such consciousness is a blend of awareness, sentiment and sacrament.

Various theories[2] of modern nationalism have been propounded. But its origins clearly owe much to the following factors: the French Revolution and the conception of 'the citizen'; the Enlightenment; the spread of education, implying centralisation and national language-formation; the oppression of ethnic groups in Europe; the oppression of groups outside Europe, and the exporting of European ideas through imperialism; and so on. Modern socialism, incidentally, often reinforces national identity, because 'the people' has to be defined nationally; and because centralisation and the welfare state increase internal cohesion and dependence. But perhaps we should note above all that industrialisation and modernisation themselves tend to dissolve intermediate bonds – intermediate that is between family and nation – and thus play a central role in the emergence of nationalism.

One other preliminary: clearly, many nations are not more or less homogeneous groups. But I shall take, for the sake of simplicity, as the classical model of a nation and a nation state one where the territory is unitary and occupied largely by people speaking one language. With few exceptions, incidentally, there are troubles where this model is not operative. But I shall take linguistic nationalism as the primary form.

First, then, let us look to the notion of a group – for a nation is a sort of group. Belonging to a group has an external definition, in the sense that we can nominate some mark or property in virtue of which members of a group are indeed members of that group. For instance: the people sitting on the one side of a lecture room are a group; or all black people; or one-armed piano players. But of course the mark which demarcates the class may not be considered specially import-ant by the members of the class. I am of medium height, but I have no very great feelings of solidarity with others of my height (though I feel *some* solidarity and I am resentful of games like basket-ball best played by giants and so discriminatory against me). So belonging to a group in a meaningful way implies an acknowledgement by the individuals of the importance of the mark which defines the group.

What does 'acknowledging the mark' mean? Briefly, it means celebrating it. Thus in acknowledging my belonging to the Scots group. I celebrate Scottishness. I can do this by recommending Burns, boasting of whisky, giving wondrous accounts of the '45 telling people how beautiful the Highlands are, wearing a kilt . . . and so on.

To celebrate is a performative act – a kind of ritual when formal-ised. Unfortunately there is no very good vocabulary to cover those acts, gestures and symbolic moves which at the formal end are ritual but at the informal end are to be found in winks, smiles, turning your back and so forth – bodily and more-than-bodily acts having an emotional significance. 'Symbolic act' is not a good phrase, because the symbolic is often identified with what is merely symbolic. So I shall on occasion employ the rather redundant expression 'performative act'.

Celebrating is a performative act which enhances what is celebrated: it as it were conveys a positive charge to the focus of celebration. Still, though it is right to look at acknowledging the mark as being a performative act, it is not just using words, but using words and other means performatively; it also involves acknowledging the focus as somehow mine or ours. So for the member of a group to acknowledge the mark which defines the group he celebrates it as his mark. 'I am proud to be a Scot' is a way of declaring my participation in the mark. (I can of course try to do the opposite, by repudiating my nationality.) My substance thus in an important way is enhanced or diminished by reference to the substance of Scotland.

Briefly then belonging to a group involves performatively acknowledging the mark. What of feelings? I assume about human life the following: that feelings are expressed performatively, and that many performative acts are intended to have feeling-effects. If I feel contempt for someone I sneer, and the sneer is an attempt to induce bad feeling, of inferiority. Sincerity is where feelings match their performative expressions.

If one were to be writing an alternative to *I and Thou*, an *Us and Them*, us-ness – the bond which makes us use 'we' – would best be seen as a mutual acknowledgement, a mutual celebration of substance, a joint performative. True us-ness implies sincerity of feeling behind such performative belonging to one another.

Consciousness then of belonging to a group involves the feelings that go with acknowledging the mark which defines the group.

But what is the mark when it comes to a national group? The simplified model we are considering involves that the folk occupy a territory and speak predominantly a given tongue. But they also have a history (typically). To understand something of this history is to understand something important about myth. For a nation of the sort we are considering is well summed up – or rather its spirit is – by the opening phrase of the great Welsh national song: Land of our Fathers. Why do we glorify the past?

Part of the reason appears to be as follows. The individual arrives in the group by birth and his belonging is performatively reinforced by education and the various and multitudinous celebrations of the mark of the group (its Scottishness, Italianness or whatever). Being born into the group though is obviously enough not a simple biological event. It involves performative aspects: the child is acknowledged as legitimate by the parents and the community, and derives therefore his identity from his father and mother. The chain of legitimation thus points backwards in time. Thus our ancestors are part of the group, and have the property of imparting the mark downwards to us.

Celebration of ancestors is then natural enough. If we celebrate our forefathers we enhance the substance of the nation, and so indirectly we enhance ourselves.

This is of some interest if we consider the great flowering of cultural and historical creativity in the 19th century in Europe. It was a period when national histories were being written, philology explored, folk music rediscovered, national-flavoured symphonies composed and so on. Ethnic consciousness was reinforced by the arts, and often the creative artist, poet or musician was seen as hero, for in giving dignity and glory to the nation he performatively diffused glory to all who belonged to the group. The most spectacular of such heroes, of course, was Wagner, and the most loved, Verdi.

Incidentally, the logic of the national hero is worth considering. He has to perform some act or acts which are positively charged. Pele, to take a modern hero, played wonderful football, helping Brazil to glittering victories. In supporting their team with lively and frenetic enthusiasm, the Brazilians conferred upon their men a glorious substance, but one linked indissolubly to those supportees, and to the nation. The cheers then of Brazilians helped to enhance the team; the team by its victories shed glory backwards upon Brazilians. It was a good exchange. Fickle supporters, incidentally, turn on their heroes, erstwhile. The losing team is abused – meaning that its substance is diminished, and by rituals of hostility the bad substance is kept away from the wider group.

To return to our emerging nations of Europe: the histories that were written became in a sense myths relating to national identity. Historiography became a kind of modern myth-making. This suggests a way in which, from one perspective, we can treat the concept of myth.

The history of a people is the real counterpart of a story. Or perhaps we should say that what is told in the story of a people reflects at least a putative series of events. I shall call that an event-pattern. The story-telling is the way the event-pattern is conveyed to us. But that 'conveying' is not just a question of the transfer of information: it is a performative act of celebrating the event-pattern; for indeed the latter is not just flat events, but ones charged with meaning. They include victories over oppression, heroic deeds and so on. A myth thus may be considered simply as a *charged story*; and in this sense, history is myth, for it is (albeit objectively and scientifically undertaken up to a point) a story which has a charge for the people for whom it is the history. Alas, however, scientific history seems often to defuse the charge.

Of course, nationalism often arises most strongly in the situation of oppression. The Greek struggle for independence against the Turks, Garibaldi's campaigns, the various phases of the Polish struggle for liberty and independence – many such examples can be cited. Thus often the history of a people is charged not just with glory but with suffering. From a performative point of view how is such suffering to be treated? It is after all celebrated in a sort of way. For one thing, the dead can be mourned. What is mourning? It is enhancing the value of the dead by weeping and other performative expressions of sadness. For death is losing the loved one: the loss is a blow which finds the response of grief, and the depth of grief is a sign of the worth of the loved one. In other words mourning enhances the dead. And the dead, solid with us in nationality, thus have a glory which they can vouchsafe to us. That is the meaning of the Cenotaph.

Thus the national story is not so much one which explains how we came to be, though it does that, as one which provides a past cement of identity and an enhancement of present substance.

History as myth is something which is conveyed performatively, for modern nationalism, in the schools. The spread of education, first among the better off, and then throughout the community, is a means of solidifying the nation through the language, and the telling, in the language, of the past story. Of course, education does much else besides. Cheating about a group's history, though indeed frequent, also has limits, since a nation needs to be 'modern' and modernity implies some deference towards objectivity and science.

Incidentally, the whole notion of modernity is an element in the mythic aspect of nationhood. Certain institutions and entities have a positive charge, from this point of view, as being concretisations of modernity: the air line, the university, the steel works, the rocket launcher, the palace of the people. Such entities have a ritual or performative function. One might regard such symbols (perhaps all symbols) as frozen acts, congealed performatives. The air line dumbly and yet eloquently tells us something: it tells you how good we are, technologically proficient, glamorously modern, organisationally impressive. In expressing modern machismo it helps to enhance the nation's substance.

All this helps us to understand Goethe's dictum about history that the best thing about it is the enthusiasm it arises. We also need to change Renan's remark that a nation is a daily plebiscite: one could say better perhaps that it is a daily sacrament – the communication of substance throughout the group through the very language itself and through the innumerable assumptions and celebrations of identity.

Let us now turn to consider the territorial aspect. It is easy for us now to believe that man is a territorial animal, since the nation-state has given us a special way of looking at the ancestral land. This becomes a kind of sacred space, from various points of view. It is the nation's home, – the place where hopefully the people are secure. It is also as the land of the ancestors the fatherland (or mother, as in Mother Russia). To tell the story of how the ancestors settled the land and defended it, developed it and beautified it, is to express the charge which the land has for the group. Its magic is enhanced because it is *ours*: 'By yon bonnie banks and by yon bonnie braes . . .' Although in modern times the numina have vanished from the streams and the forests, and the gods from the mountains, there is still something of their spirit left. The aesthetic properties of one's country (America the Beautiful) are a source of substance which we celebrate. The land too is made holy especially if it is also defended with great suffering: the blood of the dead adds solemn charge to the soil. And at the edge of the land is the frontier, to be a demarcation: woe betide the one who infringes that line.

I have used the term 'sacred' once or twice in connection with the nation's land. Sacredness in such a context appears to be a relational property: my country is sacred to me in a primary way, and only secondarily to others, who are not co-nationals. Among other things it implies that I have a duty to defend the land, and others commit an outrage in invading it. I do not, incidentally, think that sacredness is anything very special, as if one can use the conception to demarcate the religious. The point is that some spaces and people and things are sacred in the sense that they are charged in a solemn manner in such a way that a certain sort of conduct in relation to them is demanded. It is to do with depth of feeling and defined behaviour. And that behaviour has to do with enhancing or preserving the substance of what is sacred and with not diminishing it. It is thus to do with appropriate performatives.

Sometimes sacredness is in the literature more reified, as though the sacred 'irrupts' into the world, or pulsates in rocks and ikons. From a phenomenological point of view there is something to be said for saying that we have external counterparts, so to speak, to our feelings. A person with authority seems to emanate power, for instance, and a film star radiates beauty. The power exists in things to affect us, and since the sacred is solemn, it emanates a solemn, serious, deep power. This is where it is useful to use such an expression as 'charged'. When something is performatively highly charged, then it has the properties of the sacred (or its opposite). Nationhood tends to reinforce a feeling of such depth for the territory that the land becomes highly charged, and so sacred space. If the Shah takes away from Iran a casket of Iranian soil then this is to be used by him as a congealed performative whereby he celebrates his land, and mourns its passing from his power.

A nation also draws substance from its future as well as its past. The death of hope is where the future has no charge for me: likewise when a group has no spirit left and sees no future, it disintegrates in despair – like some of the smaller ethnic groups in the face of white conquest and powerful new values, good and bad. Such national accidie is, however, rare; and especially in the course of the struggle for freedom peoples have a strong interest in the future. This is partly the attraction of revolutionary ideology. The very notion of a revolution is a new start, a rite of passage, in which the humiliations of outside dominance will be replaced by the glory of a new order. A successful war of liberation, a revolution – these are purifying processes in which the old nation is put off and the new nation put on. They are collective cases of being twice-born. Indeed, one might point to great wars as of sacred significance in that the fellowship of suffering and the promise of a new deal help to give the people new solidarity and new hope.

So far in this analysis of the nation I have made use of various ideas. I think they might be useful ones in simplifying our understanding of the emotional and practical life of humankind, and of religion in particular. As a more general category than that of ritual, I have spoken of the performative act; as a more general category than that of myth I have used the idea of a charged story; and as a more general category than sacred I have used the idea of a certain sort of charge. Let me just explore this last point a little further.

Things and people can have special powers. These powers cause or suggest certain reactions of feeling and action in us. They are either beneficent, neutral or malevolent, good, indifferent or bad: or as I shall say 'positive, neutral or negative'. Thus a threatening dog has a negative charge; a wheedling one positive; one trotting past a neutral one. Typically, that is: circumstances can change this. It is a natural response to enhance or maintain positive values and to diminish or restrain negative ones – maximising the positive, minimising the negative. The sacred may be regarded simply as that which has fairly intensely positive value: it has a high positive charge.

A main type of performative act (and a typical piece of ritual) can be said to be a conveying or communication of value. Thus when I enter a church, a sacred space, I speak in whispers, do not act arrogantly or with disrespect, for example by smoking. By a kind of self-deprecation or self-restraint I reduce my value somewhat and communicate sacrificed value to what is sacred. But such proper behaviour opens up the interface between me and the sacred, and in exchange for my self-deprecation I gain the charged blessing of what is sacred. There are thus transactions across the interface between what is highly charged, sacred, and me.

This perhaps helps to illuminate the idea of mystical participation. It can either be *gaining a share of* or *being a part of*. Roughly speaking: the believer can gain a share of God (if God so permits – he can gain the grace of God, which is God's good substance in action); while the patriot is part of his nation. Thus a vital part of the mark of such belongings is the territory of the nation, and in a certain sense the land and the patriots mutually inhere. Thus from the point of view of *our* substance the invasion of our territory by hostile outsiders is a desecration and a direct attack: a desecration because the value of the land is diminished *for us*, and sacredness is *for us*; it is a direct attack because our substance is directly diminished. The nation is, so to speak, a performative transubstantiation whereby many individuals become a superindividual.

I use the word 'transubstantiation' a little advisedly. I have also on occasion used the idea of substance. I do not mean it in any technical sense, as used in philosophy. Rather by 'substance' I mean the sum or balance of performatively communicated value, as it inheres in an individual or entity. Identification with a group involves pooling part of my substance with that of others. Such a pooling is a performative matter: pledging my loyalty, etc.

Let me now illustrate some of my analysis by considering the logic of certain phenomena in religion and nationalism. I'll begin this part with an analysis of a passage from Marshal Mannerheim's memoirs.

He writes of the famous Winter War against the Soviet Union:

> May coming generations not forget the dearly bought lessons of our defensive way. They can with pride look back on the Winter War and find courage and confidence in its glorious history. That an army so inferior in numbers and equipment should have inflicted such serious defeats on an overwhelmingly powerful enemy, and, while retreating, have over and over again repelled his attacks is something for which it is hard to find a parallel in the history of war. But it is equally admirable that the Finnish people, face to face with an apparently hopeless situation, were able to resist a feeling of despair and, instead, to grow in devotion and greatness. Such a nation has earned the right to live.[3]

His words were here a celebration of heroic deeds. They are manifest in that the Finns showed disproportionate power. Perhaps the Russians may have admired the Finnish resistance, but they could not be proud of it: for pride is feeling good about what I/we have done. 'Looking back on' a past good deed is a kind of celebration-in-the-mind. We say 'looking back' by analogy with gazing at in admiration: to gaze in a certain way is to expose oneself to the impact of an object. It opens an interface, through which the power of the object flows. So, then, the Winter War has generated the positive value which flows via celebration in the mind to future generations. This enhances their Finnish substance, for they look back not on random individuals but individuals bonded performatively by consciousness of being Finnish and fighting for Finland. But why is displaying courage so good? (And incidentally, how ought Finnish courage to impress the Russians?)

Courage in war is fighting without avoiding the risks: it at least mimics fearlessness. It is prepared to meet death, the ultimate self-sacrifice. Dying for one's country is using up one's substance (or much of it, as we shall see) on behalf of the national group: performatively it enhances the substance of the nation.

Courage, effectively expressed in the business of fighting, elicits admiration often in the enemy by the following logic: combat is itself a performative struggle issuing ultimately in one side or the other acknowledging defeat, typically, and the courage of the enemy is in principle daunting. For preparedness to die makes for the effective exercise of fighting power. So an enemy's courage is impressive. That it in addition can attract praise arises from the very fact that military men in general become somewhat performatively bonded by fighting each other, and speaking from that trans-national constituency it is natural to praise its primary virtue. Also, praising an enemy is a way of enhancing one's own victory.

I have suggested too that death in battle is, if undertaken in the right spirit, a noble sacrifice, and thus communicates the individual's sacrificed value to the store of substance accruing to the nation. In fact, it might cynically be said that the more people that die for their nation without weakening the nation's capacity to sustain itself in relevant ways against other nations, the better. Provided, too, that they can be commemorated. The absolutely anonymous dead are not much use, for their death-value cannot be celebrated and thereby communicated to the nation. The commemoration in fact serves a double purpose, for it does something, through our mourning, to convey substance to the dead (so they live on in a kind of way, and so are not utterly devoid of substance, great though their sacrifice of substance had been); and it conveys their sacrificed substance to the nation.

My analysis suggests also that a nation – such as the Finnish people who according to Mannerheim has earned the right to live – is a complex performative construct, sacramentally bonded: it is perhaps like a person, for it has a body, namely the land; it has a mind, namely its population; it has a biography, namely its mythic history, its charged story; it has clothes, namely the flag, the monuments, the poetry of its tradition. It has a future. Now from a philosophical point of view such an organic, even idealist, account of a nation may be open to criticism. But phenomenologically it is vital to note that the nation is in its own strange way present to the minds of its members, and to members of other nations. Thus a nation is a phenomenological focus of loyalty, hostility, etc.

Here, as an aside, an important point emerges. A vital aspect of psychology is how such contructs as a nation enter actually into people's experience. The flow of human events in history and society, in individual living, is such that there impinge upon consciousness and feeling entities which have phenomenological reality and a special shape, independently of whether they have actual existence. Nations belong to this class of construct.

The nation as performative construct transcends the individuals who belong to it. This sometimes makes the sense of duty to the nation seem as if it is a duty to something Other. It mimics divine duty.

Here it is appropriate to see how nationalism is, and how far it is not, like a religion. Or rather, perhaps I should say 'patriotism'.

Nationalism from one point of view can be defined as the theory that each nation should have its nation-state. Patriotism is devotion to my own nation-state, and incorporates the view that my nation should have its rightful (whatever that is) place in the world. If one were to try out the six-dimensional analysis on it that I have elsewhere used,[4] one could see patriotism as involving a rather weak doctrinal dimension (already summed up as the view of my nation's rightful place); strong in myth – the charged story of my people; strong in ethics, for I have a duty to die for my country; intermittent in ritual (for I stand for the National Anthem, give suitable praise to the Royal Family or whoever, etc.); moderately strong in experience, for I feel glory as a patriot at my nation's achievements; and strong in social form, for so many institutional pressures and expressions guide me to do what I should do – pay taxes and so forth. But it is not a universal religion: it is more akin to a tribal religion. Moreover it has nothing truly transcendent.

This incidentally is why the Christian, Marxist or Buddhist – not to mention others belonging to universal viewpoints – will have a certain ultimate scepticism about patriotism. But it happens that often such ideological forms are used as reinforcements of nationalism. This is above all true of Marxism, since 'the people' inevitably gets defined in national terms where states are sovereign, and socialist centralisation strengthens immeasurably the organs of the state and so the power of the nation over against its members.

But people need the security of a group. In modern society groups intermediate between the family and the nation tend to dissolve – through industrialisation, mobility of folk, the voracious demands of the state, new communications and mores. So ethnic identity is important and should not be attacked. But (if I may permit a valuation of these matters) it ought to be transcended. To transcend is to go through something to something beyond. There used to be the patriotic bumper sticker in the U.S.A. 'America: love it or leave it.' Maybe it should have read 'Love it and leave it.' But my aim in this paper has been essentially to analyse not to judge.

This analysis has a number of components – performative acts, positive and negative charges, charged story as myth, substance, and the idea of a phenomenological construct. A nation is a superindividual which is a phenomenological construct resulting from performative acts in which individuals communicate and pool positively charged substance, including the charged space of territory and the charged story of their past.

Part III
Methodological Issues in the Study of Religion

15 Religion as a Discipline?

In 'Theology as a Discipline?',[1] Dr W. A. Whitehouse has discussed the case for theology in the university. His dissatisfaction with much of what goes on in conventional Departments of Theology ('a few harmless courses on the Bible and Christian doctrine') will be felt by many; and his proposal for small experimental Departments pointing the students towards live research work may also find support. But a much more radical view of the place of theology and religious studies is needed. The concept of a Department of Religion, rather than that of a Department of Theology, is the best answer. Perhaps some people will regard the concept as tainted because of its American associations (a red rag, it seems, to many of our John Bulls). But let us give it a good hearing.

Why is religion intellectually important? For two separate reasons: first, because it is a widespread and highly significant human phenomenon; and second, because of its claims about the nature of reality. In regard to both these sides of religion, conventional Departments of Theology display serious deficiencies. Part of the trouble is that theology lives on sufferance. True, the cunning manipulation and reinterpretation of charters have allowed it a place in universities which once would never have admitted it. But there is great sensitivity about it all around, and this has led to sad results. To be respectable, it has had to go in for tough and 'scientific' pursuits. Biblical studies are just right for this – plenty of Hebrew and Greek, textual criticism, minute historical enquiries. Church History too, being a branch of history, is undoubtedly all right. But the formulation of Christian doctrine, apologetics and the like are doubly suspect. Their methodology is obscure, and their conclusions, some may think, are prejudiced. The concentration upon the Biblical and historical side has had at least three evil consequences. First, it has restricted enquiry into religion as a human phenomenon: the non-Christian religions scarcely get a look in, and topics like the sociology and psychology of religion are regarded as largely irrelevant. Second, it has made theology rather dull for those who are interested in religious truth (and falsity). Third, theological studies are not presented in a candid way in our universities. Everybody knows very well that the Bible is selected for treatment in depth because it is fundamental to the Christian revelation. Everybody knows very well that it is no accident that the Fathers of the Church are so fully studied. But as for discussion as to whether the Bible does after all enshrine the truth and whether the formulations of the early Church are worth heeding – these are left in uncandid darkness. Yet these discussions are important; and the main issues of modern theology (largely a product, not unnaturally, of non-British theologians) are not negligible. That the universities have no quarrel with such fundamental discussion, provided that it is conducted in an open manner, is evident from the fact that it sometimes occurs in Departments of *Philosophy*.

These miseries are made worse by the fact that nearly everyone who studies theology is professionally interested and confessionally committed. Nearly all are prospective parsons and teachers of religious knowledge in schools and training colleges. The idea of going in for religious studies because they are interesting and important in themselves is largely wanting.

The cure for these evils is to rid religious studies of the grip of the Christian establishment. In the very nomenclature – Departments of Theology – it is tacitly implied that studies are devoted to Christian theology. This prevents an openness of approach, and means that interested agnostic, Jewish and other 'outsiders' are discouraged from taking up the subject. This is where the mere change of name to Religion is a blessing. Not only will it point towards a greater interest in descriptive studies, such as the sociology and psychology of religion, but also it will encourage more attention to topics such as the roots of modern atheism and agnosticism. And this in turn will generate greater concern for apologetics on the Christian side. Moreover, it should not be forgotten that the apologetic situation greatly affects the formulation of doctrine. For instance, the aftermath of the Theory of Evolution has brought an agonising reappraisal of the doctrines of the Fall and of Original Sin. In short, a Department of Religion could well do far more than present Departments of Theology to stimulate research and debate about the two fundamental aspects of religion mentioned above – its ramifications as a human phenomenon and its validity or otherwise in claiming to give us an insight into reality.

But the project might well be suspected from two angles. The theologian may feel that disestablishment is a kind of surrender, while others may be unnerved by the prospect of the candid teaching of doctrine and apologetics. Yet these objections obviously contain a paradox. For it is precisely where, in a Department of Religion, theology is liable to be subjected to the cold winds of criticism and to the need to respond to the challenge of humanism, Marxism and the like, that serious theology gets done. It is no accident that (despite all the vagaries of American education) systematic theology flourishes more luxuriantly in the States than in England, or even than in Scotland. In brief, the theologian will in fact benefit, from his own point of view, through the change. Instead of being a hole-in-the-corner affair, on the edge of a Faculty of Arts, theology can once more resume some kind of real intellectual challenge. The truth or falsity of the Christian religion, and of other religions, is a serious matter; and discussion of it should not be the academic perquisite of a special group. Even the atheist will no doubt, moreover, wish to reject the strongest, not the feeblest, statement of the religious position.

But apart from this, the theologian should surely welcome the opportunities presented by the new approach. There are many areas of enquiry to which the history and phenomenology of religion are vitally relevant. The social sciences cannot ignore the phenomenon. Asian and African Studies, now burgeoning through Hayter, need the services of the Comparative Study of Religion – a Cinderella in the present theological world. History needs Church history. Philosophy needs doctrine to get its teeth into. In countless ways, and for obvious and long-standing reasons in the nature of human culture, the study of religion can be relevant and helpful to other disciplines. But as it is, people in other Departments are discouraged by the narrow interests of theology. Moreover, it is all too easy for agnostics to slip into thinking: 'Because religion is not true, and is not important to *me*, we need not consider it in trying to understand actual human behaviour.' This is a fallacy, but a prevalent one. A Department of Religion, then, could well be a source of service to other disciplines. Already, of course, there are some theologians who do perform such services: but not on a large enough scale.

But what of the other objection? Is not religion too explosive a subject? Will not the candid presentation of doctrine and apologetics mean that the universities are betraying their duty of impartiality?

These fears are misdirected and out of date. Nobody questions the right of political scientists and political philosophers in the universities to discuss the history and principles of Marxism. If a Marxist teacher chooses to *expound* Marxism, this is no intellectual crime. Only if Marxists take over Departments of Politics and stifle open discussions is there such a crime. But again there is a paradox. The suspicious non-Christian should reflect that it is the very refusal to have an open discussion of theology that leads to the present set-up, where undoubtedly theology is an enclave of the Christian establishment. Sensitivity about the teaching of doctrine (except as mere history) is, as we saw, a main cause of the existing lack of candour in our universities about religion, and has made it all the easier for Christian scholars to keep religious studies as their special prerequisite. There is nothing terribly sinister in this, and no doubt Christian theology will always be more important in our country than, say, Muslim theology. But the suspicious non-Christian, as well as the theologian, should surely be happier with a more open approach to religion.

But yet, it may be said, even admitting that this new approach is desirable, is it practical politics? To this there are a number of answers. First, it is unclear as to what is and what is not practical politics in the new universities being set up.[2] Second, a start can be made in existing Departments of Theology by offering Religion as a subsidiary course for those reading honours in other subjects. Here co-operation with people in other disciplines may be essential, though its shape will depend on who there are and in what subjects. A course in Religion could suitably include work on the Bible and Christian doctrine; on religious and anti-religious thought in the last hundred years; and on the philosophy, psychology, sociology or comparative study of religion. Third, there is no reason why in one or two existing universities, and especially at London University, a special degree in Religion should not be established. In such ways it may be possible to attract more graduate students into the field – vital if the supply of suitable teachers of Religion is to be adequate.

Dr Whitehouse, in the article mentioned, considered how a new adventurous Department of Theology, consisting of three persons or so, could operate. This clearly presents an important kind of question. For a new university will not be likely to incorporate at the outset a fully fledged Department of Religion. What, then, could three people do effectively? In such a wide field there are many possibilities. Let us look at just one, as a sample of the range.

Consider a Department consisting of a comparative religionist, a systematic theologian and a Biblical scholar. It would then be feasible to run a three-year course with two sides to it. Thus, on the European side, one could begin with a review of the present state of Biblical studies and the demythologising movement. Quite clearly, scholars' critical questions about the historicity of the Bible are determined largely from outside – from the growth of scientific knowledge which has created problems of a philosophical and theological nature about the categories of ancient Jewish and early Christian thought. Thus the linguistic and Biblical studies could go hand in hand with an historical and critical investigation of the last hundred years of religious and anti-religious thought, including the changes in philosophical, scientific and theological views. These courses could well be supplemented by two or three others devoted to specific topics, such as creation and atonement, considered in the light of modern cosmology and psychology, and of philosophical criticisms of the Christian faith.

On the other side, and complementing these studies, a fairly extensive treatment of Eastern religions, notably Buddhism and Hinduism, would have great advantages. First, it would free the student from the European cultural tribalism which so bedevils thought about religion (and much else). Second, it would correspond to the real growth of interest in the great Eastern faiths as a possible alternative, and certainly a challenge, to Christianity. Third, out of this subject there arise in a very natural and incisive way most of the philosophical and apologetic issues which the Christian has to face. For example, the Western concept of the importance of the historical process is largely foreign to these faiths, and the notion of a personal God is altogether less prominent. This raises questions about the basis of theologies in religious experience; and so we are able to gain an insight into the sources of religion from the phenomenological point of view. In these last matters, the two sides of the course clearly come together and illuminate each other.

This is one sample. Not only would it constitute a degree course which would be lively, interesting and serious, so that the 'outsider' might well be attracted to it; but it would be quite as good a professional training as are existing theological courses. Moreover, there are obvious points of contact between such a Department of Religion and other disciplines in the university. Our sample would be, for instance, just right for a university embarking upon Asian studies.

In brief: religion is too important both as a phenomenon and in its intellectual claims to be treated as it is now in our universities. As to the claims, maybe theology is bunkum, and maybe again it is not: but whatever the truth, the claims should be intelligently presented and openly discussed. As to the phenomenon, no-one can surely deny, whatever their beliefs, that it has been and is profoundly influential – and extraordinarily interesting. In a way, it is perhaps more interesting for the agnostic than for the believer. For men do strange things under the influence of religion – strange, strange things. Who has yet given us an absolutely authentic insight into the explanations for these things? There remains so much to be understood. The study of religion has its own important contribution to make.

16 Towards an Agreed Place for Religious Studies in Higher Education

Although there are legitimate and important divergences between the university structures of England, Wales, Scotland, Northern Ireland and the Republic of Eire, there is a common sense about university standards and about the kind of research and teaching which should characterise a university. Nevertheless, there is at least one area in which there is doubt, confusion, prejudice, difficulty and sensitivity. Religious and theological studies do not fit so snugly into the common area of agreement. Yet in a way they flourish, for in various places and various ways theology is entrenched in university life. I need not now go into the historical reasons for this state of affairs, nor need I here exhibit the roots of a rather radical secularism in some universities, where theology has been excluded by charter and statute. Suffice it to say that the present rather muddled situation is the consequence of traditions and decisions which need re-thinking. I propose in this essay to make a modest contribution to such a re-thinking.

Let us begin with some distinctions. The academic study of religion can take various forms. By tradition, the form we are most used to is theology. Though descriptive, historical and linguistic studies obviously enough enter into theology, the traditional concept of theology goes well beyond them. The suggestion is that one begins from a given religious tradition, for instance the Bible as interpreted by the Church, or more widely the Bible plus the doctrinal affirmations of the Church, and one then explores, develops, systematises the given deposit of faith. I may be excused for claiming that theology is dogmatic. I do not however mean by this that theology is thereby rigid, inhumane, inflexible: there is no need to attach such pejorative flavours to the idea of dogma. It is true that theology has sometimes shown these bad characteristics: but it need not do so. By saying that it is dogmatic, I simply mean that it starts from a given revealed basis.

This, as it happens, is one of the reasons for some suspicion of theology in universities. After all, not everyone shares the Christian presupposition which makes sense of the tasks of traditional theology. Further, it is easy to speak of 'Christian' and 'the Church' as though these terms had an agreed reference. It needs no emphasising that there have been wide disagreements on these issues, so that one has to refine the concept of theology further: is it to be Roman Catholic or Protestant? Is to be Anglican or Presbyterian? And so on. The tendency in the past has been for theologies to bifurcate, one reason for denominational sensitivities which have occasionally issued, even in the setting of universities, in heresy hunts. We live in a happier age, yet there still are important cleavages about what counts as the given, dogmatic basis of theology. But more important than these disputes is the fact that, as I have said, many people both inside and outside universities are not Christians. Many are humanists, many are doubters; there are Jews, Muslims, Sikhs, Hindus in our society. For them it may be odd that so debatable a presupposition as the truth of Christian revelation should under-gird an academic discipline. I shall revert to this point shortly.

Theology in this sense can be dubbed 'dogmatic exploration'. Obviously, as I have said, such dogmatic exploration needs the services of historical, descriptive studies – of languages, of history, of archaelogy, etc. In brief, we may refer to such disciplines as 'historical exploration' (though it should be noted that sometimes they concern contemporary manifestations of religion). Under the traditional conception of theology, such historical exploration has been ancillary to dogmatic exploration.

Sometimes, however, the servant is highly influential. Though the relation of scientific history to dogmatic theology may remain in principle ancillary, one should not confuse ancillariness with lack of influence. There is always some question of how far historical exploration should modify dogmatic exploration, just as there is the question of whether the modification should run in the opposite direction. In principle, however, it seems possible for a person to pursue historical explorations of religion without being committed to anything in the way of a dogmatic basis, though presumably she should be able to enter imaginatively into religious experience; but it is hardly possible to pursue a dogmatic exploration without professing the appropriate commitment. In practice, at any rate, those who do Christian theology are Christians: they may not always be terribly

Christian, though this might presumably help. It is not feasible to assign to a person the role of exploring and expounding a credo which she does not profess.

Let us be clear about this point. I am not saying that a Christian or an agnostic cannot contribute valuably to Buddhist studies. I am only saying that anyone holding a post which requires him not merely to explore the Christian faith historically, but to develop it dogmatically has to be a Christian. For instance, the Chair of Theology at the University of Nottingham is explicitly labelled 'Christian Theology', the original intention being that this would leave it open to the University to appoint someone to a further Chair in, say, Jewish Theology. Given the label, and the assumption that the occupant has among other things to pursue a dogmatic exploration of the Christian faith, it is not feasible to appoint someone who is not in some sense a Christian. We might put the matter thus: dogmatic exploration is confessional, but historical exploration is not.

A further division in religious studies is represented, broadly, by the philosophy of religion. Philosophical questions about religion substantially have to do with criteria of truth; and sometimes also the philosopher plays directly in the same league as the dogmatic theologian. Thus, for instance, the supposed proofs of the existence of God engage the attention both of the Catholic apologist and of the philosopher; again, questions about the meaningfulness and consistency of religious affirmations can bear directly on the truth of a given faith. Moreover, philosophical questions arise whenever dogmatic conclusions seem to be confirmed or threatened by wide-ranging descriptive studies, such as the psychology and sociology of religion. There is, then, a range of enquiries concerned with the truth of religion which do not start from the dogmatic basis, though they may take such a basis seriously. At the risk of making such enquiries sound more abstract than they are, I shall call this mode of approach to questions of religious truth and value 'philosophical exploration'.

Whereas historical exploration does not directly concern the truth of religion (except where historical studies are crucially ancillary to dogmatic exploration), both dogmatic and philosophical exploration are concerned with expounding or criticising religious truths. But philosophical exploration does not presuppose particular commitment, as dogmatic exploration does.

There is another distinction which I would like to make. In religious studies, as elsewhere, some issues are highly debatable, others much less so. There are some assured results; but there are also many speculative and questionable conclusions. The possibility of such disagreements, the chance of conceptual revolutions which might resolve some of the problems, the spice of debate – these are the life-giving elements in teaching and research. Very often a high degree of debatability goes with a high degree of theory: for instance, Freudian psychology as applied to religion brings to bear on religious history and experience a battery of concepts organised into a theoretical system; the same can be said of Max Weber's work in the sociology of religion. In both cases, there is room for disagreement and debate. However, a high degree of debatability can surround particular, very concrete problems in religious history – for instance, the nest of problems surrounding the accounts of the trial of Jesus. Even so, one can see that different disciplines have in general differing degrees of debatability in regard to their content. Notoriously there is more 'debatability' about philosophical conclusions than mathematical ones, more about theoretical conclusions in sociology than about the results of textual criticism. But debatability of content can be distinguished from debatability of presupposition. When I referred earlier to the feeling that many people are liable to have about theology as a discipline, it is precisely because of its debatable presupposition, namely the revelatory nature of its basis. In so far as theology, identified with Christian dogmatic exploration, rests on a debatable presupposition, there remains a question about its place in open academic teaching and research.

It may be objected here that it is misleading to think of theology as having presuppositional debatability. After all, the attitude of faith is a kind of certitude. Can the Christian not say 'I *know* that my Redeemer liveth'. If there is here certainty and knowledge, the presupposition of theology is not open to debate. To this objection, I make two replies. First, it is commonly agreed, in the Christian tradition, whether Catholic or Protestant, that at least some of the truths of the faith cannot be proved from outside. In either case, at least an important segment of the dogmatic basis is not open to clinching or even highly probable confirmation, such as could be used to show the truth of the basis to all and sundry. Thus the very nature of faith implies that in one sense it is debatable: it is placed in an area of disagreement in relation to dispassionate evidence. Second, what is sauce for the goose is sauce for the gander. In a religiously plural world, with different persons sincerely claiming knowledge of the religious ultimate expressed in widely differing ways, the claim of Christian dogmatic exploration has to be set beside Jewish dogmatic exploration, Buddhist dogmatic exploration and so on. In principle, no vital religious tradition should be bereft of the chance to explore and amplify its basis. As we shall see, there are contingent limits which have to be set to this multiplicity of theologies in our own universities and colleges; but the principle of pluralism in dogmatic studies remains.

Now it has been implicit in the argument so far that debatability by itself is no evil: on the contrary it indicates the possibility of the fruitful interplay between different positions. But it is also implicit in the argument that debatability must lie with theories, positions, truth-claims *within* a field. It is unfortunate if a field of enquiry itself is based exclusively on one theory or position within the field of enquiry. It would, for instance, be unfortunate if psychiatry were delimited from the start as being Freudian. To be fruitful it must admit the possibility of other views. Through the criticism of existing views one makes progress. The difficulty, then, with treating dogmatic exploration as being Christian from the start, or more narrowly as Catholic or Protestant or Anglican or Presbyterian, is that it delimits the field in terms of a position within the field. But as we shall see, there are historical arguments which might contingently modify the structure of dogmatic explorations in a given milieu. But in principle, as I have said, the idea of theological pluralism is valid.

I am not here saying that all religions are equally true or that all are equally deserving of attention. It might be so: it might not. The theory that all religions point to the same truth is a conclusion within a particular sort of dogmatic exploration. It is, for instance, typically expressed in modern Hinduism. I am only here arguing that the fact of debatability in the presupposition of Christian theology needs to be recognised. It seems to be a consequence of this that dogmatic exploration should be open to other alternatives. In brief, religious studies in this respect go beyond one tradition. This brings me to a further set of distinctions I would like to make.

Since there is a variety of religions and cultures, the study of religion can take in more than one tradition. Such comparative studies can broadly take three forms. In the first place, the comparison of religions can serve a descriptive, historical function. One can note resemblances and contrasts between different doctrines, myths, experiences, developments, and so on. This can be geared to theory. One might test, for instance, the Freudian account of the genesis of religion by seeing how plausible it looks in, say, the context of Buddhism. One can test sociological theory, such as functionalist theory, over a spectrum of examples from divergent traditions. One can examine mystical experience by reference to expressions and descriptions of it in widely differing milieus. Essentially, in all this we are not directly concerned with religious truth-claims, though what is found may be highly relevant to them, just as historical exploration of the material afforded by the New Testament may be highly relevant to Christian claims.

Second, it is possible for, say, Christians to interpret other religions from the standpoint of their own dogmatic exploration. This is what we find in works as diverse as H. Kraemer's *The Christian Message in a Non-Christian World* and R. C. Zaehner's *At Sundry Times*. It is necessary, no doubt, for a theology to make sense of other religions from its own point of view. This is part of the task of interpreting the world in the light of the dogmatic basis. Though this task is sometimes subsumed under 'comparative religion' it is really a form of theology. It is not to be criticised for that. But one must always be on one's guard against confusing this job with that of bringing out the meaning and nature of other faiths from a descriptive standpoint.

This remark calls for comment. What after all does description mean here? How can one enter into the meaning of other faiths? For is this not necessary if one is to bring out their nature? Indeed, this is so. By description one must not mean a mere external recital of the facts (though this is much more important than some people think and already begins to disperse prejudices and misconceptions). In order to describe a religion one must describe what it is like to those who follow it. To do this, one must enter imaginatively into their life and experience. Thus a prerequisite of decent comparative studies is imagination and often sympathy. One does not need to be in favour of all the manifestations of religion, any more than one needs to sympathise with all such in the history of one's own faith. But one must treat the other faith seriously, and try to enter into the beauties in it perceived by its adherents. Perhaps here we neglect unduly the powerful key which is held by the history of art. So, then, description has to be in a deep sense phenomenology: one needs to penetrate into the feelings and aspirations and experiences evoked by the symbolic forms under which a religion presents itself. This is no novel thesis: it is only transferring to the sphere of religion what has long been known by anthropologists, art historians, and other students of human culture. In saying, then, that the comparative study of religion is essentially descriptive, I do not mean to say that it has only to do with a catalogue of externals and a recital of outward histories. In a sense, one enters into dialogue with what one studies. 'Studies' indeed may seem too dry a word.

However, dialogue as usually practised points to a third form of inter-religious enquiry. In entering into dialogue with the Hindu, the Christian is typically wanting to do more than understand what the Hindu has to say. He also thinks that there may be some meeting of minds, though not at all necessarily in the direction of a pan-religious syncretism. The hope, as in ecumenism, is that there may be some mutual theological modification which will at least clear away un-necessary obstacles to the messages on either side. This mutual modification shows such dialogue for what it really is: a polycentric doctrinal exploration. It is a form of theology, but not a solo – more like a jazz session, in which the different players improvise on their own themes. Dialogue, then, like the theology of other religions as described earlier, belongs to the aspect of religious studies (if that again be not too dry a phrase) dubbed earlier 'dogmatic exploration': but it is not as dogmatic as the theology of other religions, in that different dogmatic bases come into interplay. For the sake of labels, the three types of transreligious enquiry can be dubbed respectively: comparative study of religion, missiology and dialogue. Only the first of these is strictly historical and descriptive.

It needs little argument to see that the more debatable is the theoretical framework of descriptive studies, the more important are trans-religious, comparative studies. This is one of the crucial ways of checking on theories, in psychology, sociology, etc. Moreover, light can be thrown on a particular religious history by comparing and contrasting developments elsewhere. Thus the comparative study of religion should be a necessary element in what I have called the historical exploration of religion. The rather under-developed status of the comparative study of religion has hampered the work that might be done in understanding religious history, experience and institutions. I shall not now go into the complex reasons for this state of affairs: it is better to draw a veil over the many muddles and prejudices which have contributed to the under-development. But one can at least say this: preoccupation with dogmatic exploration, together with those aspects of historical enquiry which are closely ancillary to the understanding of the development of Christianity, has played an important part in this edging out of trans-religious studies.

This brings me to enunciate a first principle about religious studies, which I trust is difficult to controvert, namely this: it is not possible to confine descriptive studies of religion, and especially where there is a high theoretical content to these, to one historical tradition alone. More briefly: *the study of religion must be trans-religious.*

But of course people are not only interested in trying to understand the sociological, psychological, mythological, experiential aspects of religion from an empirical standpoint, important as such enquiries may be. As we said earlier, such theoretical approaches to religion are liable to throw up philosophical questions. And in any event, people are interested more directly in the truth-claims resting on the dogmatic bases of religion. The study of religion should not exclude such philosophical and dogmatic explorations. This is so for two reasons: one is that the truth-claims are an important aspect of what makes religion significant in people's lives; the other is that as in the history of ideas, one has to come to grips with the ideas themselves – enter into dialogue with them. For example, there are some rather inadequate histories of philosophy written by those who are not gripped by philosophical issues. To understand the development of Plato's thought, one must enter into the philosophical issues with which Plato was wrestling. But doing this is to argue philosophically. I do not say that the upshot of the history of philosophy must be critical comments, in the naughty style of Bertrand Russell. But I am saying that the history of philosophy presupposes philosophy. Likewise the best historian of science in principle is one who enters fully into the reasoning of earlier scientists. Thus it is impossible to treat the historical, descriptive study of religion without entering into a dialogue with the ideas that help to form religion. One need not be too intellectualist here: indeed one should not. For to understand the ideas one typically has to understand the living milieu of religious experience, practice, cult. But there remains a strong case for holding that it is artificial to cut historical studies off from dogmatic explorations. This leads to a second principle: *the study of religion rightly includes dogmatic exploration.*

But here comes the rub. What dogmatic basis or bases should such an exploration start from? Truth is no respecter of persons, a reason for the increasing secularism of our higher education, whatever statutes may say. One does not settle issues in zoology by appeal to tradition. The university needs to be open. Where there exists a debatable element, there should be room for debate. And as we have argued, Christian theology rests on a debatable presupposition. But at least this can be said, in terms of the previous argument: in principle, and looking at the matter still from the point of the inner logic of religion, rather than from the standpoint of practical politics doctrinal exploration should be open rather than closed. That is, there must be room for as many dogmatic explorations as may be feasible – Christian, atheistic, Buddhist and so on. In brief, a third principle: *dogmatic exploration should be trans-religious.* There is to this degree a symmetry between the requirements of truth and the requirements of description. Needless to say, philosophic exploration must in principle share the same trans-religious character. But here we begin to come up against the harsh facts of practical politics. Our universities and colleges are not just research institutes: they teach. And who do they teach? Who are those who will be engaged on the study of religion? Some will be ordinands, some will become teachers. Others may study religion out of interest alone – and presumably they ought to be satisfied with what flows from the inner logic of religious studies as above adumbrated. But those with confessional and professional interests remain an important segment of the clientele of theological and religion departments.

Another important aspect of the matter is that there are theological colleges, sometimes incorporated into the structures of otherwise secular universities. There are universities which have an explicitly religious, indeed denominational, foundation. Not for nothing did the churches do so much for so long to promote education. One might expect a Christian college or university to be trans-religious to the extent of teaching missiology or, greatly daring, the dialogue of religions. But is it not a contradiction for it to encourage doctrinal explorations of a non-Christian form? Yet is it not also a contradiction to value the dialogue without allowing its proper polycentric expression, in the shape of other doctrinal exponents to enter into dialogue with?

Since the problem arises primarily in regard to confessional and professional training, let us narrow down our questions to these: first, what is a theological college meant to be? (for a theological college is the prime exemplar of a confessional institution of higher education), and second, what is the aim of religious education in schools? (for it is towards this that the theological student who is going to teach is primarily oriented).

One way to think of a theological college is to see it as an individual writ large. This is perhaps reversing the real relation between society and the individual, but let me for the moment pursue the image. Suppose I as an individual am a Congregationalist. In so far as I attempt to explore my own position and its historical roots, I shall begin from a Congregationalist slant on life. There is nothing disreputable in this: we all start from some position. What it means is that I shall pay much attention to Congregationalist principles, though I would be a fool to pay no attention to other manifestations of the Christian tradition. I would see myself as deepening my own education as a Congregationalist. This is my kind of dogmatic exploration. Likewise a theological college is committed to its own slant, its own form of dogmatic exploration. But a condition of its doing this properly is that its members should themselves be so committed, and in this way a real organism is created. By being a voluntary association, however authoritarian (for authoritarian institutions can themselves be voluntary in basis), it gains its form of sincerity, comparable to the sincerity of the individual, in which to explore its own position.

But as we have said, truth is no respecter of persons: it is therefore no respecter of theological colleges either. What the pursuit of truth requires, and this is brought out clearly in the structure of a secular university, is that there should be no attempt to monopolise truth, no attempt to exclude counter-positions, alternative dogmas, rival theories. They all need to be explored honestly. Thus in so far as a theological college may become part of a university, or become more widely part of the fabric of higher learning, it must abide by the trans-religious principles enunciated earlier. There is no bar on dogmatic traditions: why should there be? – for there can be no bar on individuals holding particular outlooks and faiths, which they should explore as is fitting by the highest standards of sensitivity and reasonableness. But by the same token, it is not the job of the university as such, in a plural world, to set itself up as a supertheological college. This is why there is a deep need to respect the idea of the secular university. It is therefore the duty of those who find themselves in situations where a particular religious tradition is entrenched in a university, to open things out and so gradually to secularise the institution.

This might seem to some a danger. Would not religion lose out, as it seems to have done in some modern secular universities? To this I make two replies. First, if religion in terms of practical politics loses out here and there, we should not complain, since religion has sometimes put undue and wrongful pressure on education. It is only tit for tat. Second, religion in the long run should not lose out, for it is too vital a part of human history and culture to be neglected by educated men, and if the study of religion is seen to be important, so will that dialogue with its truth-claims, which I adverted to earlier, and which implies the principle of dogmatic explorations.

Of course, by speaking of 'secularisation' I do not mean the removal of religion. The secular university is so in the sense not that it is non-religious, materialistic or what have you, but in the sense that it is not of itself committed ideologically (so the University of Moscow, secular in one sense, is not secular at all in the other, and for my purposes crucial, sense). I conclude, then, that the ideal to be aimed at is of openness and pluralism in dogmatic explorations, and that this ideal should be seen clearly in universities. Theological colleges and seminaries can play a part in the fabric of higher education, but only by regarding themselves as individuals writ large who need to enter into the open, more plural situation which is the proper condition of the pursuit of understanding and truth. These constitute reasons why the term 'theology' in universities should gradually be abandoned, as enshrining the debatable presupposition that it is Anglican, or Catholic, or what have you, doctrinal exploration that determines the nature of the field. Through humility, there may lie truth.

The Humanist might complain here that it is not the job of a university to train ordinands, even in such an enlightened open fashion. The argument has perhaps made too many concessions to orthodoxy and tradition. To this I reply first that the Humanist must, like the Christian, have the courage of his convictions. Provided the teaching of religion is not closed, biased, blinkered and so inimical to the values of education itself, surely there is hope that the truth will out. Indeed, theological studies may be as productive of atheism as of faith. Second, higher education cannot be divorced from society. In a certain kind of society, there will be some who become priests and parsons: are they to be denied the right to deepen their understanding?

Nevertheless, the Humanist objection raises an important point. Since the basis for dogmatic exploration is debatable, it is unreasonable for dogmatic exploration to be too large a component of higher religious studies. There must in the first place be a reasonable place for the history of atheism and other anti-religious manifestations – a subject unduly neglected in our universities. In the second place, descriptive, historical studies should play a dominant part. This in a way is what has happened in many universities and especially so in Britain. Suspicion of the dogmatic basis has induced universities to create theology departments where a major place has been held by 'scientific' historical and linguistic studies – Greek, Hebrew, textual criticism, study of early Church history and so on. But these have been historical explorations essentially ancillary to the dogmatic basis lying hidden in the background. If my earlier argument is correct, descriptive religious studies must be much wider in their scope. They should be trans-religious, and should deal not only with Christian history, etc., but with fields such as the sociology and psychology of religion. Similarly, a strong part needs to be played by philosophical exploration. In brief, the present phase of the discussion implies the following slogan: *Pluralise the theology, prune it back, widen the scope of descriptive and historical studies!*

There are, as it happens, social and political reasons to reinforce this conclusion. Too much of our education is Western-oriented. Too little of it enables young people to cross cultural barriers sensitively. Too little takes people out of their own environment. The comparative study of religion, sociology, psychology – these are powerful tools to induce self-criticism and understanding. There remains an implicit colonialism, even perhaps in Ireland, in much of our education.

I turn now to the second question, about the aim of religious education. How are teachers to be trained who go out into schools? Well, they should be given higher education: there is no need to be too professional in orientation. Nevertheless, in the past there has been much neglect of the world outside the university into which the graduates go.

The basic question about religious education is whether its aim is to make children into Christians of a certain sort. There is a kind of fish found in the South Atlantic called the *hydromedusa syphonophora*. When two or three of these gather together, they join up, literally, one acting as tail, another does some of the propulsion and so on. They are individuals who become an organism. The problem with children is that they are in a way the reverse. They start as elements in a family. The adults take the decisions (consider baptism, for instance). But later they swim away, detach themselves. Now schools are in a sense *in loco parentis*. If the majority of parents in a given society want their children brought up as Christians, then this is what the schools do, or attempt to do. This picture implies that the school is an analogue of the theological college – a voluntary association, except of course that the volunteering is in essence done by the parents. And we have seen that in principle there is no bar to such initiation of people into a particular tradition of belief. But, as I have said, the children do not remain elements of a wider organism: there arrives the time when they take their own decisions. In this new situation, they should have something to choose, and so the results of dogmatic explorations need to be presented. But by the same token, it is wrong and ineffective to present them in a closed way. Anyone who has encountered the thirst for knowledge about Buddhism in elementary and secondary schools will see the results of an uncandid dogmatism in religious teaching. But also, whether young people do turn to a faith or not, it is vital that they should know about religion descriptively and historically. Prejudices should not come in the way of showing people an important segment of human life and experience. I conclude, then, that however dogmatically religious education may begin, it must end at the same point at which we have already arrived in discussing the logic of religious studies.

Perhaps I am optimistic in thinking that the above arguments will be generally agreed upon. What I am saying is not, however, very revolutionary, for I do not think that changes can come overnight. I am only setting something forward as an aim to be worked for, in the gradual dismantling of religious establishments in higher education. The consequences of my argument are briefly as follows.

• Let us abandon the term 'Theology' to label faculties and departments in universities.

• Let us variegate as far as possible the variety of dogmatic explorations (even if for contingent reasons, because of our history, Christianity will retain a prominent place).

• Let us develop descriptive, historical studies on a wider, trans-religious basis.

• Let us redress the balance by investing a little less effort in dogmatic explorations and their ancillaries, and more in historical explorations.

• Let us in these ways give religious studies a renewed life, in which openness, depth and insight can combine.

By an increased emphasis on the descriptive and trans-religious side, religious studies can make important contributions, not only to the education of young people, but also to researches in other disciplines. Too often now, dogmatic suspicions get in the way of a fruitful interchange between theology and sociology and psychology and history. The aims I have outlined may lead the way forward to the revitalisation of the religious sciences.

17   What is Comparative Religion?

The comparative study of religion as it is actually carried on in academic circles covers a number of different pursuits. As I shall try to show, one of these properly bears the title, while the others, though legitimate enterprises, can better be classified under such other general heads as 'history' and 'theology'. I do not think that at the present time there is a clear consensus among comparative religionists as to how one tests conclusions, nor about the methods to be used. I shall try to illustrate some of the difficulties on these scores by reference to a thesis which I myself have propounded, mainly in relation to Indian religions, and which is open to a number of criticisms.

It is useful to look at the present rôle which comparative religion plays in religious studies especially as it is conducted in Britain. Mostly it is an optional subject to be taken by students reading theology. It can, however, be taken as a separate discipline at Manchester University, and at least one new university is intending to set up a Department of Religious Studies rather different from the usual pattern in civic and ancient universities. In addition, much work in Oriental studies bears on religion, and sociologists of religion often do work which, but for the pigeon-holing of subjects, would count as the comparative study of religion. But largely, as has been said, comparative religion is tied up with theology. This accounts in part for the diversity of pursuits comprehended under the name, though the pervasiveness of religion in human history means that almost any arts or social science subject is going to have something to do with it.

Let us clear away first those pursuits which are not, in my view, properly called comparative religion, though sheltering under the umbrella. First, there is the (in this country mainly Christian) theology of other faiths. Obviously some account has to be given, by the theologian, of other faiths – as to whether they contain truth, and if

176

so in what ways. Professor R. C. Zaehner's *At Sundry Times* for instance contains a liberal, yet still Catholic, interpretation of some major world religions. George Appleton's *On the Eightfold Path* does something similar for Buddhism; Raymond Hammer's *Japan's Religious Ferment* for Japanese religions. Such works include a lot of factual material, but they tend to look at other faiths from a specifically Christian point of view. The converse is possible. Thus many of President Radhakrishnan's writings interpret Christianity from a Hindu point of view. These exercises, though legitimate, depend on prior doctrinal assumptions: they are not either purely descriptive or 'scientific'. Second, and relatedly, there is the topic known by the barbarous neologism of missiology, comprising not just the history of missions but more importantly their aims and tactics. This incorporates conclusions of a theological nature. Again legitimate, but not in the required sense descriptive and scientific. Third, and again relatedly, there is the current fashionable enterprise of the dialogue between religions, in which participants eirenically discuss mutual view-points, both for the sake of clarification and for the sake of possible arguments. This is a kind of polycentric theologising. It would have no point if each participant did not start from a prior position. These three pursuits are essentially theological. But the comparative study of religion, though in part *about* theology, is not itself theology.

What then does it aim to do? It feeds on the hope that one can make some sense of the similarities and differences between separate religious histories. This implies first that it is necessary to give a fair descriptive account of religious beliefs and practices. These are the data that may suggest accounts of why there are coincidences and variations. To give such a fair descriptive account one must suspend prior doctrinal judgements and value-prejudices (except perhaps for the higher-order principle that what is important to people is worth studying). But it is also necessary to enter sympathetically into the religious world one is considering. This involves a kind of make-believe, though it differs from the ordinary sort. The latter is such that one makes-believe that one is on the Moon, say, when one knows all the time that one is not. The former sort does not necessarily involve this conflict with what is known. Even for the committed Christian, for example, the entertaining of belief in nirvana is not *ipso facto* the entertaining of a belief which one knows to be false, for a number of reasons: for one thing, it might turn out that nirvana and the higher reaches of Christian contemplation have an affinity; for

another thing, the concept of *knowledge* does not apply straightforwardly in relation to religious loyalties. In brief, then, the descriptive
side of comparative religion is not just a recording of data: it is the
attempt at a warmly dispassionate delineation of the outer shape and
inner meaning of religious phenomena. Needless to say interpretation offered should conform to the typical interpretation given by
the adherent of another faith. One is looking at the world from the
devotee's point of view.

Would it not be enough, then, to collect accounts of faiths as given
by their adherents? Not normally, for we have an eye to comparison.
There is no guarantee that the adherent of faith A will be able to
bring out the ways in which it differs from and is similar to faith B. To
do that he must have entered at least imaginatively into faith B. Even
if he be a convert, and so can encapsulate both faiths in his own
experience, there are human troubles to consider – the zeal of the
convert, his tendency to propagandise, the small chance of warm
dispassion. There are some who can do it: many who cannot. There is
no formal prescription for selecting in advance the good comparative
religionist.

The need to straddle both sides of a comparison ought in principle
to be recognised by the historian of another religion. For naturally
one comes to another culture with certain prior views about the shape
and nature of religion. These can be misleading, as Buddhological
studies have clearly shown (the absence in Theravada Buddhism of
the worship of anything like God and disbelief in an eternal soul have
been too much for many Western scholars to stomach – they have
tried, even quite recently, to smuggle one or another of these missing
items back into the 'original gospel' of Buddhism). The best way to
deal with prior assumptions about religion (often deeply felt because
religion remains controversial) is to bring them out in the open. But
to do this is to embark on explicit comparisons. In brief it is to do a
bit of comparative religion. But in so far as the chief aim is historical,
one can still justly call the results the history of religions rather than
the comparative study thereof.

There is then already a sense in which the acquisition of the data is
comparative. But one wants to go beyond this. One wants, for
instance, to see whether one can detect any correlations within the
various dimensions or levels of religion. For example, does a certain
kind of theology go with emphasis on a certain type of religious
experience or practice? Such a question, though, is complicated by

the organic nature of religious systems of belief and practice. Thus the Christian concept of a Creator is not quite the same as the Muslim or Jewish ones, closely related as these are. For the notion of the Creator God is modified by its juxtaposition with belief in the Incarnation. Any given proposition in a doctrinal scheme has its meaning affected by what other propositions are asserted in the scheme, and of course by the atmosphere of worship, etc., that is, by the shape of religious practice which provides a milieu for the scheme of belief. This organicness of religious systems has led at least one writer (H. Kraemer) to argue that no proper comparisons between the Christian Gospel and other faiths is possible.

Now it is true that every faith is unique – it has properties not shared by other faiths. For instance, only one religion has as its chief prophet Muhammad. Only one was founded (or refounded) by the Buddha. It is true also that there are sometimes substantial differences in the content of belief and practice. Thus as we have seen no role is assigned in Theravada Buddhism for the worship of a God. Christianity alone focuses itself upon a single and exclusive Incarnation of God. But such uniquenesses by no means rule out valid comparisons, even given the organicness of religions. Sometimes there are mythological correspondences, such as the idea of a holy figure's having been born without benefit of human paternity. Sometimes more deeply there are doctrinal and experimental correspondences, such as belief in grace (as in Ramanuja and Paul) or likeness of mystical experience (as say between some Sufis and some Christian contemplatives). The organicness does not rule these out, any more than it rules out making certain comparisons between American and Rugby Football (even though these assign different meanings to terms like *goal* and have a roughly similar kind of organicness to that found in religions).

Some confusion perhaps has been caused over the question of uniqueness by the fact that it has entered into apologetic arguments. Obviously if you hold the same beliefs as everyone else, you have nothing to offer. If you think you have something to offer you are keen to stress uniqueness. Combine this with a simple appeal to revelation (not an uncommon attitude in Christianity and some other religions) and you end up thinking that in establishing uniqueness you have somehow established truth. Looking at it dispassionately, however, we must say: Yes, what you hold is in at least some respects unique. As to truth, that is another argument (and not one incidentally which lies within the province of the comparative study of religion proper, even if the latter can furnish some very suggestive and sometimes apologetically embarrassing results).

Though sensitive, then, to organicness, and hence in fact to uniqueness, the comparative religionist hopes to draw out ways in which there is some sort of explanation of likenesses and variety in religions. I take as my main example the problem of how to account for the diversity of doctrines in the Indian tradition, bearing in mind the recurrence of certain patterns of religious practice and experience. Thus some traditional systems (Jainism, Samkhya-Yoga) are atheistic, but believe in a multiplicity of eternal souls implicated in rebirth and in the possibility of release. Buddhism likewise denies a personal Creator, but does not believe in eternal souls, though it does believe in many individuals implicated in rebirth and in the possibility of release. Medieval Dualism (Dvaita) believes in everything found in the former systems, plus a personal Creator controlling the destinies of the eternal souls. Qualified non-Dualism (Visistadvaita) is very similar, but more firmly emphasises the intimate dependence of the world and souls on God. Non-Dualism only believes in a personal Creator at a lower level of truth, at the level of illusion (*māyā*). In highest truth, the soul and Brahman are identical. Realising this identity brings release. This two-decker Absolutism, as we may call it, is parallel to a main school in Mahayana Buddhism, the Madhyamika (as commonly interpreted). So we have a series of systems, ranging from atheistic soul-pluralism, through theism, to Absolutism.

On the other hand, there is a simpler set of distinctions in religious practice and experience. (Naturally here I over-simplify.) There is a contrast in the religion of the Upanishadic period between sacrificial ritual (administered by the Brahmins) and *tapas* or austerity, usually the prerogative of holy recluses. These are both rather formalistic. But they in part provide the milieu for more 'experiential' types of religion. On the one hand, there evolved the religion of *bhakti* or loving adoration of a personal God, exemplified in the *Gita* and in medieval theism. On the other hand, the practice of *yoga* was held to bring one to higher contemplative states which could be a sign of liberation. Confining our attention to the *bhakti-yoga* polarity (the polarity between devotionalism and contemplation), we may note that the two types of practice and experience can occur independently, though they can also occur together. If they occur together one may be stressed more than the other.

They can also of course appear as equals. But let us leave aside this possibility. So far the polarity yields four paths. First, there is *yoga* without *bhakti*. This is exemplified in the non-theistic systems – Jainism, *Yoga*, Theravada Buddhism. The first leans towards formalism, *tapas* being stressed. Second, there is *yoga* plus *bhakti*, with the latter rated as secondary. This is exemplified both in Shankara's non-dualism and in the central schools of the Mahayana. Third, there is *bhakti* plus *yoga*, with the latter in second place. This is exemplified in Ramanuja's theology. Fourth, there is *bhakti* without *yoga*, exemplified in some of the more fervid poets of Tamilnadu and in evangelical Christianity. It can also paradoxically be discovered in some forms of Pure Land Buddhism – paradoxically because Buddhism in origin and heart emphasises the yogic path to liberation.

This quartet of possibilities suggests immediately a thesis: that *bhakti* is correlated with theism, that *yoga* is, when by itself, correlated with non-theistic pluralism, and that the combination of *bhakti* with *yoga* with the latter in first place yields absolutism rather than theism. Necessarily the foregoing brief account is crude. But it works as a suggestive theory in comparative religion. It works outside the Indian context. Eckhart's distinction between *deitas* and *deus*, for instance, is not far removed from Śankara's theology. Some Sufis have used absolutistic language. The theory, however, may be a bit unnerving for pious Christians, for it suggests that contemplation does not have to be interpreted as union with God, etc. It also casts doubt on a simple neo-Vedantin view, that mystical experience essentially involves the realisation of the Absolute Self, though it is favourable to the notion that mystical experience is essentially the same, though contexts, intentions and interpretations differ. But the theory by itself cannot directly settle the truth claims of the various religions and doctrines.

The theory, whether it be correct or not, illustrates the point that one must go beyond comparisons and attempt some kind of explanation of likenesses and differences. It is an explanatory theory, for it tries to bring out a correlation between doctrines on the one hand and religious experiences and practices on the other; and it tries to treat the latter as dominant. But such explanations can run into a number of methodological difficulties.

First, we must be sure that definitions (e.g. of 'contemplative life', 'mysticism', 'yoga', etc.) *realistically* differentiate forms of the religious life. It is worth noting that great sloppiness has usually characterised the use of 'mysticism' and its cognates. Second, it is not so easy to know the grounds for treating one arm of a correlation as more important than the other. That is, which is explanatory of the other? Third, the attempt to generalise inevitably brings in its trail problems about description. For instance, the *lingam* in Hinduism can be assimilated to other symbols elsewhere by describing it as phallic; but this is not the description favoured by those engaged in the cult. Fourth, and connectedly, accounts of religious experience need to be sensitive to the distinction between reporting and interpretation. But it is a tricky matter drawing the line in practice. Thus there are those who distinguish between theistic mysticism and other sorts, on the ground of differences in what appears to be reporting – and yet the use of a term like 'God' in such reporting (as when the contemplative describes himself as attaining an inner apprehension of God) makes us alive to the possibility that here a whole set of beliefs grounded outside the experience are being brought to bear in its description. For the very organicness of religion means that its central concepts come 'not in utter nakedness . . . but trailing clouds of theory'.

The complexity of many of the comparative tasks is, moreover, increased by the fact that religion, in often arousing strong feeling, renders secondary sources, whether in the form of books or of the testimony of individual (and perchance highly idiosyncratic) adherents, deserving of highly critical evaluation. Religions are not often typified by the *avant garde*, and one should listen keenly for the noise of grinding axes.

Needless to say, we are at a very primitive stage in the understanding of religions and of the deeper reasons underlying the attractions of one sort of belief and practice over another. Since religion is part of the whole fabric of human cultures, the comparative study of religion must branch out into cultural history and sociology. The complexity of the enterprise means that it will only be through a co-operative effort that advances will be made. This implies that a clearer notion of the aims of such study must be developed. I have suggested in the present article that a main feature of it should be the attempt at explanatory correlations between elements in the different dimensions of religion. But since religion has its wider milieu, as has just been noted, these explanatory correlations should be extended, for example through considering the psychological and sociological roots of certain religious phenomena, and the converse, the religious roots of some psychological and social phenomena. This in turn means that psychology and sociology need the right kind of information and sensitivity to tackle religious themes. Ignorance has in the past held up a decently scientific approach to religious problems – Freud's account, for instance, of the genesis of religion is culturally very idiosyncratic. In short, the comparative study of religion is a vital ancillary to other studies, just as they can be to it.

18 Social Anthropology and the Philosophy of Religion

I

The philosophical movement known as Linguistic Analysis has, whatever criticisms may elsewhere be directed at it, the merit of encouraging philosophers to pay attention to what goes on outside the realm of technical philosophy. For the very notion that one has to pay attention to ordinary language – or rather non-philosophical language, for philosophers should be equally concerned with specialised sorts of language which do not fall under the title of 'ordinary' – means that the philosopher's task is to get clear about the nature of concepts already employed by others. The genesis of these concepts may have little or nothing to do with metaphysical theories. Thus, for example, the philosophy of science has recently been pursued with much closer attention to the history of science and to scientific theories as they actually are. The attempt to argue *a priori* to conclusions about what science ought to be like has been replaced by a realistic appraisal of the history of science.[1] By consequence, there is a paradox about Linguistic Analysis. On the one hand it may be complained that the mere investigation of words or concepts may tend to remove philosophy further than ever from the facts. On the other hand, the encouragement to philosophers to be realistic about the history of science and so forth draws philosophy closer to the facts.

II

I wish here to illustrate the importance of a similar method when it comes to the philosophy of religion. There has been a regrettable tendency in the past to philosophise about religion – to make claims about the essential nature of religion – without due attention to the facts about religion. This has been so for a number of reasons. First, metaphysics and theology have not always been easily distinguished, so that religious philosophy has tended to take the form of showing that one's own metaphysical theory really constitutes the core of the Christian faith.[2] Second, little reliable information about the great Eastern religions, and about primitive religions, was available until fairly recently to enable thinkers to see that religion is not simply to be identified with theism or polytheism.[3] Third, the Judaeo-Christian tradition, through its rather stringent emphasis upon purity of belief and its often uncompromising condemnation of idolatry and paganism, has discouraged a dispassionate interest in other forms of faith.

However, there is at the moment a growing awareness that the philosophy of religion can benefit from descriptive studies of religion, and further that philosophy itself can reciprocate by helping to clarify the concepts and methods used in the sociology, anthropology and comparative study of religion. For example, Professor Dorothy Emmet's book, *Function, Purpose and Powers* (1958), shows ways in which the study of social anthropology throws light on the nature of religious symbols.[4] Conversely, her analysis of terms like 'purpose' and 'function' as used in sociology will, one hopes, contribute something to clarity in this field. (Likewise Peter Winch's *The Idea of a Social Science* (1958).)

III

In the ensuing, I shall begin with certain remarks of Professor Evans-Pritchard in his *Nuer Religion* (1956), which raise questions about the scope of social anthropology as a means of helping us to understand religion. I shall go on to argue that many central beliefs and practices in religion are autonomous, in the sense that they are not simply to be explained in terms of social function, or of other non-rational causes – even though it is true that social facts determine in some degree the particular forms taken by religion in various societies. But to assert that certain beliefs and practices are autonomous in this sense implies that there are religious motives or reasons for holding beliefs and performing rituals. Here the philosopher may be of use in clarifying the nature of religious concepts, whether these are employed formally in beliefs and doctrines, or whether they are worked out in ritual and daily life. Conversely, such investigations of primitive religion, and often more importantly of the concepts and practices of the 'higher' religions, will enrich the philosopher's approach to religious phenomenology.

To illustrate the important connection between reasons and the explanation of human behaviour, I take an example from G. M. Carstair's in many ways excellent book *The Twice-Born* (1958), where he describes life among the upper three castes of an Indian village in Rajasthan, which for convenience he calls Deoli. He found in Deoli that people urged him continually to lock up his possessions, as otherwise he was likely to be robbed. He ignored this advice and was not robbed; and therefore concluded that his advisers were neurotically suspicious. On the other hand, when he visited the nearby Bhil tribe, to gain material for a comparison with Deoli, although he was given precisely similar advice he did not describe this as neurotic, for, as he remarks, a lot of stealing went on there. But clearly one cannot judge the rationality of such advice without some idea of the relevant crime statistics. The fact that the author was not robbed in Deoli is almost worthless as a piece of statistics. In short, in order to judge of the rationality of beliefs and actions, and conversely of their neurotic irrationality, we have to know something about the reality to which they refer or are directed. 'Reality' here is a shorthand expression for those facts which we arrive at in accordance with such procedures as there are for determining the truth.

But here we meet certain complications. First of all, people can make mistakes about reality, but their actions or beliefs can still be intelligible as being rational. For instance, men have believed that the earth is flat; but we do not have to go behind the common-sense explanations of this belief and ascribe it to psychological aberration or to the unconscious effects of the social situation. For the mistake is easily intelligible: after all, the earth seems to be flat. (Of course, a modern American who believes that the earth is flat would need investigation.) Thus, in saying that a belief is rational in the present sense, we are not asserting that it is true. But second, a deeper complication arises. What are we to make of beliefs which do not rest upon some general procedures which we ourselves recognize, but are arrived at from different *Weltanschauung*? For example, many beliefs in primitive religions, such as the Manus conception of Sir Ghost, seem foreign to our ways of thought. It is natural that social anthropologists have been tempted to dismiss such beliefs as grossly irrational and to seek for some hidden causes thereof. Again, seeing that we now know that magic does not really work, save psychologically, how can we account for its persistence in primitive societies? It is easy to slip into a way of explaining its persistence simply by reference to social functions. Now although we cannot dismiss such explanations *in toto*, it is impossible to concur in a cavalier epiphenomenalism about beliefs, motives and reasons. Thus it is first of all necessary to seek a sympathetic understanding of such beliefs. In other words, we need to clarify our ideas about the reasons which people have for various sorts of religious and magical beliefs. A similar point is made by Peter Winch:

> Although the reflective student of society . . . may find it necessary to use concepts which are not taken from the forms of activity which he is investigating, but which are taken rather from the context of his own investigation, still these technical concepts of his will imply a previous understanding of those other concepts which belong to the activities under consideration.[5]

With these preliminaries I turn to Evans-Pritchard. Evans-Pritchard, in criticising evolutionary, sociological and psychological theories of religion, writes:

> Sociological writers . . . have often treated religious conceptions, because they refer to what cannot be experienced by the senses, as a projection of the social order. This is inadmissable. That Nuer religious thought and practices are influenced by their whole social life is evident from our study of them . . . But Nuer conceptions of God cannot be reduced to, or explained by, the social order.[6]

In this, the heart of Nuer belief is autonomous and independent of social causes. A similar view about religion is expressed by Joachim Wach:

> As a reaction to the exaggerated amount of political, social and cultural influence with which religion has been credited, a tendency emerged, with the rapid development of social studies in the past century, to reverse the emphasis and to interpret religion primarily or even exclusively as a product of cultural and social forces and tendencies. Much can be said for the suggestiveness of this line of attack, and very interesting results have thus far been obtained which have helped to broaden our knowledge of the social and

economic presuppositions of religious thought and action. Yet, on the other hand, we must guard ourselves against accepting a course of enquiry too one-sided.[7]

The tenor of Evans-Pritchard's remarks and Wach's own general position both suggest that, in accounting for religion, whether primitive (in the technical sense) or not, it is necessary to understand the nature of religious experience.

A difficulty about this is that certain sorts of such experience at least have a certain degree of ineffability. Although it is absurd to assert simply that the core of religion is inexpressible,[8] since in the first place the utterly ineffable could not possibly constitute the basis of any belief whatsoever, and in the second place there are characteristic, if somewhat opaque, ways of expressing religious experience, nevertheless we can only expect that degree of precision which the subject-matter allows. Undoubtedly, there is no absolutely clear-cut way of expressing religious experience such that the point of what is being said is completely unambiguous. This is partly because at least some intimation of what the experience is like is required for understanding it,[9] and it is by no means self-evident that such intimations are universally shared. Moreover, of course, such experiences differ widely in type.

For this reason, it is wrong to accept, as Wach does, Otto's definition of religion as 'the experience of the Holy';[10] wrong at any rate on Otto's analysis of the Holy. For this notion of the *mysterium tremendum et fascinans*, which admirably fits what may be broadly described as objects of worship, hardly applies to those mystical or contemplative goals and experiences which are not given any theistic interpretation.[11] I am thinking, for instance, of the attainment of peace and insight which essentially constitutes nirvana in Theravada Buddhism. The whole atmosphere of this attainment is very different from the staggering confrontation with a theophany which constitutes the central and most impressive type of numinous experience. The numinous and mystical experiences are typologically diverse, even though this fact is obscured by the subtle integration of the two in some religions, where the mystical state is interpreted as a kind of union with, or vision of, the divine object of worship. All this becomes more obvious when the language which is used to express religious experience is examined in relation to the religious activities which surround it. On the one hand, pure phenomenology, without always explicit reference to the way in which experience is described or expressed, is suspect: for it is *through* the means of expression that we understand the experience. On the other hand, it is absurd to tear words from their context. In many cases, we can indeed say that the force of religious concepts only becomes apparent in a liturgical or ascetic setting.

Thus phenomenology and language go together, and I can appropriate and distort, perhaps, Professor J. L. Austin's term and say that there is an important task to be done in the *linguistic phenomenology* of religion.[12] This indeed is pointed out by Wach:

We need a phenomenology of the expressions of religious experience, a 'grammar' of religious experience, based on a comprehensive empirical, phenomenological and comparative study.[13]

IV

Yet it might still seem that this program of linguistic phenomenology is liable to over-emphasise the element of *belief* rather than rites in the analysis of religions. As Radcliffe-Brown says:

What really happens is that the rites and the justifying or rationalising beliefs develop together as parts of a coherent whole. But in this development it is action or the need of action that controls or determines belief rather than the other way about. The actions themselves are symbolic expressions of sentiments.

He goes on:

My suggestion is that in attempting to understand a religion it is on the rites rather than on the beliefs that we should first concentrate our attention.[14]

In this he follows Loisy, Robertson Smith and others.

These remarks naturally open up two important questions. First, in what sense can rites be said to be symbolic expressions of sentiments? And second, what is the nature of the sentiments thus symbolised? The latter question brings us back of course to the problem of how far it is legitimate to identify these sentiments with ones which have a positive social function.[15] That is, it brings us back to the question of the limitations of a *merely* sociological account of religion.

To return briefly to the first question. There is clearly a large number of ways in which language is closely integrated with behaviour, and a variety of gestures and rather formal pieces of behaviour, such as nods, smiles, frowns and winks, have a linguistic function. There is no difficulty in seeing how ritual abasements, for example, express the awe which is also expressed in verbal worship.[16] Yet it is not clear that all ritual actions are symbolic of *sentiments*. For example, to take an instance near home, the eucharistic ritual of the Christian Church may be said to symbolise, among many other things, Christ's sacrifice upon the Cross. But the latter cannot be described as a sentiment. By the same token, although in this article we shall be specially concerned to recommend attention to religious experience, it is obvious that many centrally important facts, at least in the historical religions, are supposedly actual events interpreted in a certain light, and this introduces a considerable complication into any account of religion simply based upon religious experience and the activities connected therewith. Thus, though it may well be admitted that rites often symbolise sentiments, this is by no means all that they do symbolise. With this qualification, we can go back to consider the type of sentiments symbolised by religious rituals. Perhaps it is best for our purpose to do this negatively, by considering the problem of the social function of religion.

Is it reasonable to claim that the sentiments symbolised by the rituals of primitive religion, for example, are ones which have a social function? If this can be said, it might appear plausible to agree with Durkheim's thesis that religious ritual is an expression of the unity of society and that its function is to 're-create' the society by reaffirming and strengthening the sentiments upon which the social solidarity and therefore the social order depend. Agreed, the causality whereby such a situation could obtain is quite obscure – to invoke the natural selection of societies would be extremely hazardous. Radcliffe-Brown reshapes the thesis when he writes:

> What makes and keeps a man a social animal is not some herd instinct, but the sense of dependence in the innumerable forms that it takes.[17]

Now this formula that in religion there is expressed a sense of dependence, though it may draw some support from the study of primitive religions and from theistic forms of belief, is hardly adequate as a definition, for the reason mentioned above – namely that

Theravada Buddhism, for example, does not at all centre upon belief in a numinous being or beings. It is true that *one* very important strand[18] in religious experience is a sense of dependence, if this be interpreted in terms of confrontation with powerful and holy beings.

This confrontation, it is also true, may give rise to sentiments which become integrated with, or superimposed upon, other senti- ments and features of life. Thus, for example, social rules can have a specifically religious interpretation. But that such a way of looking at them is not *necessary* has been amply illustrated in Professor Mac- beath's *Experiments in Living* (1952). He concludes his chapters on primitive morality and religion as follows:

> Profound as may be the influences which the magico-religious beliefs and practices of primitives exercise on their individual and social life, the content of their moral codes and the principles governing their social institutions were not derived from, and are not dependent on, their religion. Religion may support them; they may be given supernatural sanctions; but they are of independent origin and authority . . . .[19]

And indeed, in the development of the higher religions, we may note a tendency for independent moral insights to affect conceptions of the supernatural. Of course, it is not necessarily correct to identify social insights with conformity to moral insights; but there is at least an overlap between the two.

These remarks indicate, then, that supernatural beliefs and rituals have an independent origin, and that they are not simply to be regarded in some way as a reflection of social needs or of the social order. Naturally, the form in which we find religious beliefs and practices is considerably affected by social conditions. As Evans- Pritchard remarks:

> That Nuer religious thought and practices are influenced by their whole social life is evident from our study of them. God is con- ceived of not only as the father of all men but also under a variety of forms in relation to various groups and persons. Consequently we may say that the conception is co-ordinated to the social order.[20]

When I say that supernatural beliefs and rituals have an independent origin, I am not thereby claiming that they have a *supernatural* origin;

but simply that the reasons for religious beliefs have an autonomous status, and that just as it would be absurd to explain away a scientific theory as being the non-rational result of certain social and other conditions, so it is wrong to treat religion in a similar way.

V

One of the reasons why this procedure has been tempting to social anthropologists is the conviction of the illusory nature of religion (in particular, of primitive religions). And again, as Evans-Pritchard says, the fact that many religious entities are regarded as invisible tends in the same direction. It thus seems reasonable to think that such absurd and unempirical beliefs and practices must be the result of covert causes, and not the consequence of independent grounds or reasons for such beliefs. Thus the existence of (especially primitive) religion has been 'explained away' sociologically and psychologically.

It is here relevant to advert again to the distinction between reasons and causes – a distinction which has been given some promi-nence in recent British philosophy.[21] If one is asked 'Why do you believe P?' or 'Why did you do A?', it is usual to reply by giving reasons for the belief or action – and these have, or are supposed to have, some logical connection (not necessarily or often that of entailment) with the belief or motive of the action. Since the causality involved in rational processes is little understood and is implicated in conceptual tangles, it is only in rather peculiar cases that one can 'bypass' the ordinary kind of explanation in terms of reasons. Though psycho-analytic explanations do effect sometimes such a bypassing, they themselves ordinarily appeal to similar concepts as those we ordinarily use. For instance, unconscious motives are pictured after the model of conscious motives. However, as a general principle we can say that where a causal explanation of a belief is offered, this is an alternative to the more usual but circuitous explanation, where we talk of a person's having reasons, and so forth. All this is not to say that the distinction between causes and reasons is final, and it cer-tainly should not be invoked with the aim of showing that, as we already know how to explain human actions, psychological and physiological investigations are beside the point. Nor is it to deny, necessarily, that all human actions are the result of prior causes.[22] But it is at least a workable distinction for the present purpose.

It therefore seems sufficient, in order to rebut general theories which purport to 'explain away' religious beliefs and practices, to show that the latter have reasons and grounds in experience, which, if they do not by any means necessarily *validate* religion, nevertheless make the religious way of life under study *intelligible*.

Unfortunately we here run into a great difficulty. An attempted explaining-away of belief in scientific theories would hardly be plausible, since scientific conclusions are arrived at through recognised rational procedures. But it can scarcely be claimed that there are clearly defined methods of arriving at religious conclusions. Now although there has been, in contemporary Linguistic Analysis, a fair amount of attention paid to the 'logic' of religious statements,[23] there has been a strong strand of irrationalism running through such philosophical appraisals of religious language, especially among those who are concerned to defend religion against positive attacks. Thus Alasdair MacIntyre writes, by way of conclusion to his long essay 'The Logical Status of Religious Beliefs':

> We ought not therefore to be surprised that to accept religious belief is a matter not of argument but of conversion . . . There are no reasons to which one can appeal to evade the burden of decision.[24]

These ways of defending religion are reminiscent of Kierkegaard and link up with Existentialist apologetics, as well as with Karl Barth's uncompromising rejection of reason in religion.

Now of course such a repudiation of reason in religion can be legitimate if it is simply a reaction against certain forms of natural theology, whether they are presented in a rigidly scholastic manner[25] or in the form against which Kierkegaard himself reacted, namely the rather pretentious argumentations of Absolute Idealism. That is, it is a legitimate protest against a spurious notion of what the role of reason in religion really is. But a retreat into complete irrationalism is both unhelpful from the point of apologetics (though this is no concern of ours here) and unilluminating. It tells us little about the logic of religious statements. It is therefore unfortunate that analysis has been covertly influenced by the demands of apologetics. For our present purpose, we may note that an irrationalistic way of describing religion not only fails to introduce any insights about the religions of other cultures, but also makes it hard or impossible to draw the distinction between reasons or grounds and causes.

Furthermore, it is unrealistic to treat religious beliefs and practices in isolation from phenomenology – in other words, in isolation from religious experience. Evans-Pritchard himself, as we have seen, regards the Nuer belief in Kwoth or Spirit as an intuitive apprehension, and in line with this it is useful again to turn to Otto's classic *The Idea of the Holy* as the kind of study which helps to illuminate the field of religious apprehension, at least in regard to beliefs in gods and spirits. An appreciation of the atmosphere of belief in the holy or sacred gives us some insight into the reasons for such beliefs – the intuitions and experiences closely related to them.

VI

Where social anthropology can be of special service here, in helping to clarify our phenomenological investigations, is in showing how far the particular forms taken by rituals and beliefs are co-ordinated to the social structure. This will show what is centrally religious and what is accidental to it in the means of expression. In addition, of course, by the richness of its findings about the religions of diverse and independent societies it prevents facile generalisations about 'the true nature of religion'.

The same is true of the comparative study of religion, which on the whole has concerned itself with the so-called 'higher' religions. An important lesson to be learnt here, for the Occidental at least, is the diversity of religious concepts and practices. The study of agnostic forms of belief, such as Jainism and Theravada Buddhism, is a useful corrective to the attempt to find a single essence of religion, and to the temptation to project our own cultural presuppositions upon other societies.

Thus from two directions we see the need to attend more widely to religious phenomenology. The study of social anthropology confirms a conclusion which ought to be apparent in contemporary philosophy of religion. Perhaps the tide is turning away from mere appeals to faith towards an investigation, by philosophers and others, of religious phenomenology. This seems the only sensible way either to make religion philosophically intelligible or to gain an understanding of many of those beliefs and rituals which figure so prominently in sociological and comparative studies.

19 The Principles and Meaning of the Study of Religion

It is time that thinking about religion in the context of higher and other forms of education was clarified and reformed. I shall concentrate here on the theoretical side of the subject, but I shall not attempt to delineate in detail the social confusions and anxieties which have tended to put a question-mark over many of the theological studies in our universities. There is much to commend in what goes on elsewhere, but the fundamental basis of the study of religion has scarcely been thought out. If someone complains that my theoretical approach is divorced from the practical applications of religion or atheism, my reply is that applications presuppose understanding and clarity of aim.

What kind of discipline is the study of religion? If it tenderly embraces such figureheads as Weber, Durkheim, Lévi-Strauss, Evans-Pritchard; Otto, Pettazzoni, Eliade, van der Leeuw, Zaehner; Feuerbach, Marx, Schweitzer, Barth, Buber, Bultmann, Gogarten, Ebeling, Karl Rahner; Sartre; Aquinas, Hume, Kant, Schleiermacher, Kierkegaard, William James, John Wisdom – not to mention Isaiah, Jesus, Paul, the Buddha, Nagarjuna, Ramanuja, Muhammad and Al-Ghazzali: if it involves the consideration of all these, what form and meaning can it have?

I

Religion is concretely manifested in a variety of traditions, social structures, forms. Just as there is no colour which is not one of the colours, so there is no religion which is not a particular religion. This multiplicity of form is highly important to the establishing of the foundations of the subject, as we shall see. But there is a further complexity which needs attention.

A religion is complex, organic and subject to change. By saying that it is complex, I mean that there are, so to speak, different dimensions of religion. Thus a religion typically incorporates doctrines, myths, ethical injunctions, rituals and styles of experience, and these are all embodied and manifested in social institutions. It has, in other words, a doctrinal, a mythic, an ethical, a ritual, an experiential and a social dimension. Perhaps the study of religion has too often been over-intellectualistic, and has concentrated too much upon the doctrinal dimension of religion, and the history of religious ideas. This can involve a distortion, precisely because religions are organic. By saying that they are organic, I mean that the different elements and dimensions interpenetrate one another. Thus the meaning of doctrinal concepts has to be understood in the milieu of such activities as worship and of such personal and communal experiences as give vitality to belief. One might in this sense say that religions are 'vertically organic'; but even within one of the dimensions which I have referred to, there is a kind of 'horizontal' organicness. For instance, within the doctrinal dimension, it is not possible to understand the concept of nirvana in Buddhism, without seeing the way in which it is embedded in a whole fabric of doctrines – about the self, about the impermanence of things, about the role of the Buddha, etc. Religious concepts typically come 'not in utter nakedness / But trailing clouds of doctrine do they come'. These concepts also in part gain their meaning from their 'vertical' relationship to practices such as meditation, institutions such as the Sangha, and so forth. In brief, a religion is both complex and organic. Understanding one feature of a religion involves looking more widely at the whole, just as the meaning of a particular patch of colour in a painting is seen by reference to the rest of the painting. The attempt to describe the inter-relationships between the elements in a faith may be called a 'structural description'.

But also a religion changes, and thus a central place in religious studies must always be given to history. Indeed, the historical descriptions of religious changes themselves generate historical explanations; and in understanding a religion from the structural point of view, one tends to be driven to consider the historical origins of particular features of a faith.

But it is necessary, in describing the past, to look at it both from an inward and from an outer perspective. By this I mean that one is not only concerned with the 'outer' fact that the Buddha preached at a certain time or that Paul went on a particular voyage. One is concerned too with the inner intentions and attitudes of the participants in historical events. We might call this *the principle of inwardness*.

This means that the study of religion has some of the properties of anthropology. The anthropologist can scarcely be a mere observer of externals. To understand the meaning of the belief-system of the people with whom he is concerned, he has to engage with them. He may not belong to the group that he studies, but the encounter with people and his own imaginative capacities can lift him from the condition of not belonging to a position of imaginative participation. At least this is required in the study of religion. Some people would go further, and say that there could be no proper structural description of a faith save by those who belong to it. The only description of a religion worth having is one that comes from within, it may be said. There is an important truth contained in this thesis, and I would not wish to under-estimate the problems of entering into other men's religious beliefs, feelings and experiences. Nevertheless, the need to believe in order to understand, in this sense, can be exaggerated. Indeed, if the thesis were taken rigorously, a whole number of important studies would collapse – history, for instance, would become trapped in insuperable problems if ever the historian were concerned with the impact of more than one religious faith on any given phase of human culture. Further, if we think that only a person of the same faith or the same community can understand that faith and that community, then we must ask: What counts as the *same faith* or the *same community*? For example, the modern Christian will regard himself as belonging to a community and faith line going back to New Testament times. But the early adherents of Christianity lived in a cultural milieu highly different from our own today. This, indeed, is a main reason for self-conscious contemporary attempts within Christianity to 'de-mythologise', namely to re-present the essential meaning of New Testament myths, but without using the New Testament cultural clothing. (When I speak of myths here, of course, I do not mean the word in the vulgar sense, to indicate stories which are false, but rather to mean a certain style of expressing beliefs.) In principle, even where a linear identity of community is claimed, the exercise of understanding early phases of the community's faith involves cross-cultural understanding. To put the point crudely: Is the contemporary Christian culturally not more different from the primitive Christian than he is from the present-day Jew?

Again, in regard to the problem of understanding a religion's inwardness, it should be noted that not only are there degrees of understanding, but there are relevant forms of understanding other than the understanding of inwardness. For instance, historical and structural explanations can be relevant to the way a person expresses his inner understanding of his own religion. Belonging to a faith is no guarantee of a *superior* understanding of the religion in question, though it *helps*. A danger of appealing to the principle of inwardness is that a handle is given to artificial restrictions upon the study of religion which are common in our culture.

To sum up so far: a religion is complex, organic, subject to change. It contains both an inward and an outer aspect. Because of its changing character, the history of religion is important. Because of its complex and organic nature, the structural study of religion is important. Because of its inward nature, both historical and structural studies require imaginative participation.

I have attempted to sketch what is meant by a structural description. To some extent the very achievement of a structural description of a religion forms a kind of explanation of its particular features, for the meaning of a given element is brought out by placing it in its living and complex milieu. For instance, to understand what some Christians mean by Real Presence, one has to place this idea in the context of a fabric of ideas and of a fabric of sacramental activities and worship. But in addition to this sort of explanation, which I shall call an internal explanation, there is another kind which ranges further afield. One might, for instance, consider Freud's theory of religion as an attempt at a structural rather than an historical explanation of certain kinds of religious ideas. It is true that Freud himself had a compulsion to back his structural theory by pseudo-historical explanations as well. The tendency in anthropological, psychological and sociological studies of religion is towards such structural explanations of religious phenomena. These, clearly, also become relevant to our treatment of history. If Freud were correct about religion, which I personally partly doubt, his theory would help to explain the appeal and therefore the spread of certain cults.

But this means that the study of religion must be comparative, for the nearest thing to experimentation as a test of structural theories is seeing how they work in relation to separate cultures and historical traditions. For instance Freudian theory of religion seems to break down in Rangoon and Kandy, where Father-figures in religion are notoriously absent. Again, considering the debate about religion

between Marxists in China it is obvious that the Marxist classifications of religion which are used do not strictly apply to Chinese
religion, even if they may have applied in the West. Weber's account
of Indian religion, in the attempt to establish experimentally his
theory about religion and the rise of capitalism, is partly outmoded
because the secondary sources have changed so much. The comparative study of religion, unfortunately, is not always geared to this task
of the testing of theories, but it has nevertheless been vital to many
studies of religion, and remains so. Consider the following quotation
from Lévi-Strauss, which indicates also that some of the most exciting
problems in the social sciences arise about religion. He writes:

> Of all the chapters of religious anthropology, probably none has
> tarried to the same extent as studies of mythology. From a theor-
> etical point of view the situation remains very much the same as it
> was fifty years ago, namely chaotic. Myths are still widely inter-
> preted in conflicting ways: as collective dreams, as the outcome of
> a kind of aesthetic play, or as the basis of ritual. Mythological
> figures are considered as personified abstractions, divinised heroes
> or fallen gods. Whatever the hypothesis, the choice amounts to
> reducing mythology either to idle play or to a crude kind of
> philosophic speculation.[1]

But if Lévi-Strauss' diagnosis is correct, think what it means for a
whole range of inquiries – for anthropology itself, for biblical studies,
for some aspects of the philosophy of religion, for some areas of
literature, for some areas of history. If we have indeed failed to
understand the nature of myth, these studies to that extent rest upon
insecure foundations. Where such great problems exist, there is
bound to be excitement and the promise of fruitful advances in
understanding. Thus in the sphere of biblical studies, for various
reasons, people want to penetrate to the real meaning of early
Christian faith. But how can we do this without knowing what it is
like to look at, say, the Ascension not from a modern perspective, as
an apparently miraculous historical event, but from the perspective
of mythic thinking, where *our* distinctions between history and interpretation are not made?

   To sum up so far: the fact that the study of religion must be both
historical and structural entails that it must also be comparative.
Much is lost in understanding if the study of religion is confined
simply to one line and one tradition.

I suggested earlier that *at least* what is required for the understanding of religion is a kind of imaginative participation. I say *at least*, but one might better say that actual participation itself is a form of imaginative participation. But clearly the imaginative entering in to other people's perspectives becomes vital and necessary if the study of religion is unavoidably in part comparative. But one needs to say more about this form of participation, which involves, as I said earlier, the encounter with people. To understand others one has to understand oneself. Some of the misinterpretations of religion in anthropology, for instance, have occurred because investigators and theorists have tended to adopt the rationalistic assumptions of their particular society. It is too easy to look upon myth-oriented rituals as simply irrational. If they are treated from such a modern, technological perspective, their real significance is lost, and one is liable to invent such theories as that of Lévy-Bruhl, where a pre-logical way of thinking is ascribed to 'primitives'. The way in which one's own cultural assumptions can distort is brought out in a nice comment by Franz Steiner:

> But we need not retain Lévy-Bruhl's independent category 'primitive punishment' as opposed to the *rational* concept of punishment – as if, since the beginning of the world, there had ever been a rational punishment![2]

In brief, the understanding of others, whether in the past of one's own tradition or in other cultures, requires self-understanding – the understanding of one's own milieu. The observer is not wholly detached: in encountering others and in participating imaginatively in their life, he as it were enters into the very field which he is contemplating. In entering into that field, he himself becomes a subject of his own investigation and he must question his own assumptions. I would therefore argue that historical studies themselves, in the case of religion, need to be co-ordinated to modern structural studies. There is a continuing dialectic between the ancient and the modern, and between our culture and others.

The combination of the need for imaginative participation and the fact that the study of religion is necessarily bound up with modern structural approaches entails another important side to the whole subject. I have referred to a certain assumption about rationality in Lévy-Bruhl. One can find similar assumptions elsewhere. Thus, in regard to the sociology of religion, Talcott Parsons remarks:

Weber's theoretical analysis of the role of nonempirical ideas is in fact part of a much broader system of analytical social theory, the emergence of which can be traced in a number of sources quite independent of Weber.

Moreover not only did Weber, Durkheim, and others converge on this particular part of a theoretical system, dealing mainly with religion, but as, among other things, very important parts of the work of both men show, this common scheme of the sociology of religion is in turn part of a broader theoretical system which *includes* the economic and technological analysis of the role of empirical knowledge in relation to rationality of action.[3]

It is clear here that a certain model of the relation between scientific and empirical ideas on the one hand and those of religion on the other is implied. But such a model is, in part at least, the consequence of a certain philosophical position. Many of the notorious problems in the sociology of knowledge and in the history of ideas arise from uncertainty about the interplay between the inner logic of a branch of inquiry and the structural and historical factors in society influencing its development. Consequently, it is not possible to avoid conceptual issues in structural and historical explanations in sociology of religion and elsewhere. The question of the relation between different styles of discourse and ways of thinking is a philosophical question. It follows, therefore, that the logic of the study of religion itself impels one towards taking the philosophy of religion seriously.

But how is the philosophy of religion seriously to be conducted? It should be firmly analytic, in the sense that we should take a careful look at the nature of religious concepts and their logical and other relationships to concepts in different spheres. Thus, for instance, much depends, if we are contemplating the relation between religious concepts and those of science, on conclusions about the real significance of seemingly cosmological statements in religion. Crudely, is *Genesis* playing in the same league as Fred Hoyle? This crude question, on examination, crumbles into many lesser questions about the proper way of analysing and interpreting mythic language, etc. So the philosophy of religion must at least be strongly conceptual and analytic in its concerns. But by the same token, philosophy of religion must be realistic about its subject matter. There is a danger that one may philosophise not about religious language as it actually is and has been, but about a reconstruction of religious language as it ought to be. Thus some supposed recent analyses of religious language turn out to be partly in the nature of apologetics – either in favour of Christianity, or some other religion, or in favour of an atheistic standpoint. If philosophy of religion is to be realistic, then it must be closely related to descriptive and comparative inquiries, and also must be sensitive to the ways in which the understanding of religion changes.

This last remark could be expressed in a different way. One important mode in which a religion may change is the continuing reinterpretation of its meaning in the light of cultural and other changes. It follows from an earlier point in my argument, the point namely that a single community or faith line stretches through a diversity of cultures, that even an appearance of being static involves a changed interpretation of meaning. For instance, the theology of St Thomas Aquinas as used by many Roman Catholic theologians since Leo XIII's Encyclical *Aeterni Patris* has quite a different flavour and significance in the context of these latter days from its flavour and significance in the time of Aquinas himself. To complicate matters, a religious tradition at a given time tends to be variegated, so that different positions are held within it. Sometimes an important point about these positions is that they themselves represent criticisms of current and older interpretations of faith. This is why we sometimes want to make a distinction between empirical Christianity, say, and 'true' or 'authentic' Christianity: one who speaks thus is implicitly criticising aspects of the tradition. Further, changes in the expression of a religion themselves may be a response to external criticisms. It is, for instance, difficult to understand the nineteenth- and twentieth-century developments in Christianity in the West without paying attention to atheistic and agnostic criticisms of Christianity. To some degree, the converse is also true.

In the light of such changes and critical positions, the engagement with religion which is necessary to the project of imaginative participation (including in this, as I said earlier, actual participation) must incorporate engagement with the changing ideas of the religion one is concerned with. Here the concern is not directly descriptive or explanatory, though it is very relevant to these concerns, since the latter themselves, as I have argued, drive one towards philosophical problems about religion, which themselves in turn drive one to a realistic evaluation of religious and atheistic positions. But in being engaged with these, one is placed in the same arena. One might call this engagement with ideas and positions the 'expressive-critical' side of the study of religion. One is liable to be expressing a position within the field, or criticising a position within the field. By the principle I enunciated earlier, namely that ancient studies should always be placed in relationship to modern ones, the most natural way of incorporating the expressive-critical side of the study of religion is by treating it in the modern and even strictly contemporary context. In any event, the only direct access which we have to the inwardness of religion is in the present.

It should be noted that the expressive-critical principle implies that religious studies must always have a penumbra. If we define religion in such a way that it does not include anti-religious atheism – and there seems to be a good reason for defining it in this way, or the atheist is deprived of his anti-religion – then the study of religion itself must always move out into the consideration of positions, such as atheism, which in some respects at least play in the same league.

To sum up this phase of the argument: the descriptive and explanatory aspects of the study of religion themselves raise conceptual issues, and therefore imply the necessity of the philosophy of religion. In turn, the philosophy of religion has to take account of the changing interpretations of religious traditions and in general needs to be realistic. By the principle of imaginative participation, and so engagement with the object, philosophy of religion is bound to take seriously the expressive-critical side. To put this in another way, theological and other expressions of the contemporary tradition, together with external criticisms of these expressions, have a necessary function in the study of religion.

Since concern with the expressive-critical side has sometimes been much abused in the shaping of religious studies, I would wish to insist that, however seriously positions within the field may be taken, the shape of religious studies must not be determined by a single position within the field. I believe that no field of inquiry should have its total shape determined by a position within it. The position within the field which has determined the shape of many university studies of theology has been this – that biblical and early Church ideas and realities are normative for Christian faith, and that the task of theology is somehow to study the latter. There are at least two ways of treating this task. One is to confine inquiries to the empirical level – to turn them into historical and to some extent structural inquiries, though restricting attention primarily to the early material. The other is to accept the logic of the term 'normative' and to use the material as a basis for *expressing* the Christian faith. The former way of approaching the study of religion is defective because of its confinement to a small area of empirical data. If my argument hitherto has been persuasive, a very restricted understanding of religion, or of a particular phase of religion, is bound to accrue upon the ancient-history approach to Christianity. The second way of approaching the study of religion is at least more candid, but has a double defect: firstly it tends to be insulated from the wider understanding of religion which structural and comparative studies can bring;[4] and secondly, by the very fact that it begins from an exclusive position within the expressive-critical field, it is liable to become inhibited and even secretive in the context of academic institutions devoted to an open and critical pursuit of truth. The logic of religious studies leads to a degree of pluralism, and it is in the pluralistic situation in any case that expressions and criticisms of religious faith can be candidly and excitingly made.

The danger of the dominance of a particular position in shaping the study of religion implies that a clearer pattern of studies will always emerge if one sees the expressive-critical side as following logically from the descriptive and explanatory sides, rather than conversely. I would as a matter of fact argue that the converse logic works also. But it should not escape attention that the study of religion is so often treated by reference to a single tradition and on the basis of a particular position. Too often the deeper consideration of modern social anthropology, sociology, psychology, philosophy and history has been neglected, as though an elucidation of biblical and early Christian ideas were sufficient and as if interest in these other matters were an amateurish luxury. By the converse logic I would argue that in any event the elucidation of those early ideas requires a very ramified, modern and imaginative structure of inquiry.

I have attempted to formulate the principles for the study of religion. I have not been concerned with the application and usefulness of this study to society at large. The nerve of the argument can be summed up as follows. The study of religion must be in part historical and therefore descriptive. But the principle of inwardness must be employed, so that historical and other descriptions must incorporate descriptions of the perspectives of those who hold religious beliefs and participate in worship and other religious activities. In view of the complex and organic nature of religious belief-systems, inner description involves a form of structural description. Both historical accounts and structural descriptions in some measure function in an explanatory manner, and one is thus driven in the study of religion to wider forms of explanation, chiefly structural. These themselves need to be tested comparatively, and therefore the study of religion itself must involve some multiplicity. The principle of inwardness implies that the investigator himself must engage with the belief and positions that he seeks to understand. He thus enters the field of his own investigation, and thus must have an understanding of his own individual and cultural condition. This implies that there must always be a dialectic between ancient and modern studies and between one's own culture and others'. But also, attempts at explanation themselves generate conceptual issues, philosophical ones. This is a further reason for engagement with the expressive-critical side of religion, for philosophical approaches need to be living and realistic. Thus a necessary feature of the study of religion is the interplay from within it of expressive-critical positions, and it is in this sense that religious studies incorporate theology. But the shape of the field must not be determined from a position within it. Concretely it follows from all this that at least the following branches of study are necessary.

First, there must be history of religions, for without it there are no data for a testing of structural explanations. *Second*, there must be phenomenology of religion, in which a sound classification and understanding of elements of religion can be reached: without this the data supplied by the history of religions are unfruitful. *Third*, there must be sociology of religion and its kin, such as social anthropology and the psychology of religion; for without these our understanding of religious ideas and phenomena becomes unstructural, unselfcritical and over-intellectualistic. *Fourth*, there must be philosophy of religion, for conceptual decisions are deeply embedded in structural explanations and descriptions within the social sciences. *Fifth*, there must be engagement with modern religious and atheistic thought, for without this philosophical and structural approaches to religion become insensitive to change and to one aspect of the inwardness of description; moreover they are necessary to self-understanding, without which the attempt to understand others by engagement and imaginative participation can be grossly distorted. *Sixth*, in our culture and because modern studies of religion have so far been primarily developed in the West, the engagement with modern religious thought most naturally is tied to an understanding of the Judaeo-Christian tradition, and part of the contemporary inwardness of this tradition is that it looks to origins. Hence, there is a strong argument for maintaining a dialectic between biblical studies and modern expressive-critical positions. It happens too that such studies raise actually the problems of anachronism that beset understanding. Thus the New Testament must be seen both historically and dialectically, where the dialectic is between ancient and modern, between the origins and their re-presentation.

There are other aspects of the study of religion which ought also to be developed, but these at least seem the most necessary.

The student of religion thus needs to have historical knowledge and expertise, sensitivity and imagination in crossing cultures and time, and analytical grasp. He has to be a latter-day Leonardo. This shows why Religious Studies is neither the Queen of the Sciences nor the Knave of Arts; but it is one of the foci of the humanities and social sciences. In it some of the most engaging and perplexing problems in these disciplines have a meeting point. For to tell the truth, we are all of us far from having anything but rather superficial grasp of the multiple structures of religious faith, myths and institutions.

20 Methods and Disciplines in the Study of Religion

The second half of the twentieth century has seen a great flowering of the study of religion. There has been great growth in institutions offering courses in religion in the English-speaking world; while in Continental Europe and Scandinavia there has, in the period since 1945, not only been a restoration to vigour of the faculties of theology, but also a modest and significant advance in the history of religions, partly in the context of a widened interest in non-European cultures. At the same time, work in the social sciences has increasingly converged, in matters related to religion, upon the work of comparative religionists.

But though we may live during a period when old-fashioned rationalism is declining, and when the importance of the study of religion is more widely recognised, there is not always much clarity in the assumptions brought to bear upon it. Or at least there is much divergence of aim and method in the way in which it is approached.

This is partly because the subject is considerably shaped by the institutions in which it is embedded. Thus the existence of Faculties of Christian Theology imposes certain categories upon scholarship – for instance the division into such branches of enquiry as New Testament, Patristics, Church History, Systematic Theology, Philosophy of Religion, Comparative Religion (or History of Religions). This builds into the subject an *a priori* asymmetry in the way in which Christianity is treated as compared with the way other religious traditions are. This of course reflects the history of scholarship and the fact that classically the study of religion has been tied for the most part to the training of clergy and other specialists; and so the modern universities of Europe and America in some degree inherit the cultural assumption that Christianity should have a privileged place in the curriculum. Conversely, worry about such an arrangement sometimes leads to the exclusion of theology from the secular university. But it is not my task here to enter into the controversies surrounding this matter: but rather to look to the way in which the history of the subject affects approaches to it. Undoubtedly for many scholars there remains the assumption that their task is to be understood in the light of Christian (or Jewish or other) truth: that is, in one way or another commitment is relevant to study. We can in respect of all this point to a number of differing models.

First, there is the full-fledged model of what may be called *Constructive Traditionalism*. That is, there is the approach to the study of religion from the perspective of a given tradition – most frequently Christianity, and in particular some variety of it (Lutheranism, Roman Catholicism, etc.). Ultimately here the exploration of texts, the undertaking of a critical evaluation of them, the process of hermeneutics, the systematic exploration of doctrines and so on are geared to the constructive presentation of the tradition as expressive spiritual and intellectual truth. Ultimately the task is one of expressing rather than describing. Thus the work of such figures as Barth, Küng, Bultmann, Käsemann, Tillich, and John Robinson – to put together a variegated selection of recent theological and Biblical scholars – is in the last analysis concerned with working out Christian truth, rather than simply doing history or even debating on both sides of the question (as might happen in the context of the philosophy of religion).

Second, there may be an attitude of seeing the study of religion as primarily concerned with issues in philosophical theology – that is with the questions arising concerning the nature and existence of God (or of the Ultimate, to use a more inclusive term) as perceived in the light of the history of religion. This orientation may be called *Pluralistic Theology*. The accent is primarily on questions of truth in religion rather than on truths concerning religion.

Third, the theological tradition may be treated positivistically: that is, the essential task of the theologian is to explore and describe the history of the faith independently of truth judgements about the content of faith. Still, it is naturally the case that such an approach has its agenda set by some implicit evaluations – for instance, about the importance of particular periods and aspects of Christian, or other, history. We may call this approach *Theological Positivism*. The fact of positivism does not preclude such an approach from being critical, and making use of the various tools of modern critical historiography.

It is clear that looked at from a planetary point of view there are questions arising about such models of theology. For one thing, the very word 'theology' is a Western one. What does one use for Buddhism? Should we talk of the Buddhologian? Moreover, not all traditions are as hospitable either to Pluralism or to critical Positivism as in the modern Western tradition. Nevertheless, historians of religion have opened up critical questions about the various traditions. I do not wish to argue the point here, but it seems clear to me that every tradition will inevitably have to come to terms with such scrutiny. It matters, of course, less in some faiths than others. For instance, Buddhism is not quite so tightly wedded to history as is Christianity or Judaism, while the facts of early Islam are less in doubt than those of Judaism or Christianity. But naturally the critical positivist questions necessarily raise issues of truth in the context of what we have dubbed Pluralistic Theology and thus are liable to generate new approaches within the various forms of Constructive Traditionalism. Thus neo-Hindu theologies (such as those of Vivekanada and Radhakrishnan) can be seen as ways of coming to terms not merely with Western culture but also with modern methods of scholarship, concerning India's deep past.

The modern period has of course seen the opening up, more richly than in the past, of contacts and conversations between religious traditions. The exchange of insights between faiths has come to have the name of dialogue. It is true that dialogue could simply be a method of exchanging information and so just be a tool of historical research: but more pregnantly it has been a particular style of Pluralistic Theology, a kind of co-operative spiritual exploration of truth. Because however it does differ in style and tradition it may be useful to have a different name for it. I shall call it *Constructive Dialogue*.

But none of all this so far is what may be thought of as the scientific study of religion. It is quite true that sometimes so-called scientific studies of religion (say in sociology) conceal value – or truth – assumptions which are of an essentially theological or philosophical nature (e.g. projectionism makes certain assumptions about the truth of religious belief, typically). It is quite true also that Pluralistic Theology, Constructive Traditionalism and so forth may in fact use scientific methods in the course of their inquiries. Certainly, such great theologians as Karl Barth made use of much plain historical material and critical method. But the main thrust of their concerns was not descriptive and scientific but expressive, proclamatory, philosophical: presenting a faith-stance or a worldview.

It may be thought that there is a Science of God. In a sense perhaps there is (and to that sense I shall later come). But I think in a more obvious way the idea that there is a Science of God, a kind of Theological Science, uses the term in a Pickwickian way. Belief in God is highly debatable, only indirectly (at best) testable, a question of reaction and commitment, much bound up with value questions. Since the alternative views of the Ultimate are so various, and even include the view that there is no Ultimate, it would be rash to define a Theological Science by postulating to start with a personal God. At best we might think about a Science of the Ultimate. Now it is clear that some men claim to experience the Ultimate, and it would be wrong to neglect such experience. But because of the vagaries and strangenesses of issues about interpretation it would be better in the first instance to confine the use of the word 'scientific' to the relatively neutral investigation of phenomena, including those comprised by religious experience. In brief, then, I think it is reasonable to say that the various models I have listed above (Constructive Traditionalism through to Constructive Dialogue) do not fall, essentially, within the purview of what may be called the Scientific Study of Religion, though they may overlap with it.

Those overlaps actually are important. How can one really get the feel of a faith except by mingling among its adherents? A religion is more than texts, and the past: it is living history. This being so, a kind of dialogue with people is necessarily part of the fabric of enquiry into religion, whether Scientific or otherwise.

Again, the philosophical skills which are fashioned in the philosophy of religion are important in the empirical investigation of religion. For one thing, descriptions have to be scrutinised for assumptions. Our interpretive categories are theory-laden; often with inappropriate theory. Again, philosophy is much bound up with questions of verification and method. Moreover the whole enterprise of hermeneutical enquiry is one which requires philosophical debate. So it is idle to think one can simply do the history of religions, or the sociology of religion, or whatever, without in fact bumping up against philosophical and conceptual problems.

Moreover, the processes of critical history concerning, for example, Christian origins, vital in the task of constructive Christian theology, are relevant to other areas of religio-historical enquiry.

In brief, there is an overlap between the value-laden models for the study of religion and the relatively value-free Scientific Study of Religion.

One has, however, to be clear about this notion of the relatively value-free. It is sometimes said that it is not possible (or even desirable) to be perfectly value-free, perfectly 'objective'. The term 'objective' is an unfortunate one, because actually all science and all unravelling of the world involves a kind of interplay, even a struggle, between the inquirers and that which they are concerned to understand. The right questions have to be posed. Nature is mean about her secrets, and she is a great slaughterer of theories. Objectivity is important only in two ways – one being that by being relatively free of prejudice the inquirer may show imagination in developing new questions to pose to nature; and secondly objectivity implies the acceptance of the possible death of one's pet ideas. One should be adventurous and sagacious, but also Stoical in defeat. When we come to the human sciences, however, there is a difference of a profound kind: for it is no longer a mute nature that addresses us, but living and communicative beings. Empathy becomes important. And that means somehow adopting the American Indian proverb: 'Never judge a man till you have walked a mile in his moccasins'. Or rather: 'Never describe a man until you have walked a mile in his moccasins'. The term 'objectivity' is not usually taken to include much in the way of feeling or empathy.

So, though the Scientific Study of Religion should be relatively value-free, it has got to enter somehow into the world of values. This is part of what has come to be called the Phenomenological Method, as practised by, for instance, Kristensen and van der Leeuw. However, it happens that partly because of its particular philosophical origins in the tradition or Husserl, phenomenology of religion has also come to be bound up greatly with the search for essences: that is, with describing types of religious phenomena, and classifying them. This is to be seen in van der Leeuw's *Religion in Essence and Manifestation* and in Widengren's phenomenological work, and represents part of the whole enterprise known as the Comparative Study of Religion. It is thus probably useful for the sake of clarity to distinguish between what I have referred to above as the Phenomenological Method, which involves 'entering in' to the thought world of the believer, and Typological Phenomenology, which is an attempt to anatomise the forms of religion in a comparative manner.

The use of the term 'phenomenology' implies, as it is usually employed, a suspension of belief, a prescinding from the worldview which the investigator may happen to hold, except in so far as he may think that the investigation of religious phenomena is important, which may imply something about a worldview, though at a higher logical level. (It is in general important to pay attention to levels: thus to say that we should use empathy to enter into people's various positions is a position about positions, i.e. it belongs to a higher level.) This sometimes obscures the fact that structures are important as well as empathy. That is, since the believer views his activity against the background (or should we say from within the background) of a whole web of beliefs and resonances, the person who wishes to understand the meaning of his action needs to unravel that structure or web. For instance, what are we to make of the Buddhist laying a flower before the statue of a Buddha in Sri Lanka? To understand him it is necessary to understand his understanding of the world, and that constitutes quite a complex structure. So empathy has to be more than imaginative feeling: it has to include a delineation of structures. Consequently, there is a certain tension between the Phenomenological Method or Structured Empathy, and Typological Phenomenology, which tends to try to cut through the organic particularities of a given cultural milieu.

This tension is something which runs deeply through the territory of the history of religions. For while some of the scholars in the field are more concerned with the Comparative Study of Religion – (a phrase which comes in and out of vogue – out of vogue in so far as comparisons could be thought to be odious, and redolent of whiffs of Western imperialism and Christian superiority, the phrase falls on evil days; yet *in* vogue in so far as we wish the study of religions to make use of the opportunities for comparison and contrast, opportunities which are useful in testing various hypotheses about religion) – others again are concerned more with the history of a given tradition or culture. Thus the study of religion contains among other things the histories of various traditions, which may or may not be at one time or another in mutual historical interaction; but it also contains attempts at comparative treatment, which is necessarily cross-cultural. It is at different times important to stress uniqueness of historical development and similarities of phenomena and elements in differing cultures. The danger of separate histories is that each may fail to see certain aspects of the dynamics of religion which can be gleaned from cross-cultural comparison. The danger of the comparative study of religion is that it may bulldoze the particularities of the traditions.

Basically the Comparative Study of Religion as it is practised tends to comprise first an attempt at a world history of religions; and second various kinds of Typological Phenomenology (for instance the comparative study of mysticism, sacrifice, worship and so on). To complicate matters, it has become usual to substitute the phrase History of Religions for the Comparative Study of Religion. Sometimes, as in the work of Eliade, such History of Religions includes a special scheme of Typological Phenomenology. Actually Eliade's scheme has been remarkably fruitful, especially in raising issues about the religious and human meaning of space and time. But in addition Eliade's work, like Otto's and Wach's – to name two important forerunners – includes a general theory of existence: a kind of philosophy, one might say, compounded out of various sources including Eliade's own historical experience. Thus his Typological Phenomenology, especially in regard to views of history, is in part determined by a kind of philosophical theology. This does not mean that we have to discard the typology, but it does mean that we have to be aware, critically, of assumptions open to question and lying behind the more empirical presentations of the data. It would perhaps be ironic if having escaped from theological dogmatism as inappropriate for the Scientific Study of Religion we met it in new and more heavily disguised form in a philosophy of existence unquestioned behind the shamanism. The point is that the Science of Religion should welcome imaginative ways of looking at the data, including Eliadean ones, Marxist ones and so on; but that is not to say that what counts as the Scientific Study of Religion should be determined and defined by any one theory. For each theory should be testable in relation to the data in the field. Assuming any one theory to define the field destroys its true testability and gives it a spurious authority.

Because of the institutional evolution of the subject the Comparative Study of Religion has not always existed in close relationship to such scientific or social-scientific disciplines as the Sociology of Religion, Anthropology of Religion and Psychology of Religion. True, in the late 19th century especially the influence of anthropology was very considerable, partly because it was fashionable to speculate about the origins and evolution of religion and 'primitive' cultures were thought of also as somehow primaeval and so containing clues to the earliest phases of human culture and spirituality. Actually there seems no intrinsic reason why the History of Religions and the Sociology and Anthropology of Religion should not be treated as a single investigatory enterprise. The divergences are somewhat fortuitous. Thus the difference between sociology and anthropology represents a crude division between large and small scale societies, a difference of style of founding fathers and gurus, and a certain distinctness of methodological emphasis. But as for the scale question, this is hardly in the last resort relevant to overall theorising about society; as to the styles, they add up to differing and often competing theories which have to be tested in the same empirical market-place; and as for methods, differences are to do with feasibilities – cancer research may employ different techniques from research into the brain, but we do not thus artificially divide human functioning. Further, though obviously the concern of the social scientists is primarily with social relationships and dynamics, this is after all a major aspect of a religion and its cultural expression and milieu, so that there is in principle no absolute divide between History of Religions and the social sciences of religion.

Similarly one may see History of Religions as somewhat like economic history: the latter is history with the accent on economic aspects of existence, and the former is history with the accent on religious aspects of existence. It would be as artificial to deal with the economic history of 1979 without mentioning Khomeini as it would be to treat the religious history of the Amish without dealing with the economics of small-scale agriculture.

It may be noted also that some of the major figures in the sociology of religion have also been concerned with Typology. To take two examples: Weber and his theories of the relationship between religious and socioeconomic development; and Bryan Wilson and his attempt to classify various sects and new religious movements. This work is relevant to the often neglected point that one can have a typology of historical changes – for example what happens in cases of culture contact.

Though one might consider, reasonably, that the difference between the various disciplines (history, sociology, anthropology of religion) is somewhat artificial, it does create one advantage, in that the institutionalisation of differing approaches leads to effective intellectual lobbies against the neglect of certain areas. Thus it is easy to do the history of religions in a rather textual and 'unliving' way. The social scientists pressure us to restore balance here. A result is the renewed modern interest in the sociology of early Christianity, the attempt to look at Buddhism from the perspective of modern Asian societies, the need to analyse rites of passage in context and so on. The same can be said about some recent and rather adventitious developments. Thus in North America especially the advent in women's political activism has resulted in a burgeoning of women's studies and with that a renewed interest in the female in religion; likewise recent concerns about Blacks, Chicanos and Native Americans have led to something of a revival in the study of the religions of these people.

One major methodological issue arises especially in regard to the Sociology of Religion, and in a differing form regarding the Psychology of Religion. The tendency in these fields is for theories to be developed which are in general projectionist. Thus God and the Ultimate and the lesser entities and symbols of religious belief tend to be seen as unconscious or social projections, which then act reflexively upon society and individuals. Thus a highly sophisticated modern form of projection theory is to be found in Peter Berger's *The Sacred Canopy,* in which he claims to espouse 'methodological atheism'. It is taken as axiomatic that a scientific approach to religion cannot accept the existence of God. But the non-acceptance of the existence of God is not equivalent to the acceptance of the non-existence of God. What should be used in approaching religion is not so much the principle of methodological atheism as the principle of methodological agnosticism. It is not useful for the investigator of religion to begin by imposing assumptions drawn from his own worldview upon the subject matter. Thus the suspension of belief here required is a kind of higher-order agnosticism. Thus God or the Ultimate need neither be affirmed nor denied, but seen as something present in human experience and belief, wherever it is so present. It is only in this sense that there is a 'Science of God'. It is important that the power of religious experience and belief and the way God serves as a Focus of human activity and feeling to be recognised as factors in history and society and in individual psychology. Often the power of the Ultimate-as-experienced is underestimated by modern rationalist historians and social scientists. How important it is is not a question of validity of experience, but a matter of empirical impact. Conversely it may be that on occasions religionists have overestimated the actual impact of the Ultimate-as-experienced. So though there is not a science of God there is a sort of *science of God-as-experienced.* This is the advantage of speaking of religion as a phenomenon.

Since impacts are in principle measurable it is not surprising that much attention has been paid by some social scientists to statistical data: we can see one manifestation of this approach in the *Journal for the Scientific Study of Religion.* One of the problems arises from the way in which a suitable wedding between this and more impression-istic but empathetic phenomenology can be achieved. We see a like chasm in the psychology of religion between much of the interesting work being done in Typological Phenomenology, for example over the classification of mysticism and other forms of religious experi-ence, and the measurement of attitudes, etc., which occupies much of psychology-oriented psychology of religion. Frits Staal's sketch on how to deal with mysticism in his *Exploring Mysticism* goes some way towards achieving a synthesis; but there remain important philo-sophical problems not fully resolved either by him or by others in regard to the ways to classify inner experiences – an issue much bound up with the important, but vexed, question of the relationship between experience and interpretation. Considerable conceptual problems enter into this discussion, which has recently been carried on in the context of philosophical analysis. Lack of concern with the problem has initiated some influential works on religious experience, for instance, those by Stace and Zaehner.

For various reasons, the interplay between anthropology, depth psychology and history of religions has proved fruitful in the variety of ways myth and symbolism can be approached. There are certain congruences between structuralism, Eliade and Jung, which suggest that the analysis of religion may be a vital ingredient in any theory of human psychology. And this in turn raises an important question as to what the comparative and phenomenological study of religion ultimately aims at. Though it may be methodologically unsound to try to define the study of religion in terms of some theory within the field, and the data should be so far as possible presented in a way which is not theory-laden – for this would lead too easily and cheaply to 'confirmation' of the theory by the data – yet it may remain important for the History of Religions to supply material which can be used theoretically. Thus the following are important, though difficult areas for speculation and research: Are there in fact ar-chetypal symbols which are liable to appear independently in dif-ferent cultures? If so, what kind of explanation of this would be in order? What kinds of patterns can be found in the processes of syncretism and the creation of new religious movements in the Third World (as the many thousand in Africa) and in parts of the Western world? If the mythic mode of expressing existential relationships to the cosmos and to society have been widespread among peoples in the past and to some extent in the present, what other changes are liable to accompany the erosion of this style of thinking? To what extent do non-religious ideologies function in similar ways to traditional religious belief-systems? Can any form of projection theory be empirically confirmed? Most importantly, the confluence of anthropological and religio-historical approaches may be vital in giving us a better modern understanding of human symbolic behaviour. Curiously, though religions obviously have a vital interest in the arts and music, there has been relative neglect of the visual, musical and literary dimensions of religious consciousness. This is perhaps in part due to the kind of training typical of Western scholars – concerned often with texts and evidences, and fascinated often by doctrinal and intellectual aspects of faith. An interesting methodological question arises in regard to literature, in that novelists especially are devoted to a kind of fictional 'structured empathy' such as I described earlier. They bring out 'the feel' of what it is like to be a given person looking at the world and at others in a certain way (consider, for instance the divergent expressions of attitude delineated by Dostoievsky in the case of the brothers Karamazov). To what degree would new forms of literary presentation be relevant to the task of phenomenology? One thinks here of the novels of Eliade and Sartre as cases where more abstract analyses are clothed in particular flesh.

One can discover, in the evolution of the study of religion, a series of stages. One stage is represented by the discovery and decipherment of other cultures (I look here at the matter inevitably from the standpoint of the Western culture which gave rise to the modern study of religion). This process is still going on. There are still large numbers of important texts not yet edited and understood, and the recording of oral traditions is still only very partial. Access to the records of differing religious traditions made possible the process of comparison. Classificatory comparisons form ideally the second stage in the study of religion as a human phenomenon. The third stage is where theories whether sociological (e.g. Weber), anthropological (e.g. Tylor) or psychological (e.g. Jung) can be formulated. We remain at a rather early stage in the development of theorising about religion. Perhaps also we are at the beginning of a harvest, in which the many fruits of the extensive expansion of research in religion, especially since mid-century, can be gathered, and when the history of religions – and in a more general way the study of religion – may enter a period of greater influence, in the broader world of learning.

So far we have looked at the Scientific Study of Religion as being plural in scope, for it concerns the many traditions and the plethora of forms of religion to be discovered on the planet and in history;

and as being multi-disciplinary – for it must include not just the techniques and processes of Structured Empathy and Typological Phenomenology, but also methods drawn from history, sociology, anthropology, iconography, and so on. But there remain problems concerning the boundaries of the field. Notoriously an agreed and useful definition of religion is hard or impossible to find. Yet at the same time often scholars seem unnaturally confident as to what they mean by the Study of Religion. It is a real question as to whether the subject should consider the symbolic systems usually held in the West to lie beyond religion proper – nationalism, forms of Marxism and so on. There does seem an incongruity in treating the Taiping rebellion (or revolution) in the category of the history of religions and Maoism in another quite separate category of political history. After all, both movements were trying to resolve much the same problem of China's national identity in a time of crisis, and they have many other properties in common. It is a result of perhaps an ideological rather than a scientific divide that we put traditional religions in one basket and secular ideologies in another. It is after all ultimately an empirical matter to discover if theories worked out in regard to traditional religions also work in the case of their secular counterparts.

Thus there is an argument for saying that the Scientific Study of Religion is non-finite – that is, there is no clear boundary which we can draw around it. It simply has to be discovered in practice how far theorising goes beyond the traditional faiths. Incidentally it is quite clear that the methods of Structured Empathy are as necessary in the exploration of secular worldviews as in the case of religions proper.

Though there is increasing reason to hold that the Scientific Study of Religion should be so far as possible value-free, save in so far as in the nature of the case it has to evoke values, via the processes of empathy and phenomenology, there is little doubt that it has a reflexive effect *upon* values. For one thing, the historical approach to scriptures is bound to (and has) affected attitudes to their authority, and can nibble at their contents. Similarly knowledge of other religious traditions is bound to affect attitudes to one's own tradition. Thus a lot of ink has been spilled on the question of the uniqueness of Christianity, since from the perspective of certain theologies there is a motive to stress the difference between Christianity and other faiths; while there is something of the opposite from the perspective of modern Hinduism. The question of Christianity's likeness or unlikeness to other traditions in this or that respect is strictly an empirical question (though it may remain a debatable one). In this way empirical theses may have evaluative consequences.

The fact that the Scientific Study of Religion can have such effects is one reason why it takes a special kind of temperament to be devoted to its pursuit – a kind of passion for 'evocative dispassion'. It is, though, one of the noblest of human enterprises to try to enter imaginatively into the feelings and thoughts of others. This is an ingredient in religious methodology which has many lessons to teach in the modern world and the multicultural ambience of the planet. This is one among a number of reasons why the study of religion and religions should play a widening part in the educated person's understanding of the world. In this respect, students of Religion, like Eliade for example, may be right to call for a creative role for the history of religions. Better, however, that this role should be played not just by the history of religions, but more widely by the whole set of disciplines which in interplay make up the study of religion. All this is only perhaps a second-order way of saying that religious sentiments, ideas and institutions remain a pervasive aspect of the human world. That so often the wider study of religion – what I have called the Scientific Study of Religion – has been suspected from the side of faith and neglected from the side of reason has contributed to the lopsidedness of the human sciences.

21 The Exploration of Religion and Education

The theory and practice of religious education and more generally of the study of religion are entangled in unnecessary confusions. We shall see why. In the meantime it is, in my opinion, a straightforward task to exhibit the principles of the study – or as I should prefer to call it the exploration – of religion. True, there are some problems about defining religion and some questions about how understanding a religion is possible, but essentially these are marginal and have been unnecessarily inflated.

What then is the study or exploration of religion?[1]

First, religion means religious. It is elementary that in exploring religion we are *at least* involved in exploring religious traditions. Maybe in Britain we pay more attention to Christianity than to Buddhism, and conversely should pay more attention to Buddhism than to Christianity in Thailand or Sri Lanka. But there would be something irrational and insensitive in simply studying religion through one tradition. It would perhaps be analogous to studying political behaviour by concentrating on Wilson and Thatcher; and forgetting altogether about Brezhnev, Mao and L.B.J. So first of all the study of religion is *plural*. I do not imply that every university and school should teach concerning all possible religions. Decisions about resources and selection need, obviously, to be made.

Second, the exploration of religion ought not to be defined from a standpoint within the field. That is, it should not assume the existence of God or alternatively the non-existence of God. No doubt an explorer may believe in God or come to believe in him; or may come to be a Buddhist or a Marxist. But this does not mean that individual conclusions should be built into the shaping of the study. This has two consequences. First, the exploration would involve institutional openness (for which reason it could not be easily undertaken in a totalitarian society). Second, its methodology must involve a certain style, a phenomenological style.

220

The study has to do justice to two points – firstly that the foci of religious belief and behaviour are real, and not just abstractions; secondly that their actual existence can be made subject to *epoché*, that is, the suspension of disbelief or belief. To illustrate these two points: he who wishes to explore Hinduism will need to get a feel of the impact of Śiva and Viṣṇu upon their adherents. He fails properly to understand them if he cannot grasp their rich reality in the eyes of the faithful. But this grasp neither entails accepting nor dismissing Hindu theology. Thus though the exploration of religion can be considered from one point of view the attempt to describe and understand a certain aspect of human behaviour, from another point of view it deals with the supernatural and mysterious foci of religious behaviour.

So far then the study is seen to be plural, phenomenological and aspectual. Because feelings enter into religion often in an intense way, the exploration also needs to be empathetic (and more warmly, loving – the student of Buddhism who is alienated from it is scarcely likely to be successful). The explorer therefore needs to be equipped with a certain sort of sensitivity. One can compare the exploration of literature and poetry.

Another property of the exploration is that it is what may be called non-finite. That is, its boundaries cannot be too closely defined. For instance, some political ideologies possess a number of the properties typical of a religion – Maoism for instance has its own doctrines, ethical values, conversion experiences, rituals and so on. Though we might hesitate to call it a religion in the full sense it yet has analogies to one and so one would expect that the methods and aims character-ising religious exploration would be relevant and useful in the case of Maoism. Further, one main reason why we might wish to explore religion and religions has to do with truth. We might seek to under-stand religions in order to have a better perspective on religious truth. This being so, any system which rivals religion would have some place in the exploration of religious truth.

We may now come to the question of the point or aims of exploring religion (for the quest for truth might be one such aim – but let us leave this for the moment on one side, for it goes beyond the descriptive and empathetic level of enquiry).

The first reason for exploring religion might just be that it is interesting in itself. Exploring it might then be like listening to lovable music; we do not here need to look for further levels of motivation.

However, as well as possibly being interesting, religion is certainly important, and it is so from various perspectives. First it is so because of its extraordinary formative powers in relation to human cultures and history. Let us but take one example, perchance the most dramatic of all: within a century of the death of the Prophet Muhammad, Islam was not merely a world force, but had founded a new civilisation stretching from Spain to Central Asia. Of course, religion may not always be formative. It can be defensive and permeated by forces from outside its own fabric. Indeed one of the empirical questions always to be borne in mind is whether in a given social or historical milieu the boot is on the religious foot or some other – or since this is of course a simplistic way of expressing the matter, whether *some* of the religious factors are formative or not. For example, in contemporary Sri Lanka, the Buddhist ideology of the Sri Lanka Freedom Party is clearly one causative factor in tensions with the Tamil community – but the whole economic, historical and political scene is so complicated that any quantification of the religious factors would be impossible or misleading, unless put in the broadest possible way. But it scarcely follows from this that judgements about the importance of the religious factors should be eschewed by the contemporary analyst of the scene. Economic factors are equally hard to evaluate.

In brief, religion has importance for history, art, society, politics and so on. As such it needs to be studied by a variety of methods and disciplines: the historian, sociologist and so on can trace out the movements and structures of religion. So we may note in passing that the exploration of religion is polymethodic (in this it is like political science, economics and sociology, which are themselves likewise aspectual: in all this needless to say the various dimensions of exploration necessarily intersect).

A third main reason for exploring religion could be somewhat personal – the quest for faith and a judgement about religious truth; or conversely faith seeking understanding. In all this, the explorer does not seek only descriptive understanding, but an evaluation as well. In going beyond history he seeks a parahistorical interpretation. The relationship between the descriptive or 'scientific' exploration of religion and the truth-quest (the quest for judgements about the truth of religious claims) is of course complex. The distinction needs to be made firmly, but then transcended. I do not consider that the scientific study of religion can be divorced from philosophical and theological approaches, for reasons which will shortly appear. But on the other hand I think the dominance of theology distorts the descriptive exploration of religion. The tail of doctrine should not wag the dog of history. Much of the past narrowness of the study of religion in this country stems from the tail-ward tradition (natural in its historical evolution but needing critical transformation nevertheless). Thus establishmentarian theology has not always been hospitable to the empathetic, pluriform, non-finite exploration of religion. However, this is by the way for the moment. Now I am concerned with the logic of the study: later we can come to institutions and to education.

The reasons why even the descriptive study of religion has to come to terms with philosophy and theologies are as follows. First, certain attempts to explain religion's power over people have involved projectionist theories – such as those of Feuerbach, Marx, Freud and even Berger (or at least the Berger of *The Social Reality of Religion*). It is not possible to evaluate such theories without some philosophical insights and enquiries. Second, the intellectual history of religions needs some engagement with arguments and doctrinal claims, even if the ultimate aim may really be historical. There is a parallel with the history of philosophy – engagement with Aristotle's theory of substance helps to illuminate it. Nevertheless, one should not exaggerate the importance of philosophy and theology to the history of religion. The main reason why the truth-quest is a natural dimension to the exploration of religion is simply that individuals or groups may wish to see how the power of religion works out in relation to their own commitments (or lack of them). But people should always be as clear as possible as to the difference between exploring the truth *concerning* religion and exploring the truth *of* religion.

In brief, the main reasons for studying religion and religions are: the interest of religion, the importance of religion and the question of the truth of religion. I have argued here that the descriptive exploration of religion is more important, or at least has first logical priority, in relation to the truth-quest. How can one find truth without understanding?

It is sometimes of course said that one cannot really understand a religion without belonging to it – and this might scramble my position. But, briefly, the objection is not convincing, for various reasons. First, in fact some of the best studies of Buddhism are by non-Buddhists (and so on with other religions). In fact, the trans-religious understanding of one religion by people in another cultural tradition has never been so effective as it is now. Second, the same objection is not taken very seriously in anthropology; and anthropology involves the exploration of religion. Third, the concept of understanding has to do with degree: there are more or less profound, more or less superficial, understandings. Thus it is not an all-or-nothing-at-all matter, whereas the argument about commitment to a tradition is posed in that way. Fourth, what constitutes a tradition? Can the evangelical Christian understand easily the Irish Roman Catholic? Often proximity can itself generate alienation. Strangers may turn out to be more intelligible than siblings. Fifth, the argument about belongingness as a prerequisite of understanding (incidentally echoed by Black Studies theoreticians in the USA) has a political root: it is part of an ideology of educational power – or to put it more plainly Christian establishmentarianism in its new and rather polite form.

All this is not to underestimate the problems which may beset the explorer of religion. He may not be too sympathetic to a given tradition and needs to overcome this. He may not have encountered certain rituals: what is Vaiṣṇavism in Western India *really* like? You need hopefully to go see or at least have a film and commentary. He may not have had certain qualities of feeling and so needs to use his imagination in a special way. He may have odd images of religion (very prevalent in academe, incidentally). Really (one feels inclined to say) he needs to have had a good karma to be effective. But though there may be all these problems, they boil down to questions of experience, intelligence and predisposition – and the same applies to all other 'subjects'. I mention the difficulties partly because they have been inflated somewhat in the interests of a narrower and more traditional view of the study of religion: on the other side, the traditional study has often had very high standards, even if its logic has been a bit weak.

To sum up: the exploration of religion is in principle plural, empathetic, phenomenological, aspectual, non-finite, polymethodic and finally truth-questing (but it does not follow that the last is always not least). Its accent is above all on understanding and because of that a certain kind of fairness and a certain quality of engagement.

That is what it is. How does all this apply to education?

Education should be seamless, it goes without mention. What is done in universities and polytechnics should have the same principles as what is done in schools; and what is done in Sri Lanka should be the same in principle as in Scotland. This naturally does not mean that the same items of instruction, the same assumptions, the same nuances, should be universal: that would itself be a betrayal of universal principles. Principles need variegated applications, or else they are rightly victims of ridicule, for they betray realities.

The notion that this universality should apply to religious education in schools in the UK is not strongly felt, even in the university milieu. Perhaps it is most strongly felt in the colleges (but what will transpire on this front in relation to the present reorganisations?). It is salutary to consider the confusions in the names for the subject. I begin with terms used in higher education and move on to those employed in schools. To each term I append a micro-commentary, for I think the terminology is symptomatic of our confusions. I begin with titles used in higher education.

We find: theology, divinity, religious studies, religion, the phenomenology of religion and the principles of religion: also, biblical studies, Jewish studies, etc.

'Theology' is no doubt hallowed somewhat by tradition and is the most dominant name in the UK, though 'religion' is dominant in North America. It has two drawbacks, in my view. First, it is elliptical. If men agreed sufficiently about the nature of the *theos*, the logic might be universal. But in fact 'theology' is used in the UK to mean Christian theology, predominantly, and so there is an underlying ellipsis which not all involved would accept and which conflicts with some of the features of the exploration of religion which we have been contemplating. Second, the ineluctable nisus of the term is towards the intellectual and evaluative study of religion – not in itself to be deplored but perchance one-sided, for reasons already alluded to.

'Divinity' again is hallowed, but again is narrow and elliptical. It suggests we explore the divine: not (again) an ignoble enterprise, but one which is merely part of the operation. And by ellipsis 'divinity' avoids that essential *epoché* or suspension of belief and disbelief which the explorer must, descriptively, adopt.

'Religious studies' is a fairly recent locution in the UK. For practical purposes it is useful, as a conscious signal for a widening beyond theology. However, it is cumbrous, and there is a nice simplicity about 'religion', which is the dominant term in the USA and Canada.

'Phenomenology' and Glasgow's 'principles of religion' do no great harm but are a trifle eccentric. But they are symptoms of attempts to avoid using 'divinity' or 'theology'.

As for 'biblical studies' and so on – these represent specialisms within the wider field of the study of religion.

But consider the range at school level. We have: divinity and religious studies as above, but also religious education, religious instruction, religious knowledge, scripture, scripture knowledge.

The use of 'scripture' and 'scripture knowledge' dates from a period when the (Christian) Bible was the substance of study in schools. The use of 'knowledge' was in part an ill-conceived way of avoiding problems about differences of faith-stance between the churches and teachers.

'Religious instruction' assumes that there is agreement about a content of belief to be handed on. The term is now largely out of favour, for it goes against both the tenor of a more plural and open-minded society and the trend in educational thinking, towards exploration rather than the passivity of simply being instructed. Consequently the present vogue is to use 'religious education'.

Unfortunately this does not mesh with usage in higher education. I prefer a situation where the subject is called the same thing at different levels of education – e.g. 'history' (and where we do not really need 'historical education'). Furthermore there is acronymic trouble – the tendency to call the subject RE. This leads to illogicalities, as when people talk about 'teaching RE'. Strictly 'teaching religious education' should be teaching prospective teachers on how to teach religion. For this reason, I would prefer the use of 'religious studies' or 'religion' for the school subject.

In brief we can see a certain confusion in the babel of titles; and all this stems from problems arising from a previous assumption that Christianity, as a kind of state religion, could be taught, rather than seen as itself open to some controversy. It also meant that religion was not seen as a field of experience to be explored, but more a list of doctrinal and ethical beliefs to be imparted.

It is worth remarking, by the way, that great confusion is raised by the verb 'to teach'. *My* idea of teaching Buddhism or Christianity is to give understanding of the history, ethics, ideas, rituals, influences, developments and so on in Christianity or Buddhism. It is not to teach dogma. But the term is often thought of in the latter way. So when latterly Birmingham decides to 'teach' Communism ordinary folk (including almost everyone) think it means indoctrinating Brummie lads and lasses with Marxism.

However, what about the future? At present a kind of revolution is going on in Britain, Canada, Australia, Scandinavia and elsewhere. It is perchance no coincidence that there is less change in predominantly Catholic countries, not because the Roman Catholics are less changeful (for within the ecumenical context they are perhaps the most adventurous), but because of the more open political traditions of northern countries. In the third world, other problems and the needs of religious nationalism do not conduce to pluralism; while in the ideologically-constrictive countries there is no real question of the open exploration of religion and religions. It is, in my view, an ultimate weakness not to allow an open exploration of truth, religious or otherwise, so that, from this point of view, the new religious education is itself a contribution to human realism. Logic and institutions need to be matched; but this is the consummation of a long process of political and educational development. I now turn to the question of patterns of religious education at the school level in the UK.

Let us consider the logic of our prescription about the nature of the exploration of religion in relation to actual conditions in Britain. In other words, how can such a theory be applied?

First, a judgement has to be made about the actual importance of religion. At the moment every school has to teach it in some way or another. On the other hand, relatively few schools teach Spanish. Is religion that much more important than Spanish? I would think that the universal presence of some sort of religious education cannot irrefrageably be defended. Still, people should look coolly at the empirical problem of the influences of religion and its challenge as to truth. From this perspective, it should figure very prominently in the curriculum. Unfortunately, if the present compulsion were taken off, many – perhaps a majority – of schools would junk religious education, out of reaction, out of judgements about the intellectual status of the subject and so forth.

Second, the logic which I have tried to unfold implies that religion is or can be an area of exploration on a par with any other academic or experiential enquiry. It follows that it should get equal treatment. Now, too often, it has the privilege of compulsion and the under-privilege of lip-service – because of the relatively small amount of timetable time devoted to it. Ironically, one of the best ways of giving the subject status is through improving examination syllabuses and standards.

Third, it is necessary to recognise the shape of developing curriculum imposed by recent work in psychology – notably those researches inspired ultimately by the work of Piaget, and executed by the influential Goldman, and by, among others more recently, Hyde, Cox and Gates.[2] In brief, the main lesson is that an over-conceptual approach to religion is not educationally effective at the primary level, and this invites educationists to explore the other dimensions of religion as content for the curriculum.

Fourth, the general content should not only relate to pupils' experience, but should also relate to reality. There is a dialectical tug here. On the one hand, religion should be seen to relate (or not to relate, but if I may be Irish about it, *relationally*) to experience. This might mean a fairly narrow curricular scope. For instance, I am involved, through the Schools Council Project on Religious Education in Primary Schools, at the University of Lancaster, with some work going on in Northern Ireland schools. There is a natural tendency for teachers there, however well disposed towards a wider treatment of religion, to look to immediate problems of inter-community religious relations. In brief, they are somewhat pinned down by their own and their pupils' immediate experience. On the other hand, we have a need to widen curricula. Let us consider this in relation to world religions (so-called because of their great influences and existential challenge). It would be unrealistic to introduce young people to the rudiments of knowledge concerning religion without letting them see something of the world perspective. Whether they like it or not Buddhism is a viable alternative to Christianity and one of the three great missionary religions which the world has seen. It is part of most Asian culture from India to Japan. So even the lad in Belfast ought to glimpse it. So there is a tension between the needs of immediate experience and the duties of richer vision – but of course religious education is not alone in facing this dialectic.

Fifth, in view of the non-finite character of the exploration of religion, previously discussed, the study should embrace wider issues – it should thus be somewhat concerned with the various alternative life-styles. In this respect it can be integrated into social studies and moral education (but as regards the latter, the mistake should never be made of assuming that moral education is necessarily bound up with religion: every religion is ethical, but not all ethics are religions).

Sixth, serious consideration needs in the UK, as in other Western countries, to be given to the amount of time given to the exploration of Christianity. As the dominant traditional matrix of Western religious culture, it needs (obviously) much attention. But at the moment its exploration suffers from too many assumptions – the (by some held) assumption of its uniqueness and superiority, the sectarian assumption (namely, my form is *the* form of Christianity), the (by some held) assumption of its disastrous and constricting nature and of its superstitious lack of a scientific outlook, the parochial assumption that what it is like here is what it is like all over – and so on. Very rarely is Christianity really given the same empathetic exploration as occurs with other faiths such as Buddhism. I am very far from believing that you need commitment to teach concerning a religion – very often commitments one way or another get in the way of an exciting and rich exposition of the joys, problems and influences of a religious tradition. Therefore I would place the highest authority (and not only in this country) on the proper study of the Christian tradition.

Seventh, I think the education of adults concerning religion is vital. Too many look upon RE as a means of instilling good behaviour. Who am I to complain about good behaviour? But moral education is the job of all the school – all the community, all the nation. It is wrong to look upon religion as the handmaid of British citizenship. Others look on RE as a means of making Christians. Who am I to object? But the evangelical aim is not essentially educational. It is true that the teacher may lay forth the riches (and problems) of Christianity, and maybe of Buddhism or Judaism too; but this is not preaching.

Eighth, some consideration must be given to minorities, such as Jews, Pakistani Muslims, Sikhs and so on. This follows from the same principle already invoked regarding the importance of Christianity in a culture heavily influenced by it. True, the Sikh living here should know about Christianity, while not every Englishman absolutely *needs* to know about Sikhism. But the Sikh should be able to explore in depth his own religious and social tradition. All this reinforces the argument for pluralism, and for choice, in curricula, as recently in the new Birmingham proposals.[3]

Ninth, religious education should above all emphasise empathy and understanding. Its methods need therefore to be rich in diversity. Thus ideally people should be exposed to film, human instances of a faith, etc. Or more ideally they should be able to visit living religions in their own settings. As yet we are in a rather primitive condition, at every level of education; we need the anthropological approach to religions. Needless to say, the desirability of this approach at home is as vital as in the wider world: we scarcely understand the forms of our own Christianity, as has been remarked above.

Tenth, religious exploration should, in relating to truth-claims and evaluations, be related to home realities. For instance, what are people's real attitudes to the authority of scientists? How does it affect their actual worldview? How does this worldview affect (or fail to affect) moral and political behaviour?

I can end by remarking that the exploration of religion and religions is exciting. Its new face has many expressions. Religious studies are too important, in short, to be left to the bishops. Not that they are negligible. Far from it. Without them there might be less religion, and so less to explore.

Notes

GOD, BLISS AND MORALITY

1. A possible reply: Philosophers do not base their enlightened comments (on the nature of scientific explanation, etc.) upon discredited theories, though they may use these as a warning; why should not the philosopher similarly concentrate on examining the true religion? But criteria of truth here are so misty that it is presumptuous to pay exclusive attention to one faith.

2. As in some cases and respects an incarnate deity is a limiting form of the saintly prophet, the range of propositions of this strand is wider than here indicated; but it is convenient to focus attention on the extreme cases.

3. It is not just that each has been brought up in a certain doctrinal tradition, so that the Christian mystic for instance 'reads into' his experience Christian doctrines: there appears to be an inner plausibility in the theistic account of these matters – though I do not wish to imply by this that it is correct (nor by *this* that it is *in*-correct).

4. These predicates are applicable in often peculiar and diverse senses: *e.g.*, the mystical attainment is timeless and banishes the fear of death, while God is immortal; it is transcendent because it is unworldly, while God is in another world, *etc.* A proper exposition of these important and interesting points is, however, impossible here.

5. These are often confused, and in any case may be formulated in language where the integration of morality and religion is already taken for granted. Further, in some circles only the ghost of an argument would be permitted – where there is fundamentalist appeal to the authority of the scriptures, for example (and this is not quite like someone's being irrational in purely non-religious matters).

6. Though there are queer cases: e.g., what are we to make of the attitude of Ivan in *The Brothers Karamazov*? or of devil worship?

7. *James*, i. 27.

8. Hymn 256, Church of Scotland Hymnary.

9. Psalm 51.

10. Psalm 51.

11. Though: *(a)* certain things may be very hard to describe, e.g., a complicated piece of machinery; for the uninitiate it is too complex and unfamiliar to describe. This is contingent indescribability. *(b)* There may be 'facts' no-one can describe, because science has not yet given us the conceptual framework.

12. There are of course other uses of 'gestures' besides cases where the balance between two or more people is upset: e.g., the Hungarian who shakes his fist at a Soviet tank – a gesture of defiance (not, however, entirely unconnected in type from the unbalance cases). Also obviously, the behavioural sense. Incidentally, speech-transcending actions are clearly relevant to a discussion of religious ineffability.
13. As a commemorative plaque in the Wanderer's Ground in Johannesburg has it: 'And when the one great Scorer comes to write against your name, He marks – not how you won or lost – but how you played the game.'
14. Christ is not a sacrifice the way a lamb might be or the way Isaac was intended, in that His death on the Cross was voluntary. He was not offered by others as a sacrifice, nor is God wicked in providing a human sacrifice.
15. It is doubtful whether the God-manhood of Christ is a strict contradiction, e.g., Christ was for a time in Galilee while God is from eternity in Heaven, and Christ is God: does this constitute a contradiction? Only if Heaven and Galilee are both places in the same sense of 'place'.
16. *Romans*, vi. 4.
17. Unfortunately it is hard to see any dividing line between analogical uses of expressions in religion (i.e., non-literal but indispensable ones) and mere metaphors and allegories, etc. But one rough test is to consider how closely related a locution is to central doctrines. Some expressions in religious discourse are not, of course, non-literally used, e.g., 'god'.
18. *Gal.* v. 24.
19. The use of 'fully' and other such adverbs is significant here.
20. The third, fourth and fifth stages are: right speech, right conduct and right mode of livelihood.
21. An important segment of Buddhist spiritual exercises is concerned with the cultivation of dispositions such as universal compassion (*Visuddhimagga*, ch. iv).
22. Though the picture lost much of its appeal: one of the main motives in the development of Mahayana Buddhism was the feeling that the Hinayana aim was too self-centred.
23. William Hilton, *The Ladder of Perfection*, trans. L. Sherley-Price, London (1957).

THE CRITERIA OF RELIGIOUS IDENTITY

1. *Ṛg Veda*, I. 164.
2. This point is unaffected by theories of a primitive High God (with later degeneration into polytheism), since when we meet polytheistic religion, as in early Greece and in Vedism, there seems to be no recollection thereof and the struggle towards a simpler insight still has to be made.
3. There are many Buddhas besides Gautama of course. In the original Pali tradition he had six predecessors (*Dīgha Nikāya*, ii. 2ff.). Later, in the *Buddhavaṁsa*, he had twenty-four. The Buddhist Sanskrit writers piled on the numbers till finally 'The Buddhas are like the sands on the banks

of the Ganges' (*Lalita Vistara* 376.5; 402 and elsewhere, see Har Dayal, *The Boddhisattva Doctrine*, London (1932), pp. 24–5 and notes).
4. *Chāndogya Upan.* VI.8.7.
5. There are differing interpretations of this text; but although the non-dualism of Śankara cannot be a correct interpretation of the whole of the thought of the *Upaniṣads*, for the simple reason that it is by no means homogeneous, it undoubtedly represents a strong element therein. And it seems quite impossible to interpret *Tattvamasi* as merely asserting (as some would want to claim) that the spirit in man is of the same nature as Brahman.
6. There are different analogies to illustrate the relation of Brahman to the visible world. Thus it is sometimes said that Brahman is *beyond* the world, sometimes that it is the essence of things (*Bṛhad. Upan.*, II.1.20 – *satyasya satyam*) and hence the claim that 'Brahman is all this' (is the world: *Bṛhad. Upan.*, I.4.10–11, etc.). At any rate Brahman is hidden.
7. *Taittirīya Upan*, III.1.1, etc.
8. *Kaṭha Upan.*, II.3.17.
9. *Śvetāśvatara Upan.*, III.9.
10. Cp. *Īśa Upan.*, I.1; *Kaṭha Upan.*, II.3.3; *Śvetāśvatara Upan.*, III.2, etc.
11. *Chāndogya Upan.*, VII.24.1; *Bṛhad. Upan.*, IV.4.14; etc.
12. *Muṇḍaka Upan.*, I.1.6; etc.
13. 'He stands opposite creatures', *Śvet. Upan.*, *III.2; cp. IV.7, and Muṇḍaka Upan.*, III.1.2.
14. *Māṇḍūkya Upan.*, 7 (Radhakrishnan's translation modified).
15. From *The World*.
16. Note that this (*amata*) is one of the epithets of *nirvāṇa* even in the Pali canon, where there is no concept of a deity.
17. *Chāndogya Upan.*, III.14.3–4 (Radhakrishnan's translation modified).
18. Which I shall henceforth refer to as 'doctrinal schemes', since 'system' suggests a logical rigidity not possessed by doctrines; while 'scheme' aptly suggests composition.
19. By 'analogical' uses I mean simply non-literal yet untranslatable uses, as opposed to 'metaphorical' uses, which are non-literal but dispensable. It is of course difficult to draw a sharp line between the two, as it is also hard to draw such a line between the literal and non-literal.
20. *Īśa Upan.* 5, etc.
21. *Saṁyutta Nikāya*, 360ff., etc.
22. See R. Otto's fine comparison between Eckhart and Śankara in *Mysticism East and West*, Eng. Trans., London (1932).
23. I have attempted to give an account of the reasons for this in an article *Being and the Bible*, Review of Metaphysics, June 1956.
24. This is connected with the ontologism referred to above, but it would take us too far afield to give the full reasons for the mystical liking for cosmic necessity.
25. 'Candidate' is not here meant irreverently, nor in the normal adoptionist sense. But an incarnate Deity has to be judged by us to be such, in accordance with some criteria. This is so to speak 'logical adoptionism', and does not imply that if anyone is correctly identified with the Father he was not with the Father from the beginning.

26. *Saddharmapuṇḍarīka*, 136.4.
27. One, i.e., where moral beliefs have affected doctrines.
28. Ps. 51, vs. 17, 19.
29. See E. J. Thomas *History of Buddhist Thought*, London (1951), p. 149.
30. *Majjhima Nikāya*, i.69ff.
31. *Saddharmapuṇḍarīka*, 136.4.
32. *Avadāna Śataka* i.109, etc.
33. Divyāvadāna 48ff., etc.
34. *Majjh. Nik.* 1.157, etc.
35. See E. J. Thomas *History of Buddhist Thought*, pp. 241ff.
36. See. e.g., *Sukhāvatī Vyūha*, Sacred Books of the East, xlix, p. 15 ff.
37. See F. Edgerton, *The Bhagavad-Gita translated and interpreted*, Cambridge (Mass. 1952), p. 49; and see *Bhag. Gita*, xiv.27, etc.
38. *Mahāyāna Sūtrālaṅkāra*, 18.11.
39. *Kena Upan*, i.4.10.

NUMEN, NIRVANA, AND THE DEFINITION OF RELIGION

1. Hereafter I use 'nirvana' by itself to stand for Buddhist *nirvana*.
2. *The Idea of the Holy*, trans. J. W. Harvey, 2nd Edition, London (1950), p. 39.
3. Nirvana does, however, undergo some transformation in the Mahayana schools. For instance, on the Madhyamika view, the Absolute (*tattva, śūnya*) is the same as *prajñā* (wisdom, i.e. non-dualistic insight, *jñānam advayam*) (Madh. Karika, XXV, 19–20). This in turn is identified with the *dharmakāya* or Truth-Body of the Buddhas. Now the knowledge of the Absolute is nirvana (ibid. xviii, 5); and thus there is, *via* the Three-Body doctrine, a fairly close relation between nirvana as the attainment of non-dualistic insight and the numinous as displayed in the *sambhogakāya* and *nirmāṇakāya* of the Buddhas – in these forms the Buddhas come to be objects of worship.
4. Trans. B. L. Bruce and R. C. Payne, London (1932), p.v.
5. On contemporary feeling about this, see R. L. Slater, *Paradox and Nirvana*, Chicago (1951), p. 31.
6. *The Idea of the Holy*, p. 11.
7. E.g. U. Agga in Shwe Zan Aung's 'Dialogue on Nibbana', *Journal of the Burmese Research Society*, VIII, Pt. iii (1918), quoted in Slater, op. cit., pp. 54ff, where survival is of 'one's own mind purged from corruption'.
8. Such concepts as 'Ultimate Reality', 'Being', etc., often have a specifically religious, not just philosophical, function, and are frequently found in close connection, though also a state of tension, with notions of a personal divinity: e.g., *nirguṇam* and *saguṇam* Brahman and the chain of identities in the Mahayanist Three-Body doctrine. See Otto, *Mysticism East and West*, pp. 5 ff, and my article 'Being and the Bible', *Review of Metaphysics*, Vol. IX, no. 4 (June 1956).
9. E. J. Thomas, *The Life of Buddha as Legend and History*, London (1927), p. 20f.

10. More precisely the Buddha used the more comprehensive four-fold (*catuṣkoṭika*) negation: the *arhat* is not reborn, nor is he not reborn, nor is he both reborn and not reborn, nor is he neither reborn nor not reborn (*Majjhima Nikaya*, i. 426ff and elsewhere). As to survival, however, it would be better for the ordinary uninstructed man to mistake the body for the self (*Saṁyutta Nikāya*, ii. 95).
11. E.g. the last stage of meditation (*jhāna*) is where one is 'beyond the sphere of neither perception nor non-perception' in which there is a cessation of both perception and sensation.
12. I.e., it is not caused in any ordinary sense, though the way to it has been pointed out by the Buddha (*Milinda-Pañha*, IV. 7. 14).
13. The usual Pali term is *sa-upādisesa* as opposed to *anupādisesa nibbāna* (nirvana with and without substrate: see Buddhaghosa in *Dhammapada* Commentary, ii. 163 – *sa-upādisesa* n. is equivalent to *kilesa-vattassa khepitatta*, 'destruction of the cycle of impurity').
14. *Mysticism East and West*, p. 143.
15. *The Idea of the Holy*, pp. 58–9.
16. *Mysticism East and West*, p. 143.
17. *Systematic Theology*, Vol. I, London (1951), p. 15.
18. See L. Wittgenstein's *Philosophical Investigations*, trans. G. E. M. Anscombe, Oxford, (1953), p. 32e.
19. *Mysticism East and West*, p. 143.

MYTH AND TRANSCENDENCE

1. A version of this chapter was read as a paper at the American Philosophical Association (Western Division), April 1965, and I am grateful for the points put by the respondents, Professors Gareth Mathews and Alvin Plantinga.
2. R. B. Braithwaite, *An Empiricist's View of the Nature of Religious Belief* (Cambridge University Press, 1955).
3. Paul van Buren, *The Secular Meaning of the Gospel* (London: 1963).
4. As argued for in my *Reasons and Faiths* (London: 1958), p. 12.
5. This evidently is Paul Tillich's fear, when people talk of God's existence. Thus in D. Mackenzie Brown, *Ultimate Concern: Tillich in Dialogue* (London: 1965), p. 88, Tillich is recorded as saying: 'We can no longer speak of God easily to anybody because he will immediately question, "Does God exist?" Now the very asking of the question signifies that the symbols of God have become meaningless. For God, in the question, has become one of innumerable objects in time and space which may or may not exist. And this is not the meaning of God at all.' It is part of the burden of the present paper that it need not be the meaning of 'exists'.
6. For reasons which I advance in *Philosophers and Religious Truth* (London: 1964), Chapter III.
7. See my *Doctrine and Argument in Indian Philosophy* (London: G. Allen and Unwin 1964; New York: Humanities Press, 1964), Chapter VIII.

THE CONCEPT OF HEAVEN

1. A fuller exposition of this concept of transcendence is to be found in my article 'Myth and Transcendence' in *The Monist* (October, 1966), and chapter 5 in this volume.

LIVING LIBERATION: JIVANMUKTI AND NIRVANA

1. In his review of Rhys Davids, *Buddhism: its history and literature, Revue de l'histoire des religions* XXXVII, pp. 247–448 [see Welbon, *The Buddhist Nirvana and its Western Interpreters* (1968), p. 239 note 53].
2. This is a convenient distinction which I first made in my *Doctrine and Argument in Indian Philosophy* (1964).
3. Warder, *Indian Buddhism* (1970), p. 149.
4. Jayatilleke, *Early Buddhist Theory of Knowledge* (1959), pp. 384ff.
5. *Majjhimanikaya* 72.
6. Eliade, *Yoga: Immortality and Freedom* (1954), pp. 167–73.
7. Or Sanskrit *anupadhisesa* and *saupadhisesa*; for an interesting discussion see Welbon, *op. cit.*, pp. 208ff.
8. This point is elaborated somewhat in my *Doctrine and Argument in Indian Philosophy*.
9. In *Reasons and Faiths* (1958), chapter V.
10. See my 'The work of the Buddha and the work of Christ', in *The Saviour God*, ed. Brandon (1963).

INTERPRETATION AND MYSTICAL EXPERIENCE

1. *At Sundry Times*, p. 132.
2. *Mysticism Sacred and Profane*, pp. 191–2.
3. See my 'Mystical Experience', in *Sophia* vol. I, no. 1 (April, 1962), pp. 19ff., discussing the distinction between experience and interpretation as propounded by W. T. Stace in *Mysticism and Philosophy*, p. 37.
4. See my *Doctrine and Argument in Indian Philosophy*, ch.XII.
5. *Op. cit.* p. 37.
6. A fuller criticism is to be found in my *Doctrine and Argument in Indian Philosophy*, pp. 211ff. Zaehner's account of Buddhism is discoverable in his *At Sundry Times* (see, for example, his argument on p. 98).
7. Sutta-nipata 788: see *At Sundry Times*, pp. 98–101.
8. *At Sundry Times*, p. 101.
9. *Samyutta-nikaya*, ii, 95.
10. See *Doctrine and Argument in Indian Philosophy*, ch. X, where an analysis along these lines is worked out in some detail.
11. *Mysticism Sacred and Profane*, p. 170.
12. *Ibid*, p. 171.
13. *Mysticism Sacred and Profane*, pp. 157–8.
14. See, e.g., W. T. Stace, *Mysticism and Philosophy*, who comes to this conclusion.
15. *Ibid*. p. 193.

PROBLEMS OF THE APPLICATION OF WESTERN
TERMINOLOGY TO THERAVADA BUDDHISM, WITH
SPECIAL REFERENCE TO THE RELATIONSHIP BETWEEN
THE BUDDHA AND THE GODS

1. In the subsequent discussion, I am indebted for certain points to the
   unpublished doctoral thesis, written under my supervision, on 'A Study
   of the Gods in Early Buddhism in their mythological and social milieu as
   depicted in the Nikayas of the Pali canon', by Dr M. M. J. Marasinghe,
   of Vidyalankara University, Ceylon. (Thesis lodged in University of
   Birmingham Library, 1967.)
2. See Charles Godage, 'The Place of Indra in Early Buddhism', *University
   of Ceylon Review*, April 1945, pp. 41–72.
3. See A. B. Keith, *The Religion and Philosophy of the Veda and Upa-
   nishads*, (1925), i.p. 338.
4. *Buddhism and the Mythology of Evil*, (1962).
5. Cp. regarding the previous Buddha Vipassi, *Dīgha Nikāya*, II.37; re
   Gotama, *Majjhima Nik.* I.167f.
6. Hitherto these mysterious figures have not attracted a full-scale study.
7. Cp. *Majjhima Nik.* II.130.
8. Cp. *Saṁyutta Nikāya*, v.410 and elsewhere.
9. But by implication it helps a *god* to reverence the Buddha.
10. Except in so far as an *anagamin* may be treated as a *deva*.
11. Cp. *Digha Nikaya* 1.220 '*Atha kho so Kevaddha bhkkhu tatharūpam
    samādhim samāpajji, yathā samāhite citte Brahmayaniyo maggo patur
    ahosi*'.
12. *Niddesa* I.355ff.
13. Fully catalogued in Marasinghe, op. cit. (note I, above).
14. See *Dict. of Pali Proper Names*, ed. G. P. Malalasekara.
15. Cp. *Anguttara Nikaya* iv. 241f. and numerous other passages.
16. *Majjhima Nikaya* II.213 *Ucce sammatam kho etam, Bharadvaja, lokas-
    mim atthi devā ti*, cp. M.N. II.130.
17. Cp. the well-known passage in *Digha Nikaya*, II.75.
18. As in my *Doctrine and Argument in Indian Philosophy*, (1964), pp. 214f.
19. In his *Philosophies of India*, (1957), pp. 181f.
20. Digha Nikaya II.
21. Cp. the *Atanaiya Sutta*, and *Nipata* 39f. *Digha Nikaya* III.194ff.

BEYOND ELIADE: THE FUTURE OF THEORY IN
RELIGION

1. Guilford Dudley II, *Religion on Trial – Mircea Eliade and his critics*,
   Philadelphia, Temple University Press, 1977.
2. *Ibid.*, 126.
3. *Ibid.*, 72 from Eliade, *The Sacred and the Profane*.
4. *Ibid.*, 77.
5. This is a principal theme of my *The Science of Religion and the Sociology
   of Knowledge*, Princeton University Press, 1973.

RELIGION, MYTH AND NATIONALISM

1. Z.A.B. Zeman, *Twilight of the Hapsburgs*, (New York: Heritage Press), p. 31.
2. See especially A.D. Smith, *Theories of Nationalism*, (London: Duckworth, 1971).
3. Marshall Mannerheim, *The Memoirs of Marshal Mannerheim* tr. Count Eric Lewenhaupt, (London: Cassell, 1953), p. 373.
4. *The Religious Experience of Mankind*, (London: Collins, 1971), ch. 1.

RELIGION AS A DISCIPLINE?

1. 'Theology as a Discipline?', in *Universities Quarterly*, Vol, 16, no. 4, 1962.
2. The reference is to the new ('plate glass') universities set up in Great Britain in the 1960s.

SOCIAL ANTHROPOLOGY AND THE PHILOSOPHY OF RELIGION

1. See, for example, S.E. Toulmin, *Philosophy of Science* (1953) and N.R. Hanson, *Patterns of Discovery* (1958). The latter writes (p. 3): 'I have not hesitated to refer to events in the history of physics; these will punctuate the other arguments. This comports with my conception of the philosophy of science: namely, that profitable philosophical discussion depends upon a thorough familiarity with its history and present state.'
2. For some recent attempts in this direction, see A. Campbell Garnett, *Religion and the Moral Life* (1955), E.E. Harris, *Revelation through Reason* (1959) and F.H. Cleobury, *Christian Rationalism and Philosophical Analysis* (1959).
3. Thus Hume's pioneer work *The Natural History of Religion* concerns itself only with theism and polytheism. But even recent writers covertly identify religion with theism, e.g. I.T. Ramsey, *Religious Language* (1957), p. 46: 'We may also expect religious language to centre on "God" as a key word, an 'ultimate' of explanation. . . .'
4. Consider also various works which have been profoundly influenced by the comparative study of religions, notably W.T. Stace, *Time and Eternity* (1952), *Mysticism and Philosophy* (1962) and W. Kaufmann, *Critique of Religion and Philosophy* (1959).
5. *The Idea of a Social Science*, p. 89.
6. *Nuer Religion*, p. 320.
7. *Sociology of Religion* (1947), p. 12.
8. See T. McPherson's thesis in 'Religion as the Inexpressible' in *New Essays in Philosophical Theology*, ed A. Flew and A. MacIntyre (1955).
9. One must reject extreme formulations of this principle, such as that of

al-Ghazzali, described and endorsed by Professor R.C. Zaehner in his *At Sundry Times* (1958), pp. 12ff.

10. See J. Wach, *Sociology of Religion*, p. 13. For a criticism of essentialist definitions of religion and of Otto's definition, see my 'Numen, Nirvana and the Definition of Religion' in *Church Quarterly Review*, April-June 1959, pp. 216–25 (chapter 4 in this volume).

11. For a definition of 'mystical' in the sense indicated see my *Reasons and Faiths* (1958), pp. 55–56. Such definitions as that given by L.E. Browne, in his *The Prospects of Islam* (1944), p. 128, viz. that a mystic is 'one who believes that God is directly approachable by the human soul' hardly does justice to such forms of mysticism as those of orthodox Yoga, where the aim is not union with God, of Jainism and of Buddhism.

12. See J.L. Austin, 'A Plea for Excuses', *Proceedings of the Aristotelian Society*, N.S. Vol.1vii (1956–7), pp. 1–20. He wrote: 'We are using a sharpened awareness of words to sharpen our perception of, though not as the final arbiter of, the phenomena'. (p.8)

13. *Sociology of Religion*, p. 15.

14. *Structure and Function in Primitive Society* (1952), p. 155.

15. That is, function in the sense elaborated by Professor Emmet. She writes (*Function, Purpose and Powers*, p. 46): 'The notion of "function" is applicable where:
(a) the object of study can be considered as forming a system taken as a unitary whole.
(b) The unitary whole must be ordered as a differentiated complex, in which it is possible to talk about 'part-whole' relationships.
(c) The parts will be elements which can be shown to contribute to fulfilling the purpose for which the ordered whole has been set up, or, if it has not been purposefully set up, to maintaining it in a persisting or enduring stage.'

16. The point is touched on by Otto in his discussion of the pregnant use of silence in religious contexts, see *The Idea of the Holy* (Eng trans, 1923), App. viii, pp. 210ff.

17. *Structure and the Function in Primitive Society*, p. 176.

18. See my *Reasons and Faiths* Ch. I and following.

19. Macbeath, *Experiments in Living*, p. 350.

20. *Nuer Religion*, p. 320.

21. See R.S. Peters, *The Concept of Motivation* (1958), and also A. MacIntyre's interesting appliction of a like distinction to free will, in 'Determinism', *Mind*, pp. 28–41.

22. See, e.g., A.G.N. Flew, 'Divine Omnipotence and Human Freedom', *New Essays in Philosophical Theology*, pp. 149ff.

23. As well as the works mentioned below, see I.T. Ramsey, *Religious Language* and collections of essays contained in *Faith and Logic* (1957), ed. Basil Mitchell, and *New Essays in Philosophical Theology*. My own *Reasons and Faiths* is more a descriptive analysis than a kind of linguistic apologetics, in intention at least.

24. In *Metaphysical Beliefs* (1957), ed. Alasdair MacIntyre, p. 209.

25. See A. MacIntyre's *Difficulties in Christian Belief* (1959), p. 82.

THE PRINCIPLES AND MEANING OF THE STUDY OF RELIGION

1. *Structural Anthropology*, tr. Claire Jacobson and Brooke Grundfest Schoepf (1963), p. 207.
2. *Taboo* (1956), p. 113.
3. *Essays in Sociological Theory* (revised edition, 1954), p. 32.
4. For instance, Christian mysticism may be taken seriously, but the question of whether similar types of experience occur in, say, Buddhism is not raised.

THE EXPLORATION OF RELIGION AND EDUCATION

1. To some degree I am relying upon some earlier writings, notably *The Principles and Meaning of the Study of Religion* (1967: Inaugural Lecture); *Secular Education and the Logic of Religion* (1968); *The Phenomenon of Religion* (1973) and *The Science of Religion and the Sociology of Knowledge* (1974).
2. For an excellent survey, see K. E. Bugge (1975) 'Tendenzen and Projekte in der neueren englischen Religionspädagogik', in *Theologia Practica*, pp. 29ff.; also B. Gates (Spring 1973) 'Varieties of Religious Education', in *Religion*, pp. 52ff.
3. See John Hall on these in Donald Horder and Ninian Smart (1975), *New Movements in Religious Education*.

Index

Abelard 35
Absolute Self, doctrine of 111
Adam, fall of 100–1
Advaita 101, 102
Agga, U. 234n7
agnostic Buddhism 22, 23, 44–5
anattā doctrine 42, 47
anicca doctrine 22
Anselm 35
anthropology 197, 200, 213–14
   see also social anthropology
Appleton, G. 177
Aquinas 202
asceticism 18, 21, 22
At Sundry Times 136, 168, 177
Atman 10, 13, 42, 43, 106
   identification with Brahman 27–34,
      48, 101, 107
   nature of 29–31
Austin, J. L. 135, 189, 239n12
auto-interpretation 104–8

Barth, K. 50, 72, 193, 208, 209
beliefs 186–7, 189–94
   idealistic beliefs 22–3
Berger, P. 215, 223
bhakti 180–1
Bible
   study of 158, 163
   and transcendence doctrine 50, 53,
      59
bliss 21–2, 32
   as goal of mystics 29–30
   non-rationality of 44
Bonhoeffer 72
Brahman 13, 27
   identification with Atman 27–34, 48,
      101, 107
   nature of 28–9
Brahmanism 10
   identification in 28–34
   schemes in 13, 32
Braithwaite, R. B. 49, 235n2

Browne, L. E. 239n11
Buddha
   bodies of 26–7
   and *devas* 114–16
   and nirvana 45,46
   in Sinhalese Buddhism 126, 128–9
   in Theravada Buddhism 128
Buddhism 10, 22–3, 96–7
   and classification of mystical
      experience 105–7
   and concept of heaven 64–5
   cosmology of 91
   and definition of religion 46–8
   gods in 113–15
   and *jívanmukti* 89–90
   and liberated state 69
   Noble Eightfold Path 23
   and permanence 94–5
   religious identity in 36–8
   study of 161
   theory of impermanence in 115
   see also agnostic Buddhism,
      Mahayana Buddhism, Sinhalese
      Buddhism, Theravada Buddhism
Bugge, K. E. 240n2
Bultmann 49, 50, 72, 208

Campbell Garnett, A. 238n2
Carstair, G. M. 186
causes and reasons 192–3
celebrating 144–5
Ceylon *see* Sinhalese Buddhism
Chardin, T. de 130
Christ
   identification with the Father 20, 26,
      34–6
   incarnation and morality 20–1
   resurrection of 21
   and revelation 54–5
Christian, W. 76
*Christian Message in a Non-Christian
   World, The* 136, 168

Christianity
  and concept of heaven 61–7
  epistemological divergences in 50
  incarnation in 34,75
  and philosophy of religion 72–4
  in religious studies 158, 159, 160, 161, 164–5
  schemes in 13
  and transcendence 49–50
Cleobury, F. H. 238n2
comparative religion 78, 159, 167–9, 176–83, 199, 212–13
  and philosophy of religion 9–10
  and uniqueness of religions 179–80
Concept of Mind, The 68
constructive dialogue 209, 210
constructive traditionalism 208, 210
contemplation 24, 80, 98, 101, 102, 116
  and nirvana 122, 123
cosmos 54, 68
  in Buddhism 92–3
  God-cosmos difference 55–6, 63
courage 151–2
Cox, D. 227
creation myth 139
creativity (of God) 55–7, 58, 59
Crombie, I. C. 69
Crown of Hinduism, The 136

daily conduct, as worship 14–16
Davids, R. 236n1
Dayal, H. 233n3
demythologising 49
devas 113–15
dhamma 114, 115
dharma 95
dhātu 128
divinity 225
doctrinal schemes 9–10
  nature of 61–2
  in religions 12–13, 31–2
doctrines 62
dogma 170–1
Douglas, M. 77
Dudley, G. 131, 132–3, 134, 137, 138, 139, 140, 141, 142, 237n1
Durkheim, E. 190, 200
duty 17–18

Eckhart, M. 33, 39, 41, 181
Edgerton, F. 234n37
Eliade, M. 4, 213, 216, 217, 219, 236n6

and theory of religion 131–42
Emmet, D. 185, 239n15
Evans-Pritchard, E. E. 185, 187, 188, 191, 192, 194
Experiments in Living 191
expressive speech 16, 17
experience
  and interpretation 1–2–5
  see also mystical experience, religious experience

Fall, mythology of 100
family resemblance 12, 46–7
Farquhar, J. N. 136
Feuerbach, L. 223
Flew, A. G. N. 72, 73, 239n22
Foucault, M. 139, 140
Freud, S. 166, 167, 183, 198, 223
Function, Purpose and Powers 185

Gaillois, R. 134
Gates, B. 227, 240n2
Gautama 26, 128, 232n3
Geertz, C. 77
gestures 17, 232n12
Ghazali 109–10
God (in Christianity)
  creativity of 55–7, 58, 59
  God–cosmos difference 55, 63
  in heaven 62–5, 67, 68
  identification with Christ 20, 26, 34–6
  immanence of 59–60
  independence of 55–6, 58, 59
  and morality 19–20
  non-spatiality of 53–4, 59
  as source of holy conduct 19
  special presence of 55, 59
  transcendence of 51–60, 63
gods (in Buddhism) *see devas*
Godage, C. 237n2
Goethe 148
Goldman, R. 227
Gombrich, R. F. 125–30
groups, notion of 144–5, 153
  national groups 145–6
  and religion 81–2

Hall, J. 240n3
Hammer, R. 177
Hanson, N. R. 238n1
Harris, E. E. 238n2
heaven 61–71
  concepts of 62–7
  and concept of resurrection 66

'existentialist' view of 70
as the place of God 62–5, 67, 68
as the place of liberated souls 65, 67–9
as the place of survival 66
Hegel, F. 140
Heidegger, M. 48, 140
hetero-interpretation 104–8
Hilton, W. 232n23
Hinayana 41, 45
Hinduism 27, 73, 107, 136, 139
study of 161
history 140–2
of nations and myth 146–8
and philosophy of religion 10, 35–6, 72–3, 74, 83, 87
history of religions 79, 131, 133, 140–2, 164–5, 169
role in religious studies 196–7, 210, 212, 213–14, 216
Hume, D. 68, 238n3
humility 15, 20
Hyde, K. 227

Idea of a Social Science, The 185
identity-statements 25–6, 38–9
see also religious identity
immanence 59–60, 64, 71
immortality 69
impermanence 22, 94–5, 119–24
incarnation 13, 27
in Christianity 34, 75
and morality 20–1
independence of God 55–6, 58, 59
indescribability 17, 23n11
interpretation
auto- and hetero-interpretation 104–8
and mystical experience 102–12

Jacobson, C. 240n1
Jainism 46, 83, 90, 97
James, W. 72
Japan's Religious Ferment 177
Jayatilleke, K. N. 91, 236n4
jhānas 115, 122
jīva 90
jīvanmukti 89–97
Judaism 82
Jung, C. G. 217

Käsemann, E. 208
Kaufman, W. 238n4
Keith, A. B. 237n3

Kierkegaard, S. 193
Kitagawa, J. 131
Kraemer, H. 136, 168, 179
Kristensen, W. B. 211

Lakatos, I. 132, 133
Leach, E. 137
Lévi-Strauss, C. 199
Lévy-Bruhl, L. 136, 200
liberation 90–1, 95
heaven as place of 65, 66, 69
see also nibbāna
Ling, T. O. 114
linguistic analysis 184, 193, 201–2
linguistic phenomenology 189
'living liberation' *see jīvanmukti*
loka 92–4, 95
Long, C. 131

Macbeath 191, 239n19
MacIntyre, A. 193, 239n24, n25
Mackenzie Brown, D. 235n5
McPherson, T. 238n8
Madhyamika 95
Mahayana Buddhism 22, 34, 37, 95, 96–7, 121, 180
dualism of 96
numinous entities in 37–8
Mannerheim, M. 150–1, 152, 238n3
Maoism 73, 221
Mara 114, 115
Marasinghe, M. M. J. 237n1, n3
Marx, K. 223
Marxism 81
and patriotism 153
view of history 140
meditation 122
Miles, T. R. 69, 70
modernity 147–8
monisitic mysticism 96, 99–112
moral discourse 11, 14
morality and religion 11–24, 111–12
mourning 147
mystical experience 42
categories of 99
classification of and Buddhism 105–7
and interpretation 102–12
mystical participation 150
mysticism 20–2, 41–6, 216
defined 98–9
and notion of Atman 29–31
Otto on 41
and theism 46–8
Zaehner and theory of 99–112

see also monistic mysticism, panehenic mysticism, soul-mysticism, theistic mysticism
Mysticism East and West 41, 48
myth 137–9, 199
  creation myth 139
  and history of nations 146–8
  and idea of heaven 61–4, 67
  in Theravada Buddhism 117

nation, analysis of 144–9, 152
nationalism 143–4, 145–6
  and myth 146–7
  religion and 152–3
  and sacredness 148–9
  territorial aspect of 148
Neo-Thomists 50
nibbāna 93, 96–7, 115, 116, 122–3, 124
  see also nirvana
nirvana
  and concept of heaven 64–5
  and *jīvanmukti* 89–97
  and *loka* 93–4
  non-rationality of 44–5
  numinous aspects of 40–6
  seeing of 121, 122
  and substrate 94, 120
  and timelessness 119–24
  and transcendence 51
  transcendent nature of 51
non-rationality 44–5
non-spatiality 53–4, 59
  and God's creativity 57
  of the soul 68
Nuer Religion 187, 191
Nuer Religion 185
numinous 13, 28
  and nirvana 40–6

objectivity 211
On the Eightfold Path 177
Opposition of Religious Doctrines 76
Otto, R. 48, 188, 213, 233n22
  and numinous 40–6, 47

Pali Canon 113, 114, 115
panehenic mysticism 99
Pannenberg, W. 72
Parsons, Talcott 200
patriotism 153
Peirce, C. S. 72
performative acts 144–5, 149, 150
performative contact 135
Peters, R. S. 239n21
phenomenology 189, 194, 211–12, 225

linguistic phenomenology 189
Typological Phenomenology 211, 212, 213, 216
philosophy of religion 201–2
  and Christian theology 72–4
  and comparative religion 9–10
  and descriptive studies of religion 184–5
  and history 10, 35–6, 72–3, 74, 83
  and religious studies 165–6
  and social anthropology 185–94
  structural analysis in 75–6
  and symbolism 77–8
  task of 78–84
  see also worldviews, philosophy of
Piaget, J. 227
Plotinus 41, 140
pluralistic theology 208, 209
Popper, Karl 125, 127, 132
Precept and Practice: Traditional Buddhism in the Rural Highlands of Ceylon 125–30
prophetic experience 58–9
psychology 215, 216
puruṣa 89, 90

quietism 22, 109

Radcliffe-Brown, A. R. 189, 190
Radhakrishan, S. 136, 177
Rahner, K. 72
Ramanuja 58, 68
Ramsey, I. T. 238n3, 239n23
rationality 200–1
  and reality 186
'rationality principle' 125, 126
reality 186
rebirth 23, 90, 93, 103–4
Redfield, R. 128
relics 128
religion
  changing nature of 202
  definition of 46–8
  and family resemblance 12, 47
  inwardness of 197–8
  and morality 11–24
  and nationalism 152–3
  nature of 195–6
  tension between religions 79–83
  theory in 131–2: Eliade and 132–42; grammar of religion 133, 135
Religion in Essence and Manifestation 211
religious discourse 9

and moral discourse 11–14
  propositions in 9–10, 32
  variegation in 13–14
religious experience 81, 188, 216
  and religious beliefs 193–4
religious identity 13–14
  in Brahmanism 28–34
  in Buddhism 36–8
  in Christianity 34–6
  criteria of 25–39
religious studies 163–75
  approaches to 208–19
  changes in 158–61
  descriptive religious studies 185,
    198, 203
  dogmatic exploration in 170–1
  forms of 163–9
  history of 164–5, 169
  impartiality in 159–60
  intellectual importance of 157, 162
  principles for 195–206, 220–30
  Scientific Study of 209–11, 213,
    217–19
  see also comparative religion
religious terminology 44–5
Renan, E. 143, 148
resurrection 66
  of Christ 21
revelation 54–5, 81–2
rites, ritual 82–3, 135–6, 138, 149, 150,
    189–92
  sacrifice as 16–17
  and sentiments 190
Robinson, J. 50, 208
Russell, B. 72
Rutherford, Lord 132
Ruysbroeck 108–9
Ryle, G. 68

Sacred Canopy, The 215
sacred–profane polarity 134, 136
sacredness, and nationalism 148–9
sacrifice 16–18, 35
salvation 18, 24, 35
Samkara 95
Śankara 33, 37, 41, 44, 65, 181, 233n5
Sankhya 10, 89–90
Sartre, J. P. 217
Schleiermacher, F. 42
Scientific Study of Religion 209–11,
    213, 217–19
Self
  and Brahman 27–34, 42, 43
  concept of in mysticism 29–31

and the numinous 42
  Zaehner's translation of 106
self-indulgence 18
self-interest 17–18
sentiments 190
sin 16
Sinhalese Buddhism 125–30, 222
Slater, R. L. 234n5
Smith, A. D. 238n2
social anthropology 185–94
Social Reality of Religion, The 223
sociology 213–14
soul
  place in heaven 67–9
  theory of 65, 68
soul-mysticism 44, 47
special presence 55, 59
Staal, F. 216
Stace, W. T. 216, 236n14, 238n4
Steiner, F. 200
substance 135, 150
substrate 94, 120
śūnyatā 95, 121
Suso, H. 102–3
symbolism 77–8, 134
  of heaven 62–4, 65,66
  and rituals 189–90
syncretism 126, 127
systematic theology 75–6

Tagore, R. 42
Tathāgata 91–2, 128
theism
  and mysticism 46–8
  and transcendence 49–60
theistic mysticism 99–112
theology 72, 74, 225
  and comparative religion 176–7
  and debatability 166–7
  pluralistic theology 208, 209
  study of 157, 163–4
  systematic theology 75–6
theological positivism 208
Theravada Buddhism 92, 96–7
  gods in 113–16
  Janus-faced character of 117–18
  status of Buddha in 113–16
  and theistic transcendence 116
Thomas, E. J. 234n35, n9
Tillich, P. 46, 78, 208, 235n5
timelessness and nirvana 119–24
Tolstoy, L. 81
Toulmin, S. E. 238n1
Transcendence 49–60

and concept of heaven 63–4, 71
and creativity and independence 55–6, 58, 59
of existence 52
of human experience 51
and immanence 59–60, 64, 71
and nirvana 51, 121
and revelation 54–5
of space 52–4, 68
and special presence 55,59
and Theravada Buddhism 115, 116–17
of thought 51–2
trikāya doctrine 26–7
Trinity doctrine 69, 79
truth 223
determination of between worldviews 78–84
Turner, V. 77
Twice-Born, The 186
Twilight of the Hapsburgs, The 143
Tylor, E. B. 217
Typological Phenomenology 211, 212, 213, 216

Ultimate Reality 43
Ussher, Archbishop 138

van Buren, P. 49, 235n3
van der Leeuw, G. 134, 211
vandinavā 126, 129

Vaughan 31, 122
Void 95–6

Wach, J. 187–8, 189, 213, 239n10
Warder, A. K. 91, 236n3
Weber, M. 125, 127, 142, 166, 199, 200, 217
Whitehouse, W. A. 157, 160
Widengren, G. 211
Wilson, B. 214
Winch, P. 185, 187
Wittgenstein, L. 91, 235n18
world, concept of 53–4
worldviews 134
determination of truth between 78–84
philosophy of 74, 84–5
worship 42, 65, 69
daily conduct as 14–16
mysticism and 45

Yajnavalkya 33
yoga 180–1
Yoga 101, 102, 107, 180–1
Samkya-Yoga 89–90

Zaehner, R. C. 136, 168, 177, 216, 236n6, 239n9
and theory of mysticism 99–112
Zeman, Z. A. B. 143, 238n1
Zen 99
Zimmer 115